SOMEBODY
ELSE'S MONEY

SOMEBODY ELSE'S MONEY

THE WALROND RANCH STORY, 1883–1907

Warren Elofson

UNIVERSITY OF
CALGARY
PRESS

University of Calgary Press
2500 University Drive NW
Calgary, Alberta
Canada T2N 1N4
www.uofcpress.com

LIBRARY AND ARCHIVES CANADA CATALOGUING IN PUBLICATION

Elofson, W. M.
    Somebody else's money : the Walrond Ranch
story, 1883-1907 / Warren Elofson.

Includes bibliographical references and index.
ISBN 978-1-55238-257-8

    1. Walrond Ranch (Alta.)–History.
2. McEachran, D. (Duncan), 1841-1924.
3. Ranching–Alberta–History. 4. Alberta–History.
I. Title.

FC3670.R3E56 2009   971.23'402   C2009-903350-X

The University of Calgary Press acknowledges the support of the Alberta Foundation for the Arts for our publications. We acknowledge the financial support of the Government of Canada through the Book Publishing Industry Development Program (BPIDP) for our publishing activities. We acknowledge the financial support of the Canada Council for the Arts for our publishing program.

This book has been published with the help of a grant from the Canadian Federation for the Humanities and Social Sciences, through the Aid to Scholarly Publications Programme, using funds provided by the Social Sciences and Humanities Research Council of Canada.

Printed and bound in Canada by Marquis
∞ This book is printed on FSC Silva paper

Cover design by Melina Cusano
Page design and typesetting by Melina Cusano

TABLE OF CONTENTS

1

INTRODUCTION

The Walrond cattle ranch was one of what David Breen has labelled the four "venerable giants" of the early cattle industry in western Canada. It came into existence in 1883 in response to legislation passed two years earlier by the Conservative government in Ottawa allowing individuals or companies to lease large parcels of land in the North-West Territories at the bargain price of a cent an acre per year. This legislation was a reflection of the government's anxiety to further the aims of Sir John A. Macdonald's National Policy by providing impetus to what had been the painfully slow process of western settlement.[1] The Walrond operated on 275,640 acres in the foothills of southern Alberta to the north and west of Fort Macleod. Initially the principal financier was Sir John Walrond Walrond, a large estate owner from Bradfield Hall, near Cullompton in the English county of Devon. What Sir John had in common with the main investors in the other three operations was considerable personal wealth and Conservative party credentials either in Canada or Great Britain. The Cochrane outfit was named after its principal shareholder, Senator Mathew Cochrane, a close personal friend of the Minister of Agriculture, Sir John Pope. Cochrane leased over 300,000 acres, most of which were in the Waterton area to the south of the Walrond; the Oxley Ranch, remembered mostly for its cash flow problems, was financed by two English Conservatives, Alexander Staveley Hill, a member of parliament for Staffordshire West, and the Earl of Lathom; and the Bar U, or Northwest Cattle Company, was originally financed by the Allan family of Montreal. The head of that family, Sir Hugh Allan,[2] was the man who sparked the celebrated "Pacific scandal" by passing influence capital into the Prime Minister's party coffers in exchange for the contract to build the Canadian Pacific Railway. The four "venerable" ranches were the largest of a number of very big livestock operations that appeared in southern Alberta in the later nineteenth century. By 1884 two-thirds of all stocked land in the region was controlled by ten companies. Almost 50 per cent of that was in the hands of the largest four.[3]

The short title of this study, *Somebody Else's Money*, helps to underscore one of the central themes to be developed here. Many of the corporations that ventured into the cattle business on the Great Plains from Texas north to Alberta in the late nineteenth century were the brainchildren of dreamers. Their founders' single intention was to reap the rewards of a bountiful frontier environment quickly and with as little effort as possible; and few of them understood the challenges that lay ahead. The managing director of the Walrond, Dr. Duncan McNab McEachran, a Scottish-born veterinary surgeon from Montreal, was the person who originally coaxed Sir John Walrond and a small circle of wealthy British aristocrats and gentlemen to put their capital into the Canadian venture. From the beginning McEachran was destined to play the role of fantasy weaver. His aspirations for the ranch were very high and he had no qualms about passing them on to the others. Unfortunately, reality in the undeveloped and untamed frontier was consistently to fall short of his expectations. Rather than face the causes of this shortfall, McEachran would usually turn his back on them and convince himself that they would eventually go away. Through his letters and annual reports to the company shareholders he did what he could to persuade his investors to take a similar approach. He started by colouring the truth – not really lying, but painting conditions on the ranch in the best possible light. Then little by little his colourings became half-truths and his half-truths became untruths and his untruths became lies. Eventually, he and some of the original major shareholders felt compelled to take some rather fraudulent steps to salvage what they could for themselves. That left others to shoulder the weight of their losses.

This, then, is the story about particular individuals associated with a particular outfit. Similar stories might be told about numerous other ranches that mushroomed into existence on the Great Plains of North

America near the turn of the twentieth century. Colonel Sam Gordon, editor of the *Yellowstone Journal* in Miles City, Montana, was referring to the tendency of men like McEachran to falsify their records when he stated that the infamous winter of 1886 "was a hard winter" but "it came as a God-sent deliverance" to the managers who had been grossly underreporting their cattle losses to their shareholders. They "seized the opportunity bravely, and comprehensively charged off in one lump the accumulated mortality of four or five years. Sixty percent loss was the popular estimate. Some had to run it up higher to get even, and it is told of one truthful manager ... that he reported a loss of 125%.... The actual loss was probably thirty to fifty percent, according to localities and conditions."[4] Many of the large central Montana ranches shut down after the 1886/87 winter.[5] However, a good number in Canada and eastern, northern, and southern Montana soldiered on for up to another two decades. The Walrond ranch actively participated in the livestock industry until it succumbed to bankruptcy in 1907. As the account of that operation unfolds we will be able to view its circumstances in considerable detail and thus gain insights into McEachran's conduct that will help us to better understand the doings of many other entrepreneurs who grappled with the cattle frontier at about the same time.

This is also a story of environmental determinism. The major reason why the Walrond failed was the inability of McEachran and the men he hired to come to grips with natural and frontier conditions on the northern Great Plains. This fact too illustrates that the operation was not anomalous. Previous scholars have demonstrated that in the process of introducing production techniques to the western plains, agriculturalists in general have had a great deal of difficulty manipulating the ecosystem. In the few instances when they have seemed substantively to do so, their success has tended to prove chimerical. Thus, for instance, as Donald Worster illustrates, the oft-heralded life-generating irrigation processes in arid regions have become threatened as ground and, I would add, river water supplies have fallen to potentially disastrous levels. One might note as well that continuous irrigation in the same regions is causing minerals to seep into the topsoil, rendering increasing amounts of land saline and thus infertile. Recently, Geoff Cunfer has added considerably to Worster's illustrations by reminding us that farmers (and presumably ranchers) on the plains of North America have tended historically to achieve what he calls periods of "temporary equilibrium" with nature.[6] At such points they have attained specific agricultural objectives by conforming to nature's demands. This equilibrium normally continues until "conditions, either human or natural, change (as they always do)," at which time humans "have to adjust again." Cunfer offers this thesis as a challenge to Worster and the "declensionists." While he shows that developments have been somewhat more complex than Worster suggests, I am not so sure their views are all that conflictive. Worster has demonstrated that phenomena such as the dust bowl days of the 1930s were to a considerable degree the result of man's misguided attempts to exploit the potential of arid lands by over-use.[7] This helped to turn the soil to dust and to cause incredible wind erosion. I do not believe that Worster would argue with calling the dust bowl days a period of adjustment; nor would he necessarily deny Cunfer's point that once humans adapted to the weather and soil on the plains they were able to get a lot more out of the land. Worster's work evinces that the best agriculturalists have ever done in the struggle with nature has been when they have in a sense admitted defeat; that is, when, usually after periods of experimentation, they have learned to adapt their practices to nature's demands and given up trying to make her conform to theirs. It also warns us that supposed successes in man's struggle to manipulate nature's resources might eventually produce net losses.

The present work borrows from both of the above scholars. The period of the so-called "great ranches" on the northern Great Plains could well be described as a period of adjustment like the dust bowl days. During this period, which stretched from about 1880 to well into the first decade of the twentieth century, large companies bought up enormous cattle herds and turned them loose on the open ranges. On both sides of the Canadian-American border the vast majority of them lost money and nearly all were eventually forced out of business as their herds were decimated by wolves, the cold winter weather, prairie fires, and the diseases that spread among the animals as they mingled on the open range. In Worster's terms the ranchers failed because their practices were unsuited to the northwestern environment; to Cunfer this would surely be a period of disequilibrium when humans searched for the right methodology to exploit the natural resources of a new region. If he were writing specifically about the great ranches, Cunfer would hasten to add that the ranchers' decline ushered in the much more intensive mixed farming approach on the plains, whose longevity indicates a new era of temporary equilibrium.[8]

The primary objective here is to substantiate the first part of this argument. While I have insisted in other books that the great ranches were poorly equipped to deal with environmental pressures, I have never been able to provide detailed evidence in a close study of one operation.[9] It seems to me essential that this should be done because it speaks profoundly to the agricultural attributes of the northern Great Plains on both sides of the Canadian–American border. The Walrond ranch is an ideal subject in two ways. Firstly, it unquestionably qualifies as one of the great ranching outfits. At the height it ran over ten thousand beef cattle as well as several hundred Shire and Clydesdale horses. At the turn of the century it was the second largest ranch on the Canadian prairies, next only to the Cochrane Cattle Company. Moreover, the source materials for the Walrond are excellent. Most importantly, the company papers are in the Glenbow Archives in Calgary. The New Walrond Ranche collection contains the regular correspondence between the various managers and McEachran, who ran the company for the most part from his home in Montreal, as well as the herd count books and numerous memos about diverse subjects, including the work force and the weather.[10] The collection gives a vivid picture of the daily activities and all the various challenges the ranch had to face. Additionally, the equally fertile A.E. Cross papers in the Glenbow,[11] the Fergus Livestock and Land Company papers in three separate Montana Archives,[12] and the Powder River Ranch papers at the American Heritage Center in Laramie, Wyoming, provide ample opportunity to both verify and compare many of the circumstances and conditions on the Walrond with those elsewhere.

Numerous Canadian authorities have resisted the thesis that the great ranches on the northwestern plains were uneconomic because of their inability to accommodate environmental pressures. Breen, in his groundbreaking book, *The Canadian Prairie West and the Ranching Frontier,*

1874–1924, argues that "most big cattle companies of the early period were economically viable. Once they adjusted their grazing methods to fit the region's climatic characteristics, particularly through provision of feed supplies and shelter for unseasonable winters, big companies that were properly financed and had good local management were very successful."[13] Edward Brado in *The Cattle Kingdom*, A.B. McCullough in a well-known article, and Simon Evans in a recent and compelling book on the celebrated Bar U Ranch, repeatedly laud individuals like Senator Matthew Cochrane, George Lane, James Gordon, Robert Ironsides, and William Fares for the "flourishing" and "prosperous" livestock companies they founded.[14] Such men, they tell us, used their superior business skills to take full advantage of the elements. In enunciating this view, ranching scholars find themselves bucking the trend, so to speak, as Canadian historians in general lean more and more towards environmental theory.[15] Most recently, Clinton Evans in *The War on Weeds* leaves us with the distinct impression that western Canadian grain growers will continue to experience problems in attempting to get the best out of their land until they learn that they cannot eradicate, but must expect simply to manage, weed infestations that nature has adopted.[16]

One of the best books ever written anywhere on rural history is Paul Voisey's *Vulcan: The Making of a Prairie Community*. In this thorough study of a southern Alberta grain farming community, Voisey also uses environmental determinism to augment his central theme – that virtually no Old World institutions or cultural practices remained perfectly intact after being transported to the frontier setting. With respect to agriculture his environmental pressures come in two forms nature, referring to climate, terrain and any other natural forces that affected the way people carried on their farming operations; and frontier, referring to the special circumstances that prevailed in a new community, including a dearth of infrastructure such as fences, water wells, and efficient systems of transportation for certain types of commodities. More than any previous author Voisey makes it clear that adaptation always had to take place. A considerable adaptation, he shows us, was the one that had to be made with respect to farm size. The Canadian government, hoping to bring dense population to the West, distributed farm land in parcels of

160 acres (a quarter section) per homesteader. Very quickly this proved inappropriate, as the soil and climate in the dry belt of southern Alberta were not productive enough to sustain the family unit over the long term on such a small base. In the period of adjustment, between about 1904 and the early 1920s, numerous farmers left their holdings while others claimed and/or bought up more land in order to remain on it.[17]

Voisey also demonstrates that the really large operations were as likely to fold as the smallest ones. The optimum farm size proved to be a comparatively modest unit of about 640 acres, depending in part on conditions in specific localities.[18] The vast majority of those that were a great deal larger than that went bankrupt.[19] The reason these "bonanza farms" proved uneconomic, Voisey explains, is that grain production on the prairies was simply insufficient over the long term to offset the enormous outlays necessary for enough machinery and hired help to operate on an immense scale. Purchasing machinery normally proved appropriate not when done to expand holdings to the point where a farm became dependent on hired help, but when it was used to keep labour costs as low as possible on an optimal amount of land. This suggests that normally the farms that survived were those on which the owner, and often his wife and children, put in very long hours toiling on their own place. When they expanded their land base they did so incrementally as good harvests allowed them to upgrade their equipment, but they avoided moving into the realms of what is sometimes called "agribusiness."

In my previous work on the early ranching society of southern Alberta, Assiniboia (now southern Saskatchewan), and Montana, I have used an environmental approach much like Voisey's. I have shown how frontier conditions such as a disproportionate number of single young men and a scarcity of forage crops, outbuildings, and livestock enclosures worked along with natural elements, including bad weather and four-legged predators, to affect the livestock industry. I have also stressed the importance not just of the physical or tangible forces that controlled human behaviour but also the imaginary ones. In so doing I have moved ever so timidly into psychological history. Man felt the pressure of the western environment even before he was able to venture out into it in any significant numbers. This was because when contemplating it he was unable to control his innate propensity to dream. In the later nineteenth century people saw the western frontier in general as an unbounded commodity. "It is no doubt difficult to realize what extent of country is represented by 200,000,000 acres;" in the Canadian West alone, a correspondent wrote in the *Edinburgh Courant* in 1880, "but you will .., understand it when I tell you that the acreage of the whole United Kingdom – Scotland, England and Ireland – is only 73,153,600 [acres] or little more than one-third of the rich agricultural district in the North-West."[20] This vision induced in people the proclivity to remove the bounds that might otherwise have restrained their imaginative powers. Consequently, it became impossible for them to estimate the potential of the frontier in realistic terms.

The human imagination was an important factor in ensuring that the great ranches would initially dominate the western plains from Texas north to southern Alberta. The men who in one way or another headed up the big corporations got much of their information about this "new land" from a wealth of print and other media representations produced in eastern Canada, the eastern United States and Britain. A central message they imbibed from those materials was that the western frontier would ultimately enable virtually anyone who entered it to realize their full potential. As they learned to apply their mental and physical skills to its conditions they would become freer, more individualistic, more dexterous in both the mental and physical sense and wealthier than they had ever thought possible. The first three of these messages was presented over and over again in the print media by a host of fiction writers like dime novelists Prentice Ingraham,[21] J.F.C. Adams, and S.S. Hall and romantic novelists including George St. Rathbourne, Owen Wister, and Canada's own Ralph Connor.[22] The last message, the possibility of getting rich, was at least implied by these same authors, but it was delivered the most effectively by four well-known promotional writers – Colonel James S. Brisbin, Hiram Latham, Joseph S. McCoy, and Walter Baron von Richthofen.[23] The works of these four men told moneyed people in the East that should they invest on a large scale in western ranching they would reap phenomenal returns. They would be able simply to turn thousands of cattle loose on the rich natural pastures of the Great Plains and watch effortlessly as the animals grew, fattened, and increased their value two- and three-fold.

Unfortunately, for many of the people who initially invested in the northern plains grazing industry, the inclination to envisage the great rewards it offered caused real hardship because from the beginning it was instrumental in placing them on a collision course with the conditions both of nature and the frontier. A substantial number of the people from eastern North America and Europe who had enthusiastically imbibed the overly optimistic views presented in the print media seem to have gained a sense of destiny from reading heroic portrayals of ranchers, cowboys, and other adventurers in the dime and romantic novels, and they were induced to be inordinately free with their money by the promotional literature. They – including McEachran and Sir John Walrond – sincerely believed that:

> If $250,000 were invested in ten ranches and ranges, placing 2,000 head on each range, by selling the beeves as fast as they mature, and all the cows as soon as they were too old to breed well, and investing the receipts in young cattle, at the end of five years there would be at least 45,000 head on the ten ranges, worth at least $18.00 per head, or $810,000.[24]

What this depiction indicated to the moneyed men was not only that they could simply turn their stock loose on the open range and expect to rake in the rewards but also that the bigger their operations the more they would prosper. The secret was low costs.

> The advantages of large companies, or very large herd-owners over small ones, result from the fact that large operators can make greater savings than small operators.
>
> A man having 1,000 head of cattle will require during the whole year at least two herders, and in the busy seasons, or six months in the year, probably two more, which is equivalent to three for the whole year. A man with 5,000 head only needs

two for the whole year, and about six more for six months, equivalent to five for the whole year.

In this item the proportion of expenses between the man owning 1,000 head and the one owning 5,000 head would be three to five. So, where the small owner pays three dollars, the larger owner, who has five times as much capital invested, would pay [just] five dollars.... When the investment is still larger, the savings is greater.[25]

This attitude abounded on the ranching frontier and we see it in the pre- as well as the post–great-ranching period. "The presence of large-scale ownership and giant operations have all been part of American farming throughout the long sweep of time ...," notes Voisey. "The great slave plantations provide the most conspicuous examples, but the nineteenth-century Midwest also boasted bonanza farms. They arose in the Red River Valley, and even on the Canadian prairies, where mammoth enterprises like the great Bell farm and the Lister-Kaye farms appeared in the late nineteenth century. Because these dinosaurs soon collapsed, historians regarded them as transitory freaks of early western agriculture, but the vision that inspired them survived into the twentieth century."[26]

The Walrond experience helps to demonstrate that the big operations were no more successful in the western Canadian cattle ranching industry than they were in farming. It was not the great operations with thousands of cattle grazing over hundreds of thousands of acres but mostly those with forty to several hundred head and a few hundred to a few thousand acres that were to establish themselves on a more or less permanent basis. Most of the biggest outfits tried in the beginning to live up to the recommendations of the promoters and operate with on average about one hired worker for every thousand head of cattle. After the devastating winter of 1886/87 these ranchers realized that they were going to have to adopt a more intensive technique than they had formerly thought appropriate and they changed their operations in a number of ways. Most obviously, they started putting up more roughage for their stock and they began fencing off the open range in order to keep some of their animals near the feed during inclement weather. However, none of the big ranches made the transition from extensive to intensive agriculture. Most managed to get to the point where they were able to give more attention to their most delicate animals – the newborn calves and colts and the older gestating cows and mares – but the rest, the vast majority, continued to wander the immense ranges summer and winter. These animals succumbed in droves to harsh winters, disease, and predation.[27]

Predation and disease were both natural and frontier environmental conditions. They were natural in the sense that both germs and wolves and other four-legged predators were part of the bionetwork. They were a frontier phenomenon, as predators in general – both the two-legged and four-legged type – and certain diseases, were better able to access roaming, poorly supervised herds in an undeveloped open range system than they would have been if the stock had been confined by fences to the individual holdings of their owners. Weather, of course, is and was a natural condition. However, it too was able to make a greater impact on wandering animals than would have been the case if they had been restricted to areas that had good natural or man-made protection from fierce winter storms and that had stored feed to keep them healthy during drought or when deep snow covered the grasses. One of the factors that has become increasingly clear is the tendency of frontier ranchers to overstock their ranges. Geoff Cunfer has produced figures to substantiate his claim that the early cattlemen did not overstock American ranges in a general sense.[28] This was likely also the case in western Canada. There is no denying, however, that many cattlemen attempted to graze more livestock than their individual holdings could support.[29] As will be demonstrated, in the early days the Walrond managers ran two to three times as much stock as they should have on their lease given the extensive grazing practices they adopted.[30] This caused substantial damage to their grasslands, which in turn played a major part in their operation's financial decline. The tendency to overgraze was a product of human error, but it was obviously related to the natural environment. It was also a frontier phenomenon in the sense that people, spurred by visions of this relatively unknown land to allow their imagination to run wild, failed to recognize its limitations. "The fact of grasses curing on the ground is a … peculiarity of all the high country on the east slope of the mountains," wrote Brisbin in 1881, "and in this is found the great value of this immense range for grazing purposes…. All the flocks and herds in the world could find ample pasturage on these unoccupied plains and the mountain slopes beyond, and the time is not far distant when the largest flocks and herds will be found right here, where the grass grows and ripens untouched from one year's end to the other."[31] A year later biologist, John Macoun, supported this view in his very influential report on the Canadian West. Among other things he said that the Hand Hills area near the Red Deer River had been

> noted for its rich pastures and for the enormous herds of buffalo wandering in its neighborhood. At present the buffalo are all gone, the Indians having disappeared with them, the whole region is without inhabitants, and nothing is left but the waving grass on the hillsides and the wildfowl in the marshy flats…. Standing on a hilltop and looking over a wide area of grass covered hills and valleys – is it too much to say that here was room for millions of cattle to roam at will and get fat….[32]

Central to this view was a conviction that the vegetation in the West was superior to any other for the purpose of fattening cattle.

> The wild grasses of Manitoba and the North-West, extending to the foot of the Rocky Mountains, are famous for the nourishment they contain. They not only afford rich and ample pasturage upon which horses, cattle and sheep may thrive well, but also make an excellent quality of hay; many farmers prefer them to timothy for the latter purpose. Three varieties, the buffalo and herb grass and blue joint, after the ground has been mowed over a few times, become fine and succulent, and cure very nicely, and even the coursest variety of slough grass is similarly affected, though its improvement is not so marked…. For raising cattle and horses, this country is equal to the State

of Illinois, and of sheep-raising it is far superior. The quality of the beef and mutton raised upon our northern grasses, has been pronounced of superior excellence. Among the peculiar advantages ... the most prominent are – 1st The richness and luxuriance of the native grasses. The grass is mainly cut on the swamps and meadows, which chequer the prairies, or fringe the streams and lakes. 2nd The great extent of unoccupied land, affording for many years to come, a wide range of free pasturage. 3rd The remarkable dryness and healthfulness of the winter. The cold dry air sharpens the appetite and promotes a rapid secretion of fat, and vigorous muscular development. All point to stock-raising as one of the most important and promising of the diversified channels into which the industry of the immigrant and capitalist is to be directed.[33]

Initially, cattlemen embraced this view wholeheartedly. After his first encounter with the foothills region Duncan McEachran himself announced, "there is an inexhaustible growth of nutritious grasses. In some places it is so thick and so long as to impede the progress" of horse-drawn wagons.[34]

It was only after they had gained sufficient experience on the western ranges that cattlemen learned that such optimism was vastly overstated.[35] "It has been the fashion of Americans to boast of these uninhabited lands, to assert, with intense self-satisfaction, that we have room ... [to feed] all the oppressed of all nations," one commentator wrote after years spent grazing cattle on the plains. In the West "the grass forms a thick sod, and when the region is virgin there are but few weeds." However, if the rancher should "let this prairie be closely pastured for two years," then "weeds, rank, unwholesome, and worthless, make their appearance." In four or five years "the grass will almost disappear" and what remains is "only a field of weeds."[36] Moreover, "every rain that falls" late in the autumn "injures" the grass, "by washing out some of its nutriment." Thus by the time winter sets in the animals are in relatively poor health and do not do well. When a "hard winter" occurs "many thousands ... die."

It was during the winter of 1871/72 when grazing Texas cattle in South Dakota that this rancher had learned this lesson. He had provided no feed for his stock. "I knew, that cattle could and did winter on the plains far north and west of where I was; but … none of us knew that the tall blue-joint grass was worthless for winter feed unless it were made into hay, none of us knew that the fall rains had washed the nutriment out of it, and none of us knew that about once in ten years there is a hard winter in the far West, during which the mercury modestly retires into the bulb of the thermometer, and blizzard chases blizzard over the plains in quick succession." That year a ferocious storm started in November and "with slight interruptions, kindly allowed by Nature for the purpose of affording … opportunities to skin dead cattle," it continued until May. The losses were extremely heavy. "Hardly a herd lost less than 50 per cent, and 60, 70, and 80 per cent losses were common." That summer the "creeks were dammed with the decaying carcasses of cattle, [and] the air was heavy with the stench" of death.

The same man admitted that his own ignorance had largely been to blame for his losses but he also pointed out that in this untested land he had "had plenty of company." His neighbours had been "bright Germans, intelligent Englishmen, and keen Americans from almost every State in the Union." They were also dreamers who had imbibed the most optimistic prognostications found in the print media – "a hopeful band, young strong, and eager" and when they had gathered into their "wretched hovels o' nights," their talk had been "of cattle, cattle, cattle" and there had not been "one" who on the basis of year-round grazing, "did not firmly believe" that their "fortunes were made." One of the central messages here is that the tendency to overestimate the suitability of the western environment for grazing livestock was a major problem for the Walrond operation. Firstly, it encouraged the ranch managers to keep many of their animals fending for themselves on the open range during the winter months. Secondly, it gave them the confidence to run two and even three times as much stock on their ranges as they should have. As a result the volume and nutrition value of their grasses were negatively impacted, the health and condition of their cattle and horses declined, more of both species than would otherwise have been the case were unable to withstand winter storms and hungry wolves, and the market value of many of those that did survive suffered. These were the factors that largely determined the fate of the Walrond ranch as a business enterprise.

As the great ranches and the open range system died in the West they were replaced by a new system that was much better suited to the Great Plains – the family mixed or ranch farm. The men, and women too, who owned and operated this system were in a better position than the great ranchers to deal with the many challenges that confronted them. Within a few years they were able to fence in enough pastureland to contain their entire, much smaller, herds so that they could watch over, protect, and hand-feed them when necessary. They could also manage their pastures properly by moving their animals from one location to the other before any were too badly eaten down. Moreover, they were able to plant and harvest enough hay and green feed to get their stock through the longest, coldest winters. I have been accused of bias towards the small farms and ranches and against the so-called great ones. Nothing could be further from the truth. In pointing out that the one was better suited to conducting agriculture on the plains than the other I have simply looked at the evidence. This it seems to me corroborates Elliott West's view of the economics of small-scale agricultural production:

> The pioneer household was an economic mechanism of mutually-dependent parts ... a productive unit, often a re-markably effective and self-sustaining one. Fathers did the heaviest labor – sod busting, construction, and fence-building on a homestead ... and took off in search of other wage work when necessary. Mothers handled the multitude of domestic duties, cared for barnyard animals, gardened, and earned cash by washing, cooking, and sewing for others. Children filled in wherever they were needed ... the frontier's popular image is one of individualism and self-reliance ... but the transforma-tion of the nineteenth-century West could be more accurately pictured as a familial conquest, an occupation by tens of thou-sands of intra-dependent households.[37]

It has been in vogue since the Second World War to speak of the dangers to the family farm from large corporations that have supposedly taken hold of the land and employed efficiencies of scale to drive the smaller operations out of business. There is no question that vertically integrated giants like Cargill Beef Packers and Tyson Foods have helped to keep many producers financially dependent.[38] However, statistical evidence makes it clear that, historically, the family approach to operating ranches or farms on the plains has been the only one with any staying power. True, the size of the average agricultural holding, though still tiny by the standards of the bonanza farms and the great ranches, has risen quite a lot between the frontier period and the present. This is evident from analyses of the various figures provided by the Canadian census reports. From 1931 to 1951 most farmers in Alberta owned 200 acres or less of land.[39] By 1961 most farmers were operating 300 to 479 deeded acres.[40] In the 1980s the census reports started giving overall averages. In 1986 the average Alberta farmer owned 884 acres and by 2001 he owned just over 971 acres.[41] It is clear, moreover, that rural depopulation has been ongoing. In 1961 there were 73,212 farms in the province, in 1971 there were 62,702, in 1986 there were 57,777, in 2001 there were 53,652, and in 2006 there were 49,431.[42] 82,455 people were operating farms in Alberta in 1981, and 76,195 were doing so in 2001.[43]

However, these figures do not suggest the failure of the family farm or, as is so often decried, its replacement by corporations.[44] They simply indicate that mechanization has enabled the average family to continue to farm more land. Little by little over the decades, starting in the 1920s and even earlier, prairie farmers gave up utilizing the horse and turned to the tractor and a host of other machines. Using the great four-wheel drive tractors and self-propelled combines, balers, and windrowers as well as automatic mixing and feeding equipment, it is as easy for a modern farmer to sow his crops and look after his livestock on a 1000-acre farm today as it was for him to do so on a 200-acre operation in 1931. Presumably attempting to respond to concerns repeatedly articulated about huge companies taking over the land, the census reporters in 1971 identified all the "incorporated non-family" operations they could find in which controlling interest was "held by shareholders other than the operator and family." They found a mere 78, or .00124 per cent, of the 62,702 farms in Alberta could be described that way.[45] The same reporters found only 3,903 farms that were over 1,900 acres and only 1,862 that were over 2,880 acres.[46]

To argue that the family farm has traditionally not been threatened in the West is not, on the other hand, to glorify it or to suggest that it has been incredibly profitable. Indeed, one might argue that for much of the time it has endured in Alberta, Saskatchewan, and Montana largely because it is able to keep going in an industry which tends over much of the time to be uneconomic. The corporation ranches of the frontier period wanted to avoid investing much in labour not just because that was a prominent message from the promoters. It was also because they did the math. If at its height the Walrond had put up enough hay to feed all its cattle through a long cold winter, it would have needed to raise its labour charges more than ten-fold. It would also have needed enormous outlays of capital to purchase the extra haying and harvesting equipment it would have needed, and for building and maintaining the enormous networks of barbed wire fences and log corrals to keep the cattle accessible year round.[47]

Because the Walrond managers felt they could not afford to take such steps their herds were subject to unacceptably high death rates. In the earliest period the ranch kept some 3,500 cows for breeding purposes. The highest number of calves it ever recorded was just over 2,400 – a birth rate of about 65 per cent.[48] The average, however, was about 1,500 calves or circa 42 per cent.[49] The ranch would attempt to keep the steer calves alive for three to five years in order to get them mature, fat, and ready for the beef market. In the 1890s McEachran, figured in a death loss of 5 per cent per year on those cattle from the time they were weaned from their mothers until they were ready for slaughter.[50] However, when proper counts were taken this was always too low. By my calculations the long-term marketing rate on the Walrond was no more than 30 per cent – i.e., less than a calf for every three cows. This paled in comparison to the rate achieved by the smaller producers. The men and women who owned, say, a hundred head of cattle and who nurtured them with care and attention throughout the year, staying up day and night during calving season to act as midwife whenever a cow had difficulty delivering and making sure that each calf born during inclement weather was dried off and sheltered, could expect to get offspring from around 90 per cent of his cows. Then, after grazing, feeding, and closely attending them for three to five years, he actually *could* keep his death loss down to about 5 per cent.[51] Thus he was able eventually to market one animal for some 80 per cent of his cows. At an average price of, say, $42 per head this would give him $1,680. Mary Neth has demonstrated that in the American midwest the farmer and his wife learned in the 1920s to exist on very little money.[52] By seldom or never giving themselves proper recompense in terms of wages for all their work, by growing a large garden, keeping a few chickens and pigs for their own consumption, and selling milk and eggs for extra "pin money," they could glean enough to sustain themselves. More study needs to be done with respect to the family farm on the northern Great Plains at the turn of the century; however, it would seem reasonable to argue that with a similar approach its participants could get by on no more than $400 or $500 out of their yearly beef sales.[53] This left them over $1,100 to cover their costs of operation. By continually doing their own repair work on sowing, haying, and harvesting equipment and by improving their containment and living facilities with logs cut out of the bush, they could keep their business viable under normal circumstances. Moreover, as Professor West indicates, in years of crop failure and extremely low beef prices they could "work out" – him on one of the big ranches that were always in need of extra labour at haying or calving time, or by doing custom work with his machinery; she perhaps as a school teacher in a nearby country school or as a clerk in town. This was not living high; it was merely survival, but it was survival nonetheless – something that virtually none of the great ranches achieved.

One might argue that in a way little has changed over the years. The following is a well-known joke on the northern Great Plains: "I once asked a rancher [or farmer] what he would do if he won a million dollars. He replied 'I would keep on ranching [or farming] until it was all gone.'" People on the land invariably laugh at this joke because there is a substantial amount of truth to it. Today many farm men and women on both sides of the Canadian-American border put a lot more into their operation in terms both of energy and money than they are ever going to get out of it. In many cases the wife has worked in a nearby town most of their married life, and if you ask them where that money went they invariably tell you "into the land" or they just shrug their shoulders as if to say "who knows"? Part of the reason for low farm income is government policy and international markets. However, that the environment plays a major role is suggested by the fact that the agrarian standard of living on the northern Great Plains family-operated ranches and farms is universally low on both sides of the forty-ninth parallel.[54] The couple who have endured have done it by putting heart and soul into it and by keeping their operation to a manageable size. Most have avoided taking on any more debt than necessary and thus have expanded slowly, and primarily when there is a new generation to accommodate. In many cases, when a son who wants to farm marries, the older couple bring a mobile home onto the place for him and the new wife, and then work with the younger couple until ready to retire. At that point they move into town, making way for a new generation to take over the ancestral home.

Most of the great ranches failed because they had neither the ability nor the inclination to employ the strategies of the family farm. That is the thesis of this book and with respect to the Walrond ranch, it will be supported with clear figures and loads of documented evidence. This should play an important role in helping to clarify both the potential and limitations of agriculture on the northern Great Plains. What follows is not an exhaustive history of the Walrond cattle ranch. It is instead a thorough discussion of the economics of the large-scale grazing industry centring on that outfit. Versions of three of the twelve chapters presented here have previously been published. Much of Chapter 6 on the frontier horse business can be found in *Agricultural History*, and of Chapter 7 on the formation of the New Walrond Ranche Company and Chapter 8 on the frontier beef trade, are in *Prairie Forum*.[55] All three chapters are essential to illuminate the larger Walrond picture. Moreover, in each case, crucial evidence is presented that was not available when the article came out.

THE WALROND CATTLE RANCH:
PERSONNEL AND CHALLENGES

The land Duncan McEachran chose for the new ranch was situated in the foothills of the Rockies in southern Alberta. The area is well watered, considering that it sits on the edge of the arid plains to the east. It gets about twenty inches of precipitation annually as warm, moisture-laden air in the Prevailing Westerlies heads eastward from the coast, is forced upwards over the mountains and hills, cools, condenses to form clouds and then sheds rain or snow. Periodically, warm Chinooks occur that many early ranchers believed would enable their cattle to prosper on the open range even in the wintertime as the winds would break cold spells and melt the snow so that livestock could get at the grass below. The Walrond lease consisted of two very large blocks of land to the north of the town of Pincher Creek. The southern or "lower" piece bordered the Oldman River about eight kilometres above the town and then ran north through the Porcupine Hills. On its east side it touched up against the Peigan Indian Reserve. It measured about twenty-one kilometres east and west by some twenty-one kilometres north and south.[1] There was a gap of several kilometres between the northwestern corner of this block and the southeastern corner of the "upper" block, which measured about twenty-one kilometres north and south by some twenty-nine kilometres east and west. The western side of this piece straddled the Oldman River as it ran out of the north through the Livingstone Mountain Range. Despite the fact that precipitation is usually quite regular, much of the land in both sections is marginal for grazing as it is either too steep to retain moisture or so densely covered with bush or trees that grasses are unable to compete for either moisture or sunlight. However, there are excellent natural grasslands in the lush valley of the Oldman River and in the valleys along numerous creeks flowing out of both pieces. On the entire eastern side of the upper block, moreover, is a massive, treeless area of gently rolling hills surrounding Callum Creek, which is absolutely ideal.[2] Eventually the Walrond would own some 37,000 acres of this land.[3]

In the earliest period, however, it was the lower block that quickly became the centre of activity primarily because of the beef trade. At the time he brought the first cattle to the area Duncan McEachran got a contract with the federal government to supply both the Peigan Indians, immediately next door to the lower block, and the Blood Indians, some thirty kilometres further south and east, with regular deliveries of beef. This necessitated having numerous cattle close by as well as crews of cowboys to round up the fattest of the animals grazing nearest the reserves to be killed and delivered monthly. To facilitate this a home site known as the "lower ranch" was located on the northwest quarter of section 13, township 8, range 29, west of the 4th meridian about four miles from where Beaver Creek enters the Peigan reserve as it flows out of the Porcupine Hills.[4] A considerable amount of field cultivation and crop growing and harvesting was eventually undertaken on the lower ranch. For that reason it was sometimes referred to simply as "the farm" or "Beaver Creek farm." Beaver Creek was the largest of several streams on the lower block, and it had a wide valley well endowed with heavy growths of natural grasses and deep topsoil. Near the Peigan reserve the altitude was lower than further back in the hills, providing a lon-. ger frost-free growing season. Two more home sites were located at the north end of the lower block. One on the northeast quarter of section 19, township 29, range 9, was upstream from the lower ranch. It was called the "Beaver Creek Thoroughbred Ranche" due to the fact that purebred Clydesdale and Shire stallions were brought there to service some of the best mares that were separated out of the commercial herd at another site.[5] The Walrond acquired the quarter section through the Homestead Act of 1872. It was the only landed property the ranch actually owned in the early days.[6] In 1895 the site was abandoned, though the Walrond retained title to the land.[7] At that point the ranch took over another site nearby but on the east side of Beaver Creek, which was usually referred to as the "Loring Ranche," presumably because a settler of that name had once occupied it. It was sold in 1902.[8] One other site on the lower block – "Five Mile Ranche" – was about five kilometres straight east of the Thoroughbred Ranche on Five Mile Creek, a Beaver Creek tributary.[9] The last home site, known simply as the "upper ranch" or sometimes the "horse ranch," was located on Callum Creek. In the beginning it was used primarily for breaking and training the extra hundred or so saddle horses the cowboys needed for the spring and fall roundups. However, McEachran had a keen interest in Clydesdale and Shire draft animals, and he soon began to send out brood mares and stallions from Quebec to establish what was to become a very large commercial herd.[10] It was no doubt a reflection of his enthusiasm for that business that the upper ranch was made the main Walrond headquarters and was thus the site on which successive managers lived. From there it was possible for them to watch over both the horses and all the cattle that made their way west to the massive grasslands surrounding the creek.

Within a few years all the ranches had bunkhouses for the men and by 1894 the upper ranch had two houses – a bunkhouse for the cowboys and a somewhat grander structure for the ranch manager and his family. The former house was built on the northeast quarter of section 7, township 10, range 1, west of the 5th meridian on the east side of Callum Creek about a kilometre north and west of the point where the creek joins the Oldman River.[11] It had log walls and a "dirt and board roof" and appears to have been built in two stages as it consisted of two sections measuring sixteen feet by twenty-two feet adjoined in a T configuration. The other house was built on section 12, township 10, range 2, close by but on the west side of the creek. McEachran often stayed here with his manager and family when he was in the West, and a special room was reserved for his private use. In 1892 a small second house was built for him at the Five Mile facility so that he could stay there when he chose to oversee the eastern operations and, presumably, to be closer to Fort Macleod, a railhead and the centre of the cattle business for southern Alberta, some thirty kilometres to the east.[12] In the course of time

SOMEBODY ELSE'S MONEY

THE HIGHWAY ON THE LEFT SIDE OF THE ABOVE PHOTOGRAPH PARALLELS CALLUM CREEK, WHICH FLOWS OUT OF THE NORTH AND TURNS TOWARDS THE EAST TO JOIN THE OLD MAN RIVER NEAR THE BOTTOM OF THE PHOTOGRAPH. PHOTO BY THE AUTHOR.

SOMEBODY ELSE'S MONEY

THE VALLEY OF
BEAVER CREEK
NEAR THE NORTH
END, DEEP IN
THE PORCUPINE
HILLS. PHOTO BY
THE AUTHOR.

SOMEBODY ELSE'S MONEY

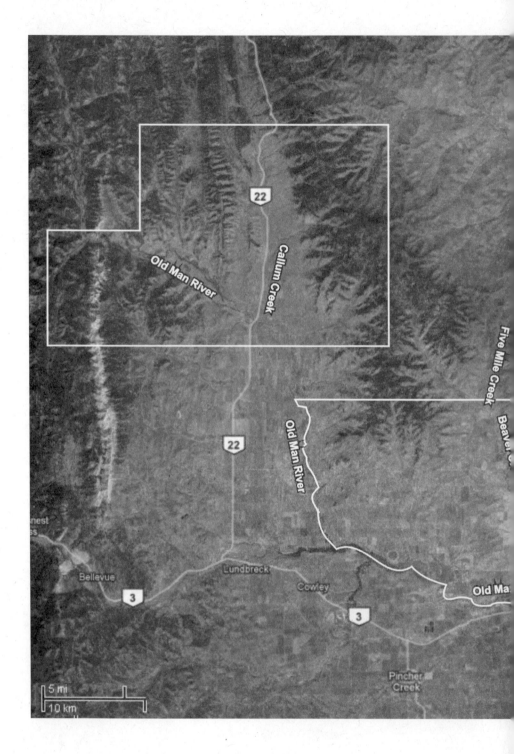

THE APPROXIMATE
BOUNDARIES OF THE
UPPER (NORTHERN)
AND LOWER (SOUTH-
ERN) WALROND
BLOCKS ARE OUTLINED
IN THIS GOOGLE PHO-
TOGRAPH. CALLUM
CREEK RANGE IS THE
LARGE TREELESS AREA
RUNNING NORTH AND
SOUTH THROUGH THE
UPPER BLOCK. IT LIES
BETWEEN THE LIVING-
STONE MOUNTAINS
ON THE WEST AND
THE PORCUPINE HILLS
ON THE EAST. BEAVER
CREEK MEANDERS
SOUTHEAST ACROSS
WHAT WAS THE
NORTHEAST CORNER
OF THE LOWER BLOCK.
IT FLOWS OUT OF THE
HEAVILY TREED SEC-
TION OF THE PORCU-
PINE HILLS AND RUNS
ACROSS THE TREELESS
SECTION TO BECOME
A TRIBUTARY OF THE
OLD MAN RIVER.

UPPER WALROND RANCH AND ROCKY MOUNTAINS, OLD MAN'S R

there were to be three different incarnations of the Walrond ranch itself: the Walrond Cattle Ranche Company, which was active from 1883 to 1888, the Walrond Ranche Company, active from 1888 to 1898, and the New Walrond Ranche Company, active from 1898 to 1907.[13] By the time the first of these companies officially came into existence, in May 1883, McEachran had been appointed its managing director. From that point forward it was he who, in every practical sense, would control the operation's approaches to raising and marketing livestock.

The Walrond was not McEachran's first western ranching endeavour. In 1881 he had taken a thousand shares in the Cochrane Ranche Company. He accepted the position of vice-president and general manager of that operation only to resign in 1883 after blizzards had devastated its cattle herds in two consecutive winters. It was during the winter of 1882 while he was still directing the Cochrane operations that McEachran came in contact with members of the Walrond interest and began negotiations to organize a new company. At that point he attempted to sell stocks he held in the Cochrane to a well-known Montana cattle merchant and rancher, T.C. Power. "By you being interested" he told Power, "I believe it would ultimately lead to upsetting a huge monopoly and securing the best half of it in our country – as I think we could do considerable wire pulling at Ottawa both with the Gov[ernment] and Syndicate."[14] By the government McEachran meant the Conservative government of Sir John A. Macdonald, with which he was on good terms.[15] By the "monopoly," he probably meant the Montana beef merchant Conrad Kohrs, who had taken over the Highland City Meat Market in Helena in the 1860s and become a rancher and trader himself in the 1870s. Along with associates in the banking industry, Kohrs had gained nearly complete control of the beef trade between Montana and Chicago.[16] The "syndicate" most likely was the group of buyers in the East who purchased the live animals and marketed them domestically or sent them by ocean steamer to be auctioned off in Liverpool, Glasgow, and London. McEachran offered to sell Power half his paid-up shares in the Cochrane operation for $150 apiece. He was not successful in this endeavour and may never have found another buyer. If so, however, it is far from certain that he was out of pocket any money. It is most likely that the shares he had received in that company were simply part of the remuneration package he attained as its employee.[17]

McEachran was in contact with the Walrond group in December 1882. Their connection was unquestionably strengthened through politics, as he was a British-born Conservative living in Canada at a time when party links fluently spanned the Atlantic Ocean. McEachran did not officially become a shareholder of the Walrond ranch until after the first cattle were delivered to its lease in the summer of 1883. There were initially seven British investors, each of whom took one share in the company worth £2,500 or $12,500. Sir John Walrond Walrond himself was in some basic respects typical of British investors whom P.J. Cain and H.G. Hopkins have described as "gentlemanly capitalists," i.e., large landholders in Britain who, to augment their image as members of the aristocratic classes in the traditional sense, were most anxious to have major landed holdings in the New World.[18] Prior to heading further west, Sir John had taken an interest in southern Manitoba. His investments in that region consisted of an 820-acre farm near the Pembina River, 1900 acres of land known as the Morris property ostensibly near Winnipeg, and a number of lots in the latter town, which he bought in partnership with a firm known as Boyle Brothers.[19] Walrond willed his Manitoba holdings to his two sons William and Arthur at approximately the time he turned his attention to the foothills of southern Alberta.[20] That living up to an image was important in Sir John's mind is suggested by the fact that at no time did he physically go out to the ranch or even take a significant part in determining its operational development. Most of the shareholders who joined Sir John in the venture had familial, personal, political, or business ties with him or with one of his close relatives. By the number of servants cited in the census reports as living in their homes, it is evident that all of them had surrounded themselves with the luxuries of life.[21] Sir John himself was descended from a gentry family that had held the estate of Bradfield from shortly after the Norman conquest in 1066. In 1913, his granddaughter-in-law, Lady Charlotte Walrond,[22] described the origins of the estate as follows:

In the years immediately after the Norman Conquest the King's great Barons commonly granted smaller manors within their own honours to be held under them by persons of somewhat lesser importance, and in process of time many of these sub-infeudations acquired most, if not all, of the privileges of the parent manors, although being non-existent at the period of the Survey, they are not to be found entered in the pages of the Doomsday Book.

One of such, respect of which the latter record is silent, is the manor of Bradfield, within the parish of Uffculm, a few miles from Cullompton and now the seat of the Honourable Lionel Walrond, M.P., and which for more than six centuries was the residence of the Walronds in direct male line; it was originally parcel of the Doomsday Manor, then known as Offacome, which became included in Walscin de Douay's great barony of Bampton.[23]

Along with being a knight, Sir John, as first Baronet Walrond, was a member of the lower rungs of the peerage, though not entitled to take a seat in the House of Lords. Of the other six shareholders three were related to him either by blood or marriage. His second child and eldest son, William Hood Walrond, later Lord Waleran, was a Captain in the Grenadier Guards, Colonel of the 1st Volunteer Battalion Devonshire Regiment, MP for East Devon 1880–85, and for the Tiverton Division 1885–1905, Junior Lord of the Treasury in the Conservative Government of Lord Salisbury from 1885 to 1886 and in 1892, and Patronage Secretary from 1895 to 1902. Sir John's son-in-law, Charles Henry Rolle Hepburn-Stuart-Forbes-Trefusis, twentieth Baron Clinton, was privileged to the House of Lords.[24] Lieutenant Colonel George Herbert Windsor-Clive was married to Clinton's sister, Gertrude Albertina Trefusis. The connection between two of the original shareholders with any of the above is not clear. Thomas Henry Goodwin Newton was a barrister, Justice of the Peace, and landowner from Henley in Arden, in the county of Warwickshire. John Goring was a "clerk in Holy orders," from the town of Wiston in Sussex.[25] The other shareholder, Lionel Richard

BRADFIELD HALL, 2008. PHOTO BY THE AUTHOR.

Cavendish Boyle, described himself as a Canadian merchant.[26] He may well be the person who introduced Sir John to Duncan McEachran. He was one of the Boyles who partnered Walrond in the purchase of the property in and around Winnipeg.[27] He also sold Walrond some of his holdings in that area.[28] One of his merchant firms, Boyle, Campbell, Burton and Company, had an office at 80 Lombard Street, London, which served as the official headquarters for the ranch and as its "agent" or "trustee" in all important legal transactions.

The "Memorandum and Articles of Association for the Walrond Cattle Ranche Limited," was drawn up and signed by the seven shareholders on 23 May 1883.[29] The Registrar of Joint Stock Companies in London registered the papers, on 29 May 1883.[30] Previously a contract had been signed by Boyle to transfer Sir John's lease on land in the Canadian Territories to the forthcoming company along with 3,900 head of cattle McEachran had purchased in his name.[31] At this point Sir John was actively lining up as many more investors as he could find in Great Britain, and by January 1884 the list of shareholders had grown from seven to nineteen.[32] Sir John had also increased his own commitment. He was now the largest shareholder with four shares worth a total of £10,000 or $50,000 Canadian; Thomas H.G. Newton and a new recruit, Lady Sarah Hotham (nee Hood), Sir John's wife's sister whose second husband had been Sir Charles Hotham, had two shares each. All the rest had one share. A core of the new recruits was related to the Walronds either directly or indirectly. There was: Sir John's fifth born child and second born son, Arthur Melville Hood Walrond;[33] Sir John's wife Lady Francis Caroline Walrond (nee Hood); Major Walter Henry Holbech, who was related firstly to Sir John's wife through her sister Sarah Hotham's first marriage to a Lieutenant-Colonel Hugh Holbech and, secondly, to one of Sir John's daughters who also married a Holbech;[34] and Reverend Horace Newton, who seems to have been related to Thomas H.G. Newton.[35] The other seven new shareholders were connected to the family through friendship and/or politics. W. Herbert Evans likely associated with the Hood family regionally. His home in Chard, Somerset, was situated just a few miles from the Hood ancestral home at Bridport in the county of Dorset; Reverend Samuel Peshall was the vicar from Thomas H.G. Newton's parish at Henley in Arden, Warwickshire;[36] and Mrs. Julia Neville Grenville was married to Lieutenant Colonel Ralph Neville Grenville, an MP from the county of Somerset.[37] Francis W. Mitchell was a prosperous "pen maker" from the city of Birmingham;[38] Arthur Constance Mitchell was a "pen maker" from London;[39] and Thomas Pakenham Law who resided at 48 Stephen's Green in Dublin, Ireland listed his occupation as "QC" or Queen's Counselor, indicative of his considerable standing in the law profession.

It was in early 1884 that McEachran took a shareholder interest in the Walrond Cattle Ranche Company. Through an agreement between him and the company signed on 1 November 1883 and registered on 25 January 1884 he accepted "fully paid up" shares in the ranch "in lieu of other remunerations and of Salary" for acting as its manager. The shares were to be worth £500 apiece and to be apportioned to him at various intervals – two on 15 November 1883, two on 15 May 1884, and one every six months thereafter until 15 May 1887. This would eventually give him ten shares worth a total of £5,000 or $25,000.[40] McEachran was also eligible for any dividends paid out to the shareholders of the company during that period. The company would pay dividends of at least 5 per cent annually. Thus in 1884, at the end of which he held four shares worth £2,500 or $10,000, he received 5 per cent of that or $500. Of course the dividend increased in value every year as the value of his shares increased until by 1887 he would be receiving at least $1,250 a year. Consequently, by the time the first version of the Walrond ranch ended McEachran was getting a total of $6,250 annually in shares and dividend. At a time when hired cowboys on the big ranches were paid on average $480 a year and senior level school teachers were paid less than $1,000 a year this was a considerable sum.[41] McEachran also, of course, got all his personal expenses paid when pursuing the ranch's interest. The only stipulation made by the company in its financial arrangement with him was that his shares should be "retained by the Company until the termination of this Agreement." This meant that McEachran was not free to sell his shares until 15 May 1887. Such a condition was not un-common with the corporation ranches.[42] The object was to ensure that the manager would continue to see his own and the company's fortunes largely as one and the same. If McEachran actually did succeed in selling the shares he had formerly held in the Cochrane outfit, Senator Matthew Cochrane may well have regretted not writing a similar clause into their arrangement.

It is likely that Sir John Walrond was prepared to give McEachran such a lucrative deal in part because he recognized that his general manager's high standing with the Conservative government of Sir John A. Macdonald could be a valuable asset. Before he took control of the ranch McEachran was already a man of considerable eminence in eastern Canada. He had graduated from the renowned Edinburgh Veterinary College in 1861 and then founded the Montreal Veterinary College and helped to found the Upper Canada Veterinary School in Toronto.[43] In 1867 he co-published the first veterinary textbook for farmers, entitled

The Canadian Horse and His Diseases, and thereafter, he wrote numerous articles and reports on the major infectious diseases affecting Canadian livestock.[44] In the 1870s McEachran was put in charge of instigating a program for the inspection of all livestock entering and leaving Canada, and in 1876 he was appointed Chief Inspector of Livestock. In 1885, he was made the first Chief Veterinary Inspector of Canada, charged with the responsibility of examining all Canadian livestock for infectious or contagious diseases. McEachran liked to underline the potential value of his influence with the Dominion government in gaining particular privileges. Indeed, it is evident that he was instrumental in procuring the Walrond leases. The act of 1881 gave individuals or companies the right to lease up to 100,000 acres. To gain access to more than that, some companies leased under more than one name. Those for the Walrond were acquired as follows: the Walrond Cattle Ranche Company Limited –100,000 acres; Sir John Walrond – 100,000 acres; Duncan McEachran – 16,640 acres; Duncan McEachran – 29,000 acres; Duncan McEachran – 30,000 acres.[45] Whether this was in accord with the letter of the 1881 legislation is difficult to know, but undoubtedly, solid Conservative credentials were useful in assuring that any objections to the practice did not achieve much headway in Ottawa.

Just as Walrond had reason to value McEachran's standing with the Macdonald government, he clearly had considerable faith in his knowledge of livestock. McEachran was the only member of the organization who inspected the herds purchased in Sir John's name, and he also did all the negotiating with respect to price. The first big deal did not go smoothly. In the spring of 1883 McEachran ordered 5,000 head from T.C. Power.[46] This was to include cows, calves, some two hundred three-year-old steers and about three breeding bulls for every hundred cows. The price was to be $25 for every animal branded by 30 June 1883. McEachran interpreted this to mean that the calves born that spring, which were as yet unbranded, were to be thrown in with their mothers free of charge. Power, who had authored the contract, would have none of that. Several letters had to be written back and forth to deal with the misunderstanding.[47] In the end the two men finally agreed that all the spring calves born after January 1883 would be free of charge as

SOMEBODY ELSE'S MONEY

McEachran wanted, but that the price for the rest of the cattle would be $32 a head. That settled, everything looked fine until it became evident that Power was not going to be able to completely fulfill his end of the bargain. The two men agreed that once the calves were deducted from the total, 3,900 animals were to be delivered and paid for rather than 5,000. The cattle were to come from Power's Judith Cattle Company ranch at Warm Springs. However, when Power's men sorted through the cattle on the ranch they managed to find only 3,125 that were appropriate for the sale.[48] McEachran was extremely impatient to bring the Walrond into full production and he seems to have been most disappointed when informed of this.

Ostensibly, Power feared that he could be held responsible for failing to live up to the contract and perhaps sued for damages. Thus, he sent instructions to his partners at Fort Benton that McEachran was not to be allowed to take possession of the cattle until he paid for them in full by bond along with any duty that would be charged at the border.[49] McEachran had already paid a deposit of $21,000. Therefore he still owed another $79,000. He agreed to pay another $50,000 when the cattle drive started out of Fort Benton but he was not happy to do so. "In complying with your demand for the payment the sum of $50,000 for the band of cattle now opposite Benton, on your threat to prevent them being crossed unless said sum is paid, I beg to inform you that such demand is not in accordance with the letter or spirit of the contract entered into by us and on paying you this sum I do so under protest and soley [sic] with a view to prevent injury to the cattle from being held where they are without sufficient food and to avoid further delay and loss and I do so protesting as above without prejudice to my rights in the contract."[50] When McEachran discovered that his Montana broker was holding him responsible for paying any customs duties assessed at the border he shot off another angry letter. "I call your attention," he wrote, "to the fact that I was informed that the assessments on the herd of cattle purchased by me to be delivered at shoots [sic, he meant chutes] provided for branding on this ranche and which delivery is about to commence today, and learning from you that said assessment has not been paid or arranged for, I hereby notify you that in receiving the cattle as per our agreement

..., I in no way whatever assume any responsibility for the payment of said assessment or any other charges which may be made or leveyed [sic] against the said herd."[51]

This latter issue eventually dissipated as no customs charges were actually ever levied on the cattle. Had they been, conflict almost certainly would have flared up again. All cattle imported to Canada from the United States that were not to be kept for at least two years were subject to a 20.5 per cent *ad valorem* tax. This should have exempted the younger breeding stock and their calves and the yearlings. However, steers that were over two years old might have been taxed, as the Walrond practice would be to market a lot of these cattle at three to four years of age. Similarly the aged cows could have been taxed. There were a lot of very old cows in the Walrond's first Montana purchases, and many of them were to be sold to Indian bands in years to come.[52] However, all the big lease operations evaded the tax. It is difficult to believe that their relationship with the Macdonald Conservatives was not a factor.

Historians like to repeat the well-worn adage that trust was the basis of the early cattle business and that a man's word and a handshake were all that were necessary to conclude some of the big deals that were undertaken.[53] The problem here, however, was that Power and McEachran did not trust each other. Power, at first, was afraid to allow the cattle to leave without a substantial payment for fear that McEachran would ultimately fail to honour his commitments in full. McEachran, on the other hand, did not want to pay out the contract completely at that stage because he feared Power would not live up to his responsibilities. Along with the cattle, Power provided saddles and harness, wagons, cooking facilities, and provisions for the first Walrond drive north. McEachran asked him to supply "mowing machines" as well, so that his men would be able to cut hay.[54] Power found twenty-five horses for the drive, but McEachran knew he would need more to operate the ranch and he brought in about a dozen from Montreal along with ten Short Horn bulls.[55] These animals were shipped together by steamer across the Great Lakes to Chicago, and then carried by rail from Chicago to St. Paul, Minnesota, and then by steamer again up the Missouri River to Fort Benton.[56] In future the Walrond would replenish its saddle horse supply primarily from Montana, where it was able to find the larger animals all ranchers on the northern Great Plains required when working cattle in the winter time through deep coverings of snow.[57] The first Walrond cattle drive was very successful in comparison to the Cochrane's celebrated disastrous drives of 1881 and 1882.[58] Realizing that part of the problem in the latter cases had been that the cattle were not put on the trail to the Calgary area until late in the season and, therefore, were subjected to fierce early winter storms, McEachran got his animals on their way as quickly as possible. The cattle started out near the beginning of July 1883 and by 21 September McEachran reported that he was "happy to say we got the herd in good order."[59]

In the end McEachran was very pleased with the cattle he obtained from his Montana buyer.[60] He ordered more and in the fall of 1884 would try to market slaughter steers through Power.[61] He was unsuccessful in both cases, however, and two other merchant companies with which he was familiar, Poindexter and Orr and I.G. Baker, brokered most of the rest of the stock he bought in Montana in later years. Both companies also worked out of Fort Benton.[62] Among the men who trailed the Walrond herds to Canada in 1883, the leader was Jim Patterson, who had spent years on the ranching frontier in Montana. Once all the cattle were safely on the Walrond he became the ranch's first foreman. It is likely that Power originally recommended Patterson as McEachran had repeatedly asked him to find him "an experienced cattleman to put in charge."[63] Another man who rode the trail with the first Walrond cattle was William Bell. McEachran had made Bell's acquaintance previously, apparently in Canada, and he insisted that he ride along on at least the first drive.[64] Bell was to become the ranch "clerk" in charge of keeping the books and regularly reporting all important developments to McEachran in Montreal.[65] George W. "Doc" Frields from Fort Macleod became the first on-site general manager.[66] A number of the men who helped out on the various drives were encouraged by Frields and Patterson to stay on to work the cattle year round. These American cowboys brought their riding, roping, cutting, and herding skills with them and they became the role models for the "greenhorns" from Britain and eastern Canada who joined their ranks later on.[67]

In attempting to establish the financial viability of any of the great ranches it is extremely important to be aware of one basic fact about the men they were forced to rely on. Many were not, generally speaking, the sterling sorts glorified over and over again in nineteenth-century dime and romantic novels or on twentieth-century celluloid. They were mostly single, young, and male, and therefore a good proportion of them were less settled and less reliable than many of us would like to think. True, some who worked for part of their career on the Walrond were well known for their cowboy skills. Jim Patterson, himself, was widely lauded for his prowess with both cattle and six-shooter. After his stint on the Walrond he moved on to take over the same position on the Cochrane outfit. Later he was appointed Dominion Livestock Inspector at Winnipeg.[68] Charlie Raymond, a Texan, was equally acclaimed for his ability to ride bucking broncos and rope animals from the saddle. John Lamar, the cattle foreman in the 1890s, was known for his "cow sense" and, like Patterson, his gunmanship. Old-time cowboys used to tell tales of how he could ride at full gallop and shoot the head off a prairie chicken. They also believed that "nothing still or moving could escape his lasso." Johnny Franklin came to Canada from Texas in the early 1890s. He enjoyed "the rare distinction of having never been thrown from any horse."[69] Unfortunately, however, skill at a particular trade does not necessarily suggest a willingness to shoulder a great deal of responsibility. Many of the young men who populated the ranching frontier often had difficulty placing their careers above their urge to fulfill basic animal instincts. Once the summer roundups came to an end each fall, cowhands were laid off by all the large outfits. "Calf branding was finished yesterday and was pretty fair but not up to expectations I have not got the exact tally but it is about 1400," Bell reported in July 1888, "I am paying off the extra men today and will go to MacLeod with them this afternoon."[70] These men usually headed to the numerous bars and whorehouses on the frontier to quickly spend their summer wages. "When paid," a Montana rancher once noted, "their habit was to immediately ride off" to the nearest saloon "and spend all they had on drinking, gambling and having ... a right good time. They returned after every dollar had been squandered and started piling up for the next orgy."[71] The Walrond managers noted this tendency among their own hired help. In January 1899 Warnock told McEachran about one of the men named Brown who wanted badly to go back to England. "Out of the wages paid him since coming here I don't think he has saved a dollar!" Warnock opined, "he lost one cheque by giving it to Jeff Dans to take to town and get it cashed for him. Jeff went to town, cashed the cheque, got drunk, stayed in town and spent the money." He "has not come back to work since."[72]

Considerable numbers of the employees on the big ranches were also capable of the kind of violence Canadians have tended to believe occurred almost exclusively in the American West. In 1904 Jesse Hinman pulled his gun to settle a conflict arising out of a card game in a bar in Pincher Creek. He shot "intently but with poor aim" at a man known as "Rattlesnake Pete." Having missed he clobbered the man over the head with his six-shooter. Hinman was later sentenced to five years in prison. In the same year a "cowpuncher" from Claresholm and one from Pincher Creek went on separate drunken shooting sprees in their respective towns. Fortunately, the men were both arrested, apparently before anyone was hurt.[73] There is a good chance that the individuals involved in all three of these incidents worked on the Walrond at some point, as the towns in which the incidents occurred were near the ranch. Others unquestionably did. In 1885 there was a gunfight in a corral on the ranch when two of the cowboys named Thompson and Charlie Wright "both pulled their revolvers at the same moment." Thompson was hit in the shoulder and Wright evaded arrest by making a hasty exit across the line to Montana.[74] In November 1895 John Lamar and Gilbert McKay, a former Walrond employee, got into a heated dispute apparently involving a mutual female acquaintance. Some days later McKay rode out to the ranch and challenged Lamar to a gunfight. Lamar was unarmed, but eventually losing his temper he went into the house and strapped on his six-shooters. When he came out Mckay was still waiting and he immediately went for his gun. However, Lamar beat his assailant to the draw, shooting him "in arm and body and toppling him out of his saddle."[75] Miraculously McKay survived after a stint in a North-West Mounted Police hospital. Another gunfight involving several of the ranch's cowhands occurred in the late spring or early summer of 1900, probably in a saloon in Pincher Creek or Fort Macleod. In July David Warnock told McEachran about a skirmish involving their man Tom Miles. Miles was thought to be dead "from the effects of his wound" and some "Pincher Creek men have been killed."[76] Five or so months later Warnock reported that "Miles is back looking very well and quite recovered from his wounds.... He made a narrow escape of sharing Morden and Carr's fate, the bullet missing his spine by less than one inch. He says Johnston's arm is recovering under medicine treatment."[77]

Far from acting as conscientious employees, men such as these would often find themselves tempted into a life of crime, particularly when they were laid off and out of money. Their misdeeds involved, among other things, the rustling of roaming livestock.[78] McEachran was well aware of this. In his own reminiscences about the ranching business in 1923 he paid the usual compliments to the "genial whole-souled" cowboys who, while they tended to "gamble and drink away their earnings," were "generous to a fault, honourable and trustworthy and loyal" to their employers. However, he also singled out for condemnation the "cowboy of the newspaper and the novel writer," the "good for nothing ... black sheep, who will do no good anywhere." This man, often "very much wanted by the officers of the law, at home, and therefore armed with a six-shooter, bowie knife, and the usual paraphernalia of the 'bad man' ... migrates to the far west where he indulges in all his wild extravagances, 'goes broke,' perhaps becomes a horse thief and consequently an outlaw."[79] The big ranchers at times expressed deep frustrations about cowboy rustling.[80] "There seems to be a great deal of horse stealing going on and a number of ... breeders have lost a good many horses since last Autumn," Warnock told McEachran in 1901. "Some arrests have been made lately and I hope convictions will follow."[81] In the spring of the same year, Clay Fallis, who had once worked on the Walrond, and a partner, were being hunted by the police for stealing fifty-nine head of cattle from the Cochrane ranch to the south. At the same time "a young fellow named Collyns" was sentenced to "three years penal servitude for stealing two steers the property of a High River Rancher."[82] In 1904 the *Nanton News* reported that Charlie McLaughlin was arrested and sentenced to seven years in jail. Thus, the report announced, both horses and cattle are at long last protected from "one old offender."[83] L.V. Kelly believed that stiff sentences handed out to cowboy rustlers in 1903 had still "not resulted ... in any marked reduction of boldness or frequency." Twenty prisoners, sentenced to terms varying from one to ten years, had been sent up from the Macleod district alone during the previous year, "but the docket for 1904 was as populous as before."[84] Of course, not all the cowboy rustling was the work of hired hands. Some of the perpetrators were professional outlaws and settlers. However, the involvement of men who at one time or another were employed on one or more of the bigger ranches is beyond doubt. Indeed, this was the case with two of the most notorious outlaws on the northwestern plains. Henry Ieuch, better known as "Dutch Henry," and Frank "Slim" or "Left-handed" Jones, got into the business by taking the livestock of their employers in the Big Muddy region of Assiniboia.[85]

There is no reason to think that the Walrond's hands were any more trustworthy than those on the other spreads and, while a proportion of them may well have done a good job, there can be little doubt that the company suffered financially from the depredations of others. How much this cost in a given year is impossible to estimate, as under the circumstances of the open range, roaming animals could be taken in ones and twos without detection. But as will be demonstrated, when the operation took counts of its cattle it almost always came up short of expectations. Rustling, and much of it by its own employees, should be seen as one of the reasons.

The Walrond Cattle Ranche normally employed about eleven men in the busy summertime when the two roundups were undertaken – the first in the spring to brand and castrate the new calves; the second in the fall to do the same to the calves born after the first roundup, and to separate out fat cattle that were ready to be sent to market. In the winter, when the cattle were left largely to their own resources, about half these men were laid off.[86] The ranch had two main sources of income. There was the annual sale of fat cattle at the end of the summer grazing season to local merchants such as I.G. Baker and Company or William Roper Hull and to brokers such as Gordon and Ironsides of Winnipeg who supplied more distant markets in eastern Canada and Great Britain.[87]

More important in the early years, however, were the contracts with the Department of Indian Affairs to supply beef to the Blood and Peigan Indians. The Indian contracts involved delivering sixty to seventy head monthly to the Blood reserve and thirty-five to forty to the Peigans.[88] Four men were dedicated to this. Because it was paid on the basis of net dressed weight for the contracts (i.e., the weight of the carcass after the hide, inner organs, head, and feet had been removed), the company had to supply a man and an assistant to slaughter, butcher, and hang the cattle. To deliver the carcasses in this state the men built holding corrals close to where animals belonging to the ranch were grazing. Each month the fattest of these animals were rounded up and slaughtered. In the beginning the men employed to butcher the animals usually stayed at a cabin on or close to the lower ranch. "Black bros. will not board the men for the summer as they say it will not pay them to do so. So I got them a cooking outfit and grub and they will board themselves," Bell wrote in 1887. "For the present they will use Black's cabin, stable and corral. They will have to move across the river before high water and camp there … for the greater part of the summer." We had "Damien and Lamar build a corral joining the slaughter pen. Damien will also build a small corral for his horses and we will have to build some sort of a cabin for them to use while the streams are up. Clay and his Indian will move down to the agency as soon as the grass gets good. They will live in the Ross cabin and hold the cattle" there.[89] In time, however, killing facilities were built on the lower ranch.[90] Then the animals were probably all slaughtered there and delivered by horse and wagon.

As the above words illustrate, along with the American and British hands, the ranch, at times, hired one or two Natives who had become proficient in the arts of the cowboy. It should not be lauded too loudly for this, however, as there was a considerable discrepancy between white and Native wages. The white riders were paid on average $35–40 a month.[91] On 9 April 1887 Bell informed his boss in Montreal that "we have now two Indians herding, Damien has one at the Bloods" helping to bring in cattle for the beef contract, "and we have one herding the beef cattle" for the Peigan tribe, "at Beaver creek." Bell was very pleased that these men were hired at a bargain basement price. "We give them twenty dollars per month each and board and they furnish their own horses."[92] In later years Native hunters paid by the stock associations and the Northwest Territories government were to be instrumental in helping the ranchers deal with the very serious threat to their cattle and horse herds posed by wolves. However, there appears to have been little love between them. "A more lazy, filthy race could scarcely be imagined," McEachran wrote in a published account of his first journey west.[93]

There often were tensions between various ranchers and Native groups, and it is beyond question that some Indians at times also posed a predation threat. In the 1890s Warnock told McEachran that "about twenty Blood Indians are under arrest for killing Cochrane's cattle. They had killed a large number to procure tongues for the Sun Dance."[94] Years later McEachran told a Mounted Police commander, "on Friday afternoon when we arrived at Tennessee coulee I found the Piegan [sic] Indians corralling a WR doggie steer. I watched them corral him and when I rode up and asked them what they were doing they informed me that they were going to kill him" as the animal was disfigured by a well-known disease normally referred to as "lump" or "big" jaw. "On telling them whose property the steer was they looked surprised and explained that … the Police had told them that they might kill any big jaws they found and they led me to believe that they had already killed some." McEachran was unmoved by the explanation. "Had I not been short-handed," he said, "I would have sent for you and had the whole gang arrested. To allow these Indians to camp there – on Tennessee creek … for weeks at a time without … men to oversee them is I think a strong temptation to commit depredations on cattle and something will have to be done."[95] Tennessee Creek was in the heart of the lower block to the west of Beaver Creek.

Along with the various men on the Walrond ranches there were usually also at least two hired women. Their job was to cook and clean for the cowboys. Usually the woman was the wife of one of the men and she was normally paid on a par with the Native workers.[96] "I note in the ranch books that former married employees of the company were paid at the rate of 60.00 per month" the onsite manager told McEachran in the 1890s. The <Shrocks> "were offered that wage to go to the Quorn

Ranche and also by Garrett of Pincher Creek, but I did not say anything about wages when I sent for them. I do not think that 60.00 would be too much to allow them – 35.00 for the man and 25 for the woman. That will be a saving of 20.00 per month in actual cash besides the economy practiced by both the man and the woman in their respective departments. The woman besides cooking will wash the company's … linen and do your washing when at the ranche. The man will save a large sum annually in blacksmith bills."[97]

The woman who perhaps stayed the longest was Annie Warnock, the wife of Dr. David Warnock, who like McEachran was a Scottish-born and educated veterinarian. He joined the operation in the late 1880s or early 1890s and stayed with it until December 1902.[98] At first his main responsibility was to manage the Clydesdale and Shire horses and then, in the late 1890s he was appointed onsite manager of the entire ranching operation.[99] Annie (née Whitlaw) was born in Ontario and then came West with her parents to farm near the Walrond. She lived with Warnock in the main ranch house from October 1897 when they were married.[100] Annie gave birth to a girl, Seslie, on 4 May 1900. She seems to have lived a rather gentile life, as the ranch normally employed at least one domestic servant for her home on Callum Creek. At the time of the 1901 census, an English girl, Bessie Haimur, was living at the Walrond headquarters.[101] Bessie, like the wives employed with cowhand husbands, did the cooking and cleaning. Annie must have been in charge of the main household, and she entertained the guests who came out to visit, including the well-heeled stockholders from the East.[102] After the Warnocks left, John Connachy was appointed manager, and he and his wife, Jean, lived in the house. The operation then also kept a Chinese cook named Wam Wing.[103]

The explanation of what the frontier environment did to the status of women in general is complex. There can be little doubt, however, that in many cases women found their status augmented by it. There were two reasons for this. One was the gender imbalance. Women gained power and status in the early West simply because men so greatly outnumbered them. Females from all levels of society were in a sense placed on a pedestal by males who vied for their attentions and/or bowed to their right to set standards of civil and moral decency.[104] Some also felt their stature augmented as they took on incredibly daunting tasks. As only limited information exists about the Walrond women, the best the historian can do to get a glimpse of their daily lives is focus on some of their peers. One was the wife of James Fergus in central Montana. When he first started ranching Fergus had a very traditional view of the position of women in the home. This is seen in a long letter he wrote to his wife Pamelia in 1879 some two years before she was to join him on the open range in Fergus County. In that letter he lectured Pamelia on her duty to be both more demure in crossing boundaries appropriate to her gender and more obsequious to her husband. "I have not had an opportunity to give you my private opinion of the disgraceful scene that took place before" some of our friends "and your own family at dinner one day last week," he wrote. "You made use of such language as never fails to disgrace or at the very least lower a female in the estimation of all respectable people." Fergus explained that the right to this type of behaviour belonged to men alone. "Profane language is allowable to men by common usage, but when used by a woman it is generally allowed that she only has to add drinking and then she is prepared to become a public woman. They are the only women whom anybody expects to hear swear and even some of them have never stooped so low."[105]

One of the things that is evident in this letter is that more than anything else Fergus was bothered by his wife's unwillingness to give into his will or to the authority he felt he had a right to assume as the head of the family. "On the day in question," I also told you that "a certain article of food was too salt," he wrote. "A good woman would have felt sorry that such was the case, would say that she would try to be more careful in the future.... In place of that you ... said it was not too salt." This was wrong mainly because it was a wife's duty to give in to her husband's judgment. If the head of the family believed the food was too salty "it was your duty to" change it. Fergus ended his diatribe with a not-so-thinly-veiled threat to end their relationship. "I would never come near such a person [as you] if circumstances did not compel me, I would let you find some lower element in which to practice your contrary nature and your profanity."[106]

After he brought Pamelia out to the ranch at Armels and Box Elder Creeks in central Montana, however, Fergus's attitude changed almost overnight. The couple seems never to have become emotionally very close, but they formed an enduring bond based on more practical considerations. Here in the wilderness where her efforts and energy were so necessary Pamelia became her husband's true partner. "Madam fails less than I do," Fergus told a friend when his own health faltered in 1883, "works hard, doing nearly all the work for nine men, makes butter, raises chickens, has flowers and plants in doors and out and is always busy."[107] When free of those duties she made carpets out of rags, braided rugs and made patchwork quilts and "always kept the purse." She also became very independent, looking after the ranch on the numerous times when James was away. During one of those times some sixteen Crow warriors stopped by. They were angry over an earlier mistreatment by white men and they showed it. However, Pamelia dealt with them "so cleverly, that, while they were at the ranch … they were friendly and grateful when they left, and no collision of any sort … occurred."[108]

Quite clearly Fergus learned to appreciate the active role his wife took in a frontier setting where supplies and services of almost every kind were wanting. At her death he told a friend that she "and I were always together and thought far more of each other than we did when we were young."[109] Most of the Walrond women who were employees along with their husbands must have worked very hard, and we can be sure that when the monthly pay was issued, it went directly to the husband rather than to them. On the other hand, given the relative scarcity of their gender and the fact that there was no one else to handle the tasks they were required to undertake, they must have been in a position to command a certain amount of respect, and not just from their husbands. "One and all" of the men who worked on the Fergus outfit "loved" Pamelia and would "do anything for her."[110] Another rancher's wife testified that her ability to maintain the household, take care of barnyard animals, and help with the ranch work gave her satisfaction and a sense of self-worth: "I do think that this is the best sort of life," she wrote. "One feels so much better and happier.… Of course, washing dishes, scrubbing floors, and all the rest of it, does sound and seem a great hardship to people at home; but … it doesn't seem so when you do it. I know I would not exchange my happy, free, busy, healthy life out here, for the weariness and *ennui* that makes so many girls at home miserable."[111] Anecdotal evidence suggests that ranching women set an example that gave frontier women in other walks of life more self-esteem and assertiveness than they might otherwise have had. It was well known, for instance, that Nancy Russell was very aggressive and effective in managing the career of her celebrated cowboy artist husband, Charlie. Most of the latter's closest friends believed that he "was not only much more successful" through her "business like methods but far happier."[112] The substantial duties the women who worked on the Walrond fulfilled, the fact that the salary they commanded, however small, added significantly to their family income, and the realization that their husband's value as an employee depended in part on his relationship with them must have provided some degree of empowerment. To say as much is not necessarily to suggest that the workload they were expected to carry in cleaning, feeding, and doing the laundry for several men was balanced. It does indicate, however, that in contemplating their lives one needs to consider the positive as well as the negative aspects.

Besides the cowboys, one or two Indians, and a couple of women on the ranch at any time, two or three individuals held supervisory posts. They were paid better than the others. Foremen got from $60 to over $80 a month depending on their credentials.[113] The clerk during Bell's years was probably paid at least that much and the onsite manager got from $100 to $150 a month. In April 1883 McEachran told T.C. Power that he was willing to pay a ranch manager "$1,000 for the first year, $1,200 for the second year and $1,500 for the third year." The amount paid the clerk, and the cattle and horse managers, also increased with time.[114] These men had fairly heavy responsibilities. The company initially ran a basic herd of 8,000 to over 9,000 head of cattle plus an annual calf crop that could vary from about 1,300 to over 2,000 depending on the weather and other conditions.[115] One of the jobs of the foreman and onsite manager was to attempt to keep track of the herd numbers as the months and years went by. This was extremely difficult throughout the open range period simply because the large majority of the animals at any one time were scattered across the land and extremely difficult to count.

Attempts to do so were occasionally made during the roundup. The usual practice was for the cowboys to move out onto the open range and gather as many of the cattle as could be found in a given pasture area, separate out all the steers and dry cows that were ready to be sent to market, and then brand and castrate any calves that had been born too late to be processed in the spring roundup. All the cattle would then be herded into specially constructed log corrals and enumerated as they exited through a gate at the end of a chute. There were two problems with this. Firstly, it was hard on the herd. Cattle that have been out on the range and separated from human contact for an extended period of time become feral. They are easily alarmed during the gathering process, and the extra stress of being chased into a small enclosure normally makes them very fearful. They become anxious, mill around a lot, and howl out their displeasure in loud mooing or baying sounds. During the whole of the process they stop eating and often lose weight. It was for that reason that one year when a count was attempted cattle buyer Archie Mclean, who had contracted to purchase the slaughter animals by the head, was very "annoyed" about the fat animals "being handled through corrals and chutes."[116] The other difficulty was that the counts were seldom incredibly precise. There were three reasons for this. Firstly, in gathering the animals the cowboys would often miss a number of them in thick forests or in very rough topography. (Note the two following photos of the Livingstone Range and the Porcupine Hills.) Secondly, since they rounded up all the animals in a particular area and then let the majority go before moving on to another area, some were likely to be counted at least twice. In later years the men learned to deal with the latter problem by marking the cattle with a bit of paint as they counted them.[117] In the beginning, however, they do not seem to have foreseen the need. The other problem was that on running down a chute the wild animals would panic in their quest for freedom, try to push past each other and often explode through the gate at the end, two or three at a time. This could easily confuse the counter. A "rough count" was attempted, ostensibly without success, in 1885 and more successfully in 1888. The latter one put the total number of cattle at 9,605, of which 1,386 were newborn calves.[118]

The first Walrond company utilized the most extensive practices possible. The ranch hired cowboys at about the ratio the promoters had recommended (one to a thousand head of stock), and the vast majority of the cattle were left to fend for themselves most of the time on the open range. Except during the two roundups most of the hired men largely watched them from the saddle and tried to prevent them from straying too far from the ranch's leased lands. One of the secrets to success the promoters had stated over and over again was to keep costs as low as possible. Along with employing only a skeleton workforce this meant avoiding investing in a lot of equipment to put up feed. The ranch was involved in a small amount of plant husbandry from the beginning. Besides mowing and stacking wild hay the men planted and mowed oats for green feed. "Farming operations have gone on very well considering the weather and we have now between thirty and forty acres plowed," Bell reported in the spring of 1887. "We have not sowed any yet owing partly to the weather and party to not being able to get seed but we will begin sowing in a few days"[119] However, the acreages under crop were far too small to produce enough roughage for any livestock over and above the work and saddle horses that were kept around the home corrals for regular use and for a few old cows with small suckling calves that were likely to die if not sheltered and attended closely when the weather was unco-operative.[120] Oats were sown in May, before the spring roundup, and the green feed was put up along with the wild hay during the weeks between the roundups.[121]

Of course, in the beginning some extra hands had to be employed to build basic infrastructure. Initially, along with housing, corrals, chutes, and squeezes were constructed at all the ranch sites so that animals could be branded or otherwise attended to when they first came in on the early drives from Montana and from the roundups. Soon stables were added in which to house the work and/or riding horses that at any one time were being used on a regular basis. Much of this work was done by contractors – small ranchers living nearby who were efficient with hammer and saw. They would agree to construct a particular facility for a certain amount stated in writing before the job was undertaken.[122] The years of the Walrond Cattle Ranche Company were the principal building period, but

SOMEBODY ELSE'S MONEY

SOMEBODY ELSE'S MONEY

some construction would continue to be necessary thereafter as greater sophistication was being incorporated into ranching practices. Years later when trying to market the ranch, McEachran would tell a prospective buyer that "we have ... cultivated and fenced lands.... Then we have buildings, lots of them, large stables, equine house, poultry house, implement sheds, corrals etc, implements of all kinds ... about 41 miles of good fencing etc."[123]

Generally speaking, within a few years of starting the first version of the Walrond ranch Duncan McEachran and Sir John Walrond could take satisfaction from the knowledge that they had accomplished a lot. They had enlisted a group of well-heeled investors and hundreds of thousand of dollars in finance capital; they had purchased a basic herd of cattle in Montana and moved them, along with the men, expertise, and equipment to operate a great new cattle empire, to the foothills of southern Alberta; they had also secured lines of communication in Montana that would enable McEachran to purchase more stock and perhaps even to do some marketing in the future;[124] and they had been able to achieve what was expected to be a lucrative outlet for their beef through contracts with the Department of Indian Affairs to regularly supply both the Peigan and Blood reserves with fresh meat. There is one very important ingredient that neither of them seems to have realized their new company required, however. To be successful it needed the undivided attention of a leader. This person needed to be someone special – someone willing to devote virtually all his energies not just to planning but also to personally seeing all the work each year to completion. One of the arguments in the next chapter will be that while McEachran alone was positioned to fulfill that role he lacked both the necessary attributes and the will.

THE WALROND CATTLE RANCH:
UPPER MANAGEMENT

Good management is vital to the survival of ranches and farms on the northwestern plains. This is the case today and it was at least equally so during the frontier period. A major disadvantage the Walrond ranch was hampered with from the beginning was that Duncan McEachran's management style was flawed in two rather obvious ways. Firstly, he had an abrasive and overbearing personality, which alienated many of his contemporaries, and, secondly, he attempted to control the entire Walrond operation for the most part from his home thousands of kilometres away in Montreal. If the first of these shortcomings was specifically a Walrond problem, numerous other great ranches on both sides of the Canadian/American border suffered from the second.

Among many of his western contemporaries McEachran was considered high-handed and arrogant. This may in part have been from envy at his eminent credentials. It was also related to his tendency to get involved in rather virulent and emotive quarrels with people with whom he disagreed. Of these conflicts the ones that brought him the most criticism centred on a number of so-called "squatters" who settled on the Walrond's lands. All the leases given out by the Dominion government prior to 1886 were "closed."[1] That meant that no outsiders could legally settle on them without the permission of the leaseholder. Nevertheless, when individual homesteaders started to trickle into the foothills region, some of them, by accident or design, located on one or the other of these leases. This was generally frowned upon by the leaseholders, but most of them eventually turned a blind eye to it primarily because they understood that there was a good deal of public sympathy for the smaller farmers and ranchers. It seems to have been based on antipathy for the select owners of the great spreads who were thought to have unfairly reserved huge pieces of prime agricultural land primarily through their connections in Ottawa.[2] The big men were aware as well of the more tangible threat that a disgruntled squatter might set their grazing lands on fire.[3] McEachran alone tried to force all squatters off his land. His usual practice in dealing with them was to call on the courts to issue eviction notices.[4] This always caused resentment and in time it immersed him in four well-publicized conflicts that sealed his image as a bully.

In the early 1880s two brothers, James and Anthony Dixon, settled on separate quarters several kilometres north of the town of Pincher Creek on the south end of the lower Walrond ranch. In 1890, McEachran had them served with a statement of claim demanding that the land be returned to him and prohibiting them from cutting hay or erecting fences. This prevented the Dixons from putting up feed for their live-stock and forced them to hire a herder to keep the Walrond cattle out of their crops. It seems undeniable that they had a moral right to the land. It had first been occupied in 1880, prior to the Walrond lease, by a man named George McKay. The Dixons bought out McKay on 26 June 1884 and then finished building a house, some granaries, corrals, and cattle sheds. They also broke twenty-six acres of land and put up two miles of fences to keep their cattle from straying. C.E.D. Woods, the editor of the *Macleod Gazette* who always took the settlers' side against leaseholders, estimated that the improvements were worth about $1,500 and noted that prior to the dispute Dr. McEachran had visited the Dixons and made no objection to their right to the land.[5] The doctor's "position cannot have a little authority and law on his side without grossly abusing it," Wood asserted, "and without setting the whole country by the ears, it is time that he should be deprived of both." McEachran persisted, however, and eventually the Dixons were forced to give up their holdings without recompense.

Some eight years later a similar case led to "a bitter grievance" being "aired" against McEachran. In 1883 J.D. O'Neil settled on the Walrond range, "picked a quarter, erected a two storey house and a good barn" and built corrals. He then went east for his family and during the return trip he happened to meet McEachran on the train and he pleaded for permission to "homestead where he had built." McEachran refused either to grant O'Neil and his family the permission or to pay any sort of compensation for the improvements. Bitterly, O'Neil was forced to take another homestead near Calgary.[6]

In both of these cases McEachran carefully worked within the law. In one dispute, however, he demonstrated that he was prepared to go beyond legal means when he felt it necessary to achieve his ends. In 1890, Robert Dunbar was informed by the Department of the Interior that his homestead patent on land that was part of the Walrond lease had been cancelled, and shortly thereafter McEachran formally instructed him to leave. Dunbar's land had first been leased to a John Hollies. In 1888 the Hollies lease had been terminated as a consequence of a government effort to cut down on land speculation. The Walrond had agreed to take over the lease in exchange for 29,000 acres near Fort Macleod that the government wanted for settlement.[7] The Hollies lease had not been closed, but the Department of the Interior's position, and the one strenuously put forward by McEachran, was that since the Walrond had given up a holding that had been acquired under the original 1881 legislation in exchange for this land, it should be subject to the provisions of the earlier legislation. Therefore it was closed to settlement. When Dunbar received the eviction notice, however, he must have been incredulous. He had been on the site since 1882.[8] With the help of two sons who had joined him the following year, Dunbar had built a home, plowed some land, and begun grazing cattle. Moreover, his right to the land must have seemed as defensible in law as McEachran's. A patent had been granted him in 1888 and pre-emption rights given.[9] His sons had then built a house and settled near him.[10]

Dunbar refused to leave, and in late July 1891 cowboys from the Walrond outfit rode out to the house his sons had built and pulled it down. John Lamar wrote to McEachran a few days after the incident: "we met [one of the Dunbars] ... on our way over, and we told him what we was going to do and he forbid us doing it but we went ahead and pulled it down all the same. The whole tribe of them are boiling over with wrath."[11] The Dunbars were powerless to stop the cowboys because they were badly outnumbered and they undoubtedly knew of Lamar's proficiency with a six-shooter.[12] On 25 September 1891 several opposition MPs questioned Edgar Dewdney, then Minister of the Interior, in the House of Commons as to why settlers had been turned off land to which they had received homestead rights.[13] Dewdney admitted that the Dunbar brothers had been on the land since the early 1880s and had been granted a patent, but this, he said, had been a mistake.[14] The conflict appears finally to have been resolved when the Dunbars were offered compensation by the government for their land and improvements.[15]

It is indicative of local opinion that on another occasion when a squatter had the nerve to stand up to McEachran it was the squatter who received the lion's share of public support. Sometime in the 1880s Dave Cochrane, a retired North West Mounted Policeman, settled on Walrond range. As the Dunbar case was unfolding, McEachran ordered Cochrane off his land and, as usual, without compensation. However, when the latter threatened to set fire to the Walrond pastures McEachran agreed to turn the matter over to arbitration. Three neighbouring ranchers, Lew Murray, who had once worked for the Walrond,[16] John Herron, and Billy Hyde, were selected as arbitrators. Almost certainly sensing public opinion, the three men ruled that Cochrane should leave but that first McEachran should pay him the comparatively large sum of $2,700 for his improvements.[17] The fact that this was considered a defeat for McEachran brought him no empathy in the foothills region. Later, with the urging of Wood, twenty-five settlers in the Porcupine Hills petitioned the House of Commons to cancel the ranch's lease and open all the others for homesteading.[18] "Probably no single man or company was ever more thoroughly unpopular," Wood asserted in one of his editorials, "if the Walrond ranche company chooses to dig its own grave, and then deliberately walk into it, it is no one's business but its own."[19] It was the realization that the system was unpopular as well as a barrier to dense settlement that would prompt the Dominion government to announce cancellation of all the original big leases in 1896.[20]

The fights with settlers were the most prolonged and widely publicized that McEachran found himself in, but there were a number of others. When, for instance, he disagreed with some of the actions of the Southwest Stock Association, he separated from it rancorously. "I find that we were taxed the sum of $410.40 for the association last year," he wrote to the president, "and as I cannot learn from any source that we derive any corresponding benefit from our connection with it, and particularly as there seems no disposition to endeavour to increase its usefulness, I beg hereby to with-draw the name of this Company from membership."[21] About the same time McEachran got into a heated dispute with Wood over the question of the seriousness of an outbreak of the dreaded cattle disease known as the mange. When McEachran claimed that after a mild outbreak the disease "had entirely disappeared," Wood accused him of a cover-up. He charged that the Dominion Livestock Inspector had based his declaration on the condition of the Walrond cattle alone, thus implying that he was concerned only about his own animals when he should be leading a campaign to stamp out the disease. When very serious outbreaks were to severely damage roaming herds in later years Wood's remarks would appear most pertinent.[22]

"Vigorous" exchanges of "editorials and letters" kept controversy between Wood and McEachran alive through the 1880s and into the following decade,[23] and there can be little doubt that all these incidents negatively affected the Walrond's relationship with neighbouring ranchers. In 1891 someone apparently incensed over McEachran's unbending attitude towards settlement fired several shots at one of the ranch houses. According to Edward Brado, ranch/settler relations deteriorated to the point where the Mounties were forced for a time to provide McEachran with protection.[24] The greatest negative aspect of this for the Walrond ranch was that it increased its exposure to rustling. The impact of settler rustling on the cattle herds of all the big operations appears to have been an even bigger problem than cowhand predation during the open range period. As all the herds were able to wander miles away from their owners' holdings and mix and mingle with other herds, homesteaders and squatters alike were consistently tempted to take strays that did not belong to them, particularly if the animals were unbranded. The settlers could be particularly ruthless when they felt that they or their kind had any substantial grievances against a specific operation. McEachran must have realized this, as it had been made clear to the Cochrane ranch even while he was still associated with it.

The Cochrane turned its initial herd loose on its first lease west of Calgary in the fall of 1881. The cattle had been branded only superficially before the drive north from Montana, and the following spring the manager, Major James Walker, set out with his cowhands to round them up and brand them properly. In gathering the cattle the cowboys were assisted by settlers in the district, who seem to have been a bit awed by the big ranch and therefore to have got some satisfaction from helping out. Many also had unbranded cattle scattered on the range that they hoped to retrieve. They soon realized that the Cochrane had no intention of helping them. One rancher owned a cow and calf that he had "made pets of" and kept around his home place. He saw the animals being swept into the corrals and roped for branding. With strong support from one of the foremen the rancher objected. Reflecting McEachran's attitude, however, Walker refused to be moved and the animals were processed with the rest. This lost the Cochrane the support of the settlers, who immediately stopped helping and began heading home. In the days that followed some of them rustled every Cochrane animal they could find. "Many a secret coulee, many a distant ravine and sidehill [sic], still held" the ranch's cattle "and these settlers knew the country much better than the Cochrane men did." They "kept on gleaning, until a very respectable number ... were diverted to individual ranches, without the exchange of a dollar."[25]

Over the years numerous incidents described in the newspapers showed that prejudices against the big ranchers continued to grow. In 1904, for instance, James Shea from the High River area was convicted of stealing and rebranding horses. He stated that "the big men had continually stolen from him" and he was simply "getting even."[26] The Walrond was subject to a great deal of pillaging and there is little doubt that local biases made it significantly worse than it would otherwise have been. In his history of the ranching frontier, L.V. Kelly applied his considerable literary and satirical flare to describing several telling incidents involving Walrond stock. In 1892 he notes "a cow bearing the distinctive WR ... brand was seen on the range lavishing huge affection on a calf that carried a 77 hair brand, and returned the affection of the mature mammal with great vigor, wiggling his tail and gamboling around in the excess of great family joy." There was little question that the two animals were "mother and child, despite the man-made evidence to the contrary in the shape of dissimilar brands." John Mitchell, who owned the 77 ranch, "was arrested and tried on the charge of stealing the calf." He was acquitted for lack of clear proof against him.[27] Several years later "an elderly lady, named Broulette, mother of a number of sons who were well-known among the Southern stockmen, had been deprived of support from this offspring by the interception of the law, which took several of them away from her and sent them to the penitentiary for irregularities with regard to other people's stock." At that point the lady had no one to support her, so, when John Elgin, "an elderly settler of over fifty years, came into her life, she fell madly in love with him and they married." Winter was approaching and their love "needed something more than kisses to keep soul in body." Consequently, the bride and groom went "on a short moonlit honeymoon trip" during which they stole a Walrond steer. The two were arrested, and each was sentenced to five years in jail.[28] In August 1896 William Morgan, a rather "'intensive' breeder," settled on Halfbreed Creek near Walrond pastures. At that time he had eighteen cows, four calves, and eighteen steers. "On November 2nd, 1896 Mr. Morgan had a herd of eighty-nine head, by police count, including eighteen calves. These remarkable indications of breeding possibilities … astounded the Police but brought no other results, because in a prosecution the Crown must prove ownership before they can make a case." A little later Morgan "and a man named Conger, both of whom had been under police surveillance as a result of the prolific increase" in their herd, "were arrested and charged with stealing a calf from a cow that had a 'W' brand, but the case was dismissed, the learned judge holding that the prosecution had not proven" guilt.[29]

Other examples of this kind of rustling are not difficult to find.[30] Even more disturbing is evidence that beef merchant Patrick Burns might have been complicit, along with a number of lesser cattlemen, in some sort of organized cattle theft that involved altering brands and adding new ones. In 1892 D.H. Andrews of the Stair ranch wrote to the

Glengarry Ranch Company with some rather serious charges. "We have found one of our three year old steers, branded 76 and plain earmark … vented with your brand and also with Mr. Burns's brand on it. I hear you have delivered a number of cattle to Mr. Burns during the spring months and that most of them were killed before the spring round up" and also that "three other firms have found their cattle branded as our steer has been."[31] While no charges appear to have been laid against Burns or the Glengarry operation there can be little doubt that something devious was going on. About eight years later the Walrond employees found evidence of the same sort of thing with their cattle. On 12 November 1900 Warnock wrote an angry and accusatory letter to Burns about a steer marked with his brand and the Walrond brand. "Your explanation is that he is one of the steers purchased from us in 1897," and branded at Cayley, where the fatter animals were loaded onto railway cars for shipment to a slaughter plant.

> As far as I am aware no WR cattle were branded at Cayley or anywhere else. The only delivery made at Cayley was the last turnover in 1897 and those cattle were not branded [with your brand]. We arrived at Cayley with the cattle at noon on November 1st and the same day shipped 103 head, and Mr. Lane [your agent] handed me a cheque in payment for the whole bunch. Next morning the balance of 165 head started en route to Namaka... We sent a man to assist in driving the cattle to Namaka. When I asked Mr. Lane what was going to be done with the cattle taken to Namaka, he informed me that they would be held and fed there until shipped to Calgary and slaughtered. If any of these cattle were branded at Namaka we were not notified, and would not have consented to their being branded without being vented [i.e., having the existing brands obliterated with a hot iron]. It is possible that the steer … [was] sold to you by someone who had no right to him. We have never made a practice of selling cattle to be branded and turned loose and if we did we would most certainly see that they were vented. I should be pleased to learn from you

whether any of the cattle referred to were branded at Namaka, and whether any more are supposed to be on the range.[32]

Warnock had similar concerns about sales to beef merchants Gordon and Ironsides of Winnipeg, with whom Burns was forging a close working relationship.[33] In 1898 he asked cattle buyer A.J. McLean to send him a statement of the numbers of animals he had purchased from the Walrond and the points from which they had been shipped. His "object," he said, was "to straighten out some shipments of Gordon and Ironsides, in which W.R. cattle were found," presumably by the brand inspectors. The Winnipeg buyers were not being co-operative and the dates of their shipments did not seem to coincide with the dates on which Walrond cattle had been sold.[34] By this time settlement was bringing a lot more small ranchers and farmers to the foothills, and Warnock understood that they could pilfer unattended stock a few at a time more or less at will to rebrand and sell. It is an illustration of his concern that soon after he wrote the letter to Burns he placed an ad in the local paper warning "cattle shippers and others ... against receiving any cattle of our brand from anyone who does not produce written authority to deliver such." He also offered a $200 reward for "the conviction of anyone guilty of appropriating, killing, branding, selling or shipping unlawfully cattle or horses belonging to us."[35] The fact that this ad singled out "shippers" tells us that Warnock himself was far from convinced that people like Burns and Gordon and Ironsides were guiltless. Warnock later told his boss he disliked dealing with Burns and from that point on the ranch would not do so until forced to liquidate its entire stock after the disastrous winter of 1906/07.[36] By then Burns and his Winnipeg associates were to have gained almost total control of the beef trade.

Evidence suggests that rustling continued to increase as homesteading on the plains proceeded. As late as the autumn of 1906 a police report from the Lethbridge area stated that rustling appeared to have increased in the past year and that it was the settler who was most responsible for it. From the rapid growth "of some of the herds in this district, and from the numerous reports received," the problem seemed to be getting worse, the report noted; "this is not the same class of work as is done by ...

[those], who take chances and drive their ill-gotten gains north for sale." In this case a settler or homesteader "rides the ranges with a running iron strapped to his saddle generally in stormy weather and picks up calves which have arrived at the age to be easily weaned from their mothers. It is only a work of a few minutes for these experts to rope the calf and drive it to some place where it is held till it would not be claimed by the mother, or recognized by the owner."[37]

McEachran's personality thus worked against the eventual success of the Walrond ranch. The manner in which he actually ran the ranch, or his management technique, was even more problematic. Until his retirement as the Dominion Livestock Inspector in 1902 his usual practice was to actually be on the ranch for only a week or two once or twice each year. Even after he retired he might only be there for a couple of four- to six-week periods. Because of this he had to leave the Walrond's fortunes most of the time in the hands of hired men. Present day ranchers and farmers will testify that this approach seldom works, and not just because of the wage expense or the problem of theft. On the northern plains, where growing seasons are short, weather unpredictable, especially in the spring and fall months, and winters severe, agriculture requires a hands-on approach. Someone with a vested interest needs to be on the job, particularly at peak performance periods, to see that the work gets done properly. As John W. Bennett notes:

> The seasonal round of ranching everywhere is governed by the needs of the livestock population. It is a full year of activities since cows, unlike crops, do not have a dormant season. ... The winter season was ... a period of constant inspection and feeding in which the rancher had to tour his pasture areas delivering ... hay and keeping the water sources open and running. In unusually inclement weather he would need to move his herd into more sheltered areas. If the winter was very cold, he might run short of hay, and have to seek out supplies he could buy. Spring is the time of calving, and summer the period of weaning and branding and the constant manipulation of the herds to ensure adequate natural pasture. Fall ...

for the "cow-calf" rancher, was the time of sell off of spring calves ... but some ranchers wintered their calves to get higher prices for the heavier animals in spring. Some ranchers mixed the two regimes. In any case, the animals need care the year round.[38]

It might be added that during mating season the cattle producer also needed to be out on his pastures seeing that enough bulls were mingling, as they should with the cows so that breeding could proceed efficiently and the calves would be born early the next spring. He also needed to ensure that certain bulls mixed with certain cows so that bloodlines were retained and improved. And he had to be careful to closely monitor all his cows so he knew which ones were not engendering top quality offspring on a regular basis and thus should be sold so the money could be turned into new and better animals rather than going to waste.

It was also essential for the rancher to keep costs on things like fencing supplies and equipment, medicines, harness, horses, tack, and feed as low as possible and to avoid waste. The point is that to be successful the ranch, then as now, needed to be attended to by someone who really, genuinely cared. That someone is normally the owner and his family rather than a hired man whose relationship with the operation is based strictly on wages and who cannot feel the same sense of urgency – either to make a profit or simply to survive. As noted above, between 1883 and 1907 McEachran always had a second-in-command on the place. Presumably the men who filled that position were considered very capable. David Warnock, who was the horse manager in the late 1880s and much of the 1890s and the onsite general manager from 1898 to 1903, was well educated and intelligent. He was married and settled, he knew livestock and their needs, and he was relatively conscientious. He had some money of his own but, interestingly, he refused an invitation from McEachran to invest in the Walrond and, at times, he showed a tendency to evade responsibility for problems on the ranch.[39] When, for instance, a count of the cattle came up well short of expectations his prime concern seemed to be to avoid the blame. In a letter to McEachran over which he agonized for some time, and which he rewrote at least once, he first tried to downplay the shortage by arguing that the men counting the cattle had missed 10 per cent of the herd because of poor weather. Then he contended that "we are short principally in cows ranging from six to ten years old." This enabled him to propose that the shortage was "largely due to the ravages of wolves," before he had become the manager. His estimation that it was mainly the older cows that were deficient is dubious. Accurately estimating the percentages of cattle in various age categories in a particular herd is hard even for practised veterans and under the best of conditions. In the circumstances of the open range, it was next to impossible. To further underscore the point that much of the shortage had occurred before he took over control, Warnock also reminded his boss that earlier winters had been "severe, and the loss among breeding stock may have been heavier than we realized." Finally, indirectly emphasizing that he himself had at least once warned that the contracts to sell beef to the Indians were hurting the ranch's cash flows,[40] he noted that before he had become onsite manager "hay was fed to beef cattle" for those contracts "which perhaps could have been more profitably fed to weak cows."[41]

Most modern cattlemen know that it is next to impossible to find someone to nurture their animals with the requisite attention to detail. Hired men, even conscientious ones, which Warnock appears to have been, just cannot care quite as much as the man who is concerned about the question of whether or not he is actually making any money.[42] The difference is that the owner far more than his employee is traumatized by the thought of the value of his livestock inventory fading. To all appearances Warnock tried to do a good job, but, given his tendency to rationalize, one suspects that when riding among the cattle during cold and stormy weather his concern for the stock might have been compromised by the thought of the warmth and comfort of the house he had left. Of course, the size of the ranch and the fact that the animals were spread out over vast distances dictated that Warnock had to rely on his cowpunchers to do much of the monitoring. This made the chance of the job being done properly even less likely.

When cows were calving in stormy weather, it was necessary to have men riding night and day amongst them conscientiously looking for newborn animals to make sure they were being sheltered and nurtured properly. When wolves were a major problem, some men had to be designated to spend long spells keeping the beasts at bay. Rationalizations such as "I haven't seen many new calves (or wolves) tonight – might as well call it a day," or "I haven't checked the south pasture recently but things will probably be okay over there till morning" were not good enough. One feels quite certain that many of the workers on the larger, corporate spreads were susceptible to such reasoning; and despite all the hype about their dedication and loyalty it seems beyond doubt that the worst of them actually stole some of the cattle for which they were supposed to be caring. To grapple with this problem, someone who, like McEachran, had a financial stake in the Walrond should consistently have been around to ensure that the best men were attending to their duties and the worst were singled out and released.

James Fergus and his son Andrew's livestock operation, though modest by the Walrond's standards, eventually became one of the bigger outfits in Montana.[43] Their approach, typical of that of many family units on the Great Plains, provides an instructive contrast to McEachran's. Fergus seldom made much money. He complained many times about the losses he sustained from a plethora of sources. "It is," he once said, "hard scratch to make both ends meet raising cattle and horses now on bank interest with water fenced up, losing so many by wolves, hard winters ... thieves and mud holes in spring."[44] He once told his half-brother William that he was so worried about his debts that he and his wife were "not spending a dime that we can get along without. I have not a decent pair of [boots] or shoes.... Mrs. Fergus is the same and our house needs many things but we go without rather than go any further into debt."[45] Yet the ranch remained in family hands until son Andrew finally decided to sell out when he reached retirement age.[46] One reason the Fergus outfit survived while many great ranches did not is that James and Andrew lived and laboured on the ranch themselves. During his lifetime James agonized over every penny spent and tried as much as possible to moderate every loss his company took from both natural and market forces. Moreover, as we have seen, he worked in full partnership with his wife, Pamelia.[47]

The Ferguses relied on hired men too, but they kept a close watch on them. When James figured they were being recalcitrant he had no qualms about intervening. In March 1899, for instance, when he was well into his eighties and suffering all the infirmities that come with age,[48] he caught some of the crew loitering. "I went into the Bunk house yesterday and found one man cleaning harness something he done before and six doing nothing. Among them Johnson our foreman and one of our men, the rest were outsiders. I done a little talking, took Johnson into my room and done a little talking to him." Johnson told me that "the roads and grounds were so icy he could not ride." I told him, "it was not icy enough to keep him from helping to clean harness." Johnson said "he was not hired to clean harness," to which I replied, "he was hired to work and must do it."[49]

Along with his loose management practices and difficult personality, Duncan McEachran had one other significant, though less obvious, weakness – an eternal optimism, which he tended to articulate whenever it seemed likely to serve his own private interests. Alfred Earnest Cross once told Billy Cochrane that he was "very glad" Cochrane believed "the price of beef would be up, as I cannot make up my mind even yet that it is going to be very high. McEachran has a habit of talking in rather an extravagant way especially about the cattle business."[50] Cross's assessment was well founded. This is illustrated in a letter McEachran wrote in 1882 to tempt T.C. Power to buy half his shares in the Cochrane organization. In the letter he grossly underplayed the horrendous death losses the ranch was known recently to have suffered and blamed them on his onsite manager, though he, himself, was to some considerable degree responsible.[51] Then he cited the long list of resources the ranch now had to call on. Everything is now "in good shape, we put 8,500" cattle "or there about on last year, this year we bought from Poindexter and Orr 4,300 or there about of cattle nearly pure short horn, besides several small lots of steers from Baker & Co. and others – and about 125 ample Hereford and Angus bulls – besides 80 short horn.... We have also about 500 horses, 167 mares new served this summer, 2 Thoroughbred stallions – 2 Imported Clydes, and a Spanish Jack. We are entitled to and must get 10,000 acres of land at $1.25 per acre" from the Canadian government, "the only company which will get this privilege. We have also two coal mining rights on the range where we have unlimited coal fields."[52] McEachran went on to surpass the most outrageously optimistic estimates of the promotional literature by predicting that "if we get through this winter all safe it will make at least from all sources, fifty-per cent on the investment per annum – exclusive of lands or coal butts of which in the near future will be very profitable. By this you will see that" if you become a shareholder, "it will pay you both directly and indirectly and I trust that this is not the only good thing I will be able to turn in your way and which you can reciprocate."

Even as McEachran wrote the above letter the Cochrane herds were being overwhelmed a second time by fierce blizzards and he was involved in negotiations to join the Walrond group.[53] In February 1883, he was still claiming that the losses "are very much exaggerated.... So far as we now know" they "will not exceed two per cent on the whole stock and that only on the Pilgrim cattle" (yearling steers brought in from the East).[54] "There have been no losses on the range cattle so far as yet reported," and our new manager "keeps nothing from us." It was soon to become common knowledge that this and the previous winter had destroyed over three-quarters of the Cochrane stock and that McEachran was no longer associated with it.[55]

In truth McEachran should be seen as a promoter rather than a rancher in the traditional sense. This statement will be illustrated here in a number of ways, but for now one more example will perhaps suffice. Sometime between the First World War and his death in 1924 he was to go on an urgent campaign to sell the Walrond ranch. By that time the operation was completely insolvent. Its cattle herds had been reduced to almost nothing by inclement weather, predators, and disease, and its resources were far short of what was required to pay off even its own shareholders.[56] Yet McEachran repeated virtually all the assessments and faulty reasoning of Brisbin, McCoy, Richthofen, and Latham in a pamphlet he wrote to attract buyers.[57] He began by exploiting these writers' myths about the grasslands. In western Canada there is, he noted, "a vast area of the land forming the foothills of the Rockies extending from the base of the mountains eastward a hundred miles or more, and from the

Boundary Line northward for three or four hundred."[58] This region has "soil of the heaviest black loam several feet deep, the natural grasses of the richest and most nutritious quality, which not only grow luxuriantly during summer, but owing to the dryness of the climate, cure on their stalks and retain their nutritive qualities similar to hay during the winter."[59]

Though he had by then lost thousands of cattle to winter storms – particularly during the infamous winter of 1906/07 – McEachran announced that cattle and horses could be left to "run out the entire year finding their own food and shelter."[60] He also reiterated the importance of size: "a herd of 10,000 head will be proportionately more profitable than one of 3000," because the outlay for "wages, supplies … corrals, stables, wagons, mowers, [and] rakes," will be more or less constant. "And except during the 'round-up'"[61] the bigger operation will require "only one or two more men" while "the cash return from the sale of steers will be three and a third times as much and the increase in calves correspondingly larger. It is no exaggeration to say that the sun does not shine on a country better adapted to stockraising, on a large scale, than Alberta. Spring is early and usually mild, summer is never very hot... The rain fall is such as to insure abundance of grass while running streams and never failing springs abound everywhere in the foot-hills and on the open prairie, lakes and marshes afford ample water at all seasons excepting winter when they are frozen over."[62] In order to resist pro-settler policies in Ottawa McEachran had over the years almost certainly helped promote the view that the region was not capable of producing regular crops.[63] This did not stop him from describing what was then left of the Walrond ranch as "about 39,000 acres of free-hold land not excelled in Alberta" for "mixed farming" as well as ranching.[64]

McEachran's tendency to dream unrealistically was significant in bringing the Walrond Ranche Company to life as it was unquestionably an important factor in persuading Sir John Walrond and other investors to support the project in the first place. As the next chapter will demonstrate, there can be no doubt that the same tendencies helped to create cash shortages that would eventually put the Walrond out of business. The clearest indication of this is McEachran's policy of paying dividends to his shareholders in years that were obviously very bad for the ranch as well as those that appeared quite good. McEachran was not alone in adopting this policy. He was just one of a number of ranch managers on the Great Plains who got themselves into a position where they felt they had no other option.

THE FIRST GREAT KILLING WINTER

While Sir John Walrond and Duncan McEachran could enjoy the sensation of watching their planning and work come to fruition on the Walrond ranch in the 1880s, they must also have felt somewhat uneasy as discomfiting signs soon presented themselves. Firstly, the price of beef in Canada continued a slow but steady decline that was not to let up until the turn of the twentieth century. Canadian historians like to emphasize the importance of the so-called "beef bonanza" in stimulating the rise of the western cattle industry in this country.[1] In fact the only such event that occurred took place in the 1870s, ending within a few years, well before men like Matthew Cochrane and Sir John Walrond ever contemplated entering the business. Between 1870 and 1873 average yearly prices nationally for live steers ranged from 7.8 to 7.21 cents a pound. They then dropped to 5.8 cents in 1874, to 5.75 cents in 1883, to 4.3 cents in 1887 and then all the way down to 3.02 cents in 1896.[2] While they thus watched prices weaken consistently over the course of their first five years it must have seemed equally worrisome to everyone with a financial stake in the company that the expected rapid natural increase in herd size, which all the promoters had predicted, did not materialize. Unable most years to get a precise tally of the overall numbers of cattle in the herds, foreman Jim Patterson did manage to count the newborn calves, since the crews had to brand and/or castrate the animals one at a time as they conducted the roundups. His reports showed the annual calf crop actually declining almost every year. From 1885 to 1887 the total numbers branded in the annual spring and fall roundups fell from 2,407 to 1,464, or by nearly 40 per cent – this despite the fact that McEachran continued to augment his herds with Montana stock.[3]

There are several explanations for this. In the first place, despite McEachran's positive remarks in the one letter to Power, there were initially a high percentage of old and/or poorly bred cows in the first herds brought in from Montana. To upgrade the overall quality Patterson sent a lot of these animals to slaughter.[4] What made this particularly economic in his mind was that the contracts the Walrond and other ranches got from the Department of Indian Affairs gave them the right to sell meat of almost any quality for Native consumption. The ranchers got the same price per pound for the meat from old, "stringy," and even diseased cows that they got for good, young steer meat. The department seems to have realized that since the buffalo had disappeared and the alternative for the Indians was starvation, they were unlikely to complain about quality. This was also, of course, a great way to help the earliest ranchers get started and thus to open the West to settlement. The ranchers themselves saw this as a real advantage. Bell once told his boss that "when you can get the price of a good steer for a cow over ten or twelve years of age you had much better let her go even if you buy young cows to replace them." Remember, he said, "the [original] herd contained a large number of old cows and we understood that one of the chief benefits the company would derive from the contract" to supply the Indians, "would be to turn them into money and get the herd cleaned up."[5]

As a disproportionate number of cows were sent to slaughter in this period the annual calf crop obviously had to be affected. Another obstacle to successful calving on the frontier was the high percentage of cows that gave birth during the fall, winter, and early spring when the weather could be extremely harsh. The reason for this was that the bulls were left with them throughout the year and thus it was impossible for ranchers to control the time of conception. Naturally enough a greater percentage of the out–of–season calves succumbed to the elements than would have been the case if they had been born in the late spring or early summer. Moreover, since many were born at a time of year when the grass was covered with snow, the mothers often had difficulty taking on enough nutrition from grazing to recuperate after calving and thus to sustain both themselves and their offspring. Most modern cattlemen in the foothills region ensure that their calves are born sometime between the beginning of March and late May. This is relatively easy to achieve. They know that the bovine gestation period is nine months so they put their bulls with the herds in July and then remove them in late August or early September. A difficulty for any frontier rancher who wanted to time his calving was that because there were no fences separating his herds from those of his neighbours, he could still not prevent indiscriminate fraternization between his cows and "scrub" bulls owned by other ranchers who refused to adopt the same system.[6] McEachran attempted to get the cattlemen in the Pincher Creek district to co-operate in timing their breeding but to no avail. "I find quite a difference of opinion exists as to the taking up of the bulls," he wrote to his head office in July 1887, "the Pincher Creek district are so much in favour of it, although they were the people who were so much opposed to it when I first proposed it, that now they have applied to the N.W. Council to make Pincher Creek a Bull district, so that they can force every one within the district and ten miles around it to take them up.... There is no range in the country as well supplied with good young bulls as ours."[7] However, the measure was eventually dropped, in part, it would seem, because of the impossibility of getting all the neighbours to cooperate.

Also responsible for the failure of the plan, and every bit as important, was that it would have meant the sudden loss in the introductory year of all the late calves. When the Walrond was getting around 1,400 calves a year it usually got between 400 and 650 out of season. Those that survived long enough were branded and counted with the rest. Had breeding suddenly been timed in a given year in order to prevent all the non-seasonal cows from being bred, none of them would have produced a calf and the overall calf count that year would have been proportionately even lower than usual. McEachran would have felt uncomfortable reporting this to his shareholders, particularly as he had led them to expect the weather to be mild year round and had convinced them that the Walrond herd would keep pace with the marvellous rates of growth predicted in the promotional literature. "Pulling the bulls won't work and is not practicable," Bell told him. First, he said, we don't have the necessary facilities to pen up the bulls for part of the year and "besides taking them out [even] in the latter part of Oct[ober] and the early part of Nov[ember] would mean no calves after July – do you really want that?"[8] The answer quite clearly was "no." At this early stage, when experience on the northern Great Plains had not yet convinced them that long inclement periods were a fact of prairie life, it was easier for McEachran and his men to cling to the belief that the heavy losses they were experiencing would prove anomalous.

In the 1890s, when they would finally come to the conclusion that severe winter weather was the norm, a majority of the ranchers in the area would agree to co-operate in timing their breeding and they would build the requisite infrastructure to pen up their bulls. However, they were never able to achieve total co-operation and their efforts proved only marginally successful.[9] In the late winter of 1902 David Warnock told McEachran that "a few calves are beginning to appear on the range but these are brought in as found and are being sheltered. The cows must have been served by bulls running loose in Willow Creek district last spring. Quite a number ... were found running at large."[10]

A decline in calf numbers was also what a rancher today would expect were he to leave his breeding stock to wander alone and unsuper-vised most of the time. When giving birth pregnant cows, particularly young ones, often need human intervention to pull calves that have got too big in the womb and thus are a challenge to the birth canal. If that is lacking, the birthing process can often be so difficult that both calf and would-be mother die in the process. Ranchers and farmers who have adopted a much more intensive system in the modern period than the Walrond and other big frontier ranches utilized put their cows in small pastures during calving season, hand feed them and watch them day and night, treating each newborn animal as a precious commodity. Conse-quently calving rates of 90 per cent and even better are not uncommon.

Environmental conditions that periodically threatened all roam-ing livestock were the other factor in declining calf numbers. As noted previously, predation was particularly problematic on the Walrond. As we will see, diseases that spread easily as numerous herds mingled over great distances also took their toll. Above all, extreme weather exacted a high price. The Walrond's calf crop fell consistently in this period, but the biggest drop was after its first really devastating winter – that of 1886/87. The destruction that rained down on steers, heifers, cows, calves, and bulls alike was described by Bell in the spring of 1887 when he sent the "monthly statements and stock sheets" to Montreal. "You will notice that I have not given the numbers dead," he wrote, "there is so many dead around both of our own and other peoples" that a proper count is impossible to achieve.

> Besides the cattle are greatly scattered. Quite a number crossed the river during the bad weather and are now scattered in over Freeze Out and the country about there and when the mild weather came a great many crossed the hills onto Willow Creek, Meadow Creek[11] and the country about there so that all I could do would be to make a guess and I do not see that there would be any benefit derived from my doing that. The loss I think will be about 10% of the whole though of course much varies in some classes of stock.... The chief losses will be on cows calves and bulls. The loss among bulls ... will be especially severe as they went into the winter in poor condition."[12]

Three weeks later Bell reported that the situation had deteriorated. "The bad weather during the first part of the month had pretty serious effect on the cattle," he wrote, "as they were not in condition to stand it and as it came during the first rush of calving it killed quite a number of both cows and calves."[13]

McEachran at first attempted to play down the devastation in his own reports to his directors and shareholders.[14] However, once the spring roundup was over he realized that the calf numbers could not be refuted. He was required by contract to provide "an annual Statement of the Affairs of the Company in Canada with certified inventories of the cattle and horses and other live and dead stock of or belonging to the Company with balance sheet shewing assets and liabilities and receipts and any expenditures." The annual statement was to be verified by auditors appointed by the board of directors. This should have meant that accountants were required to go out to the ranch and count and estimate the value of every last animal and even measure and estimate the worth of any other liquid assets on the ranch, including hay and green feed. However, that obviously was out of the question. Most years the only record that could realistically be utilized was Patterson's little black book in which he placed a mark every time a calf was branded.

McEachran thus had to report exactly how many calves were born. His disquiet is evinced in a letter to the company accounting firm in London. "We finished the round up last night here and I regret to say the number of calves fall far short even of what I anticipated, making every allowance for winter and spring losses. The number actually branded is 965 with probably a hundred unbranded being too young. The number of dry cows in every roundup is enormous." Every ranch but the Co-chrane "is in the same position" and many are "even worse off. I fear our losses have been greater than we at first thought but only in cows and heifers – probably 18 per cent of them – but the steers and adult she stock and on bulls – 5 per cent will cover it."[15] The count book actually gives the total number of calves processed in the July roundup as 996.[16] It should be noted that the 1887 spring roundup was undertaken about two weeks late and, therefore, relatively speaking, more of the pregnant cows than would otherwise have been the case had given birth. In other words the losses were even worse than on the surface it appeared. As usual the ranch conducted a second roundup to brand the calves that were born too late for the spring gathering. It too was disappointing. After care-fully looking over the cow herd in September, Bell told the company secretary-treasurer, James G. Ross, that "calf branding will commence in a few days and I will be able to tell how it turns out pretty soon.... The prospects are that it will turn out well in proportion to the spring branding but not nearly up to our average, possibly one half as much as the spring branding."[17] His estimate was about right. That fall 468 head were branded. This might be compared with 558 in the fall of 1885 and 646 in the fall of 1886.[18]

Whether McEachran purposely held back the spring roundup in order to make the disaster look less devastating than it really was is impossible to know for sure. Viewed against his later actions, however, it does not seem improbable. In his letter to the accountants he admitted that his earlier estimation of death losses in the herd generally was far too low, and he attempted to rationalize it: "Shortly after arriving here I rode industriously over the range, in all places where ... [cattle] were said to be lying dead," and I "could not count many hundreds of carcasses, and supposing I had only seen half of them" I felt "justified in believing that not over 2/3 of these were ours. Hence I could not believe that our loss was heavy. Yet it is a fact that we are short of cattle – to a larger extent than the carcasses would represent." He also pointed out that he was not the only one who had been guilty of underestimating the disaster. "Mr. Godsol of Pincher Creek who had about 800 head gathered only 400 and he assures me that he kept account of the dead ones as far as he could and has not been able to trace the shortage in that way."

The Cochrane ranch, which by this time had moved from west of Calgary to the Waterton area some twenty-five kilometres south of the lower block, was reported to have come through the 1887 winter relatively unscathed. Interestingly, it occurred to McEachran that the family could simply be "cooking" the books. "It is a curious fact," he said, "that the Cochrane cattle wintered safely last winter on a range where stock of no kind were even known or imagined to be able to exist.... I have a suspicion that they are 'borrowing' at this year, and the actual facts are not given as I believe" William F. Cochrane, "who is now in not very robust health, since an accident last summer, did hope to put it on the market this year."[19] One thing is clear: McEachran was correct in his assumption that all other neighbouring outfits were very severely affected. Years later A.E. Cross told one of his contemporaries that "the custom" when the open range system first unfolded in western Canada "was not to feed almost any cattle which I was influenced by. The following winter was the most severe known in the country. My cattle drifted south in the storms with a large number of new cattle on the range, forming a block in a small part of the country, the consequence was we lost from 25 to 50 per cent of our cattle principally our breeding stock. The calf branding for the next and a few following years was very small, so we were greatly crippled, and had to turn to the horses for a revenue."[20] Many years after writing that letter Cross offered the opinion that "few of the ranchers lost less than 40 per cent, some losing 100, many losing 75 per cent."[21]

The heavy impact of the 1886/87 winter has of late been disavowed by historians, some of whom seem to fear that it might somehow tarnish the great ranchers' image.[22] For that reason it would seem reasonable to quote one more authority from the period. In 1913 local journalist L.V. Kelly called upon all his remarkable literary talents to describe it.

Clustering in the coulees or huddling on the open, the animals suffered and died in enormous numbers. Some, breast-high in packed and crusted banks, died as they stood; some who were sheltered somewhat by bluffs or coulees starved pitifully, ravenously searching for food until the frost had reached their vitals. The bodies of great steers were found in the spring, heaps of them, with their throats and stomachs punctured and torn by sharp splinters from dried and frozen branches and chunks of wood which they had swallowed in their anguish. The coulees showed the most bodies in the spring, for naturally the animals sought their shelter, crowding close together for the warmth of each others' bodies. One would succumb, others would crowd in on that body, others would drop, and when the winter broke the bodies lay piled six and eight deep all up the bottoms of the ravines. Hundreds of the animals, helplessly endeavouring to find sustenance, sucked the hair from the hides of their dead comrades, dying finally with their throats, mouths and stomachs lined with it. Though the ranchers and cowboys performed prodigies of endurance, riding wide and far and hard in their supreme efforts to save such of the herds as they could, they did little good, being only able to watch their stock perish and hope for a break in the weather that never came until nearly the first of March.... The loss in Alberta was a fearful blow to the stockmen, but the cattle people of Montana, Wyoming and Dakota suffered even more severely, many men being forced entirely out of the business

... twenty thousand cattle died in the country north of the Old Man's River alone.[23]

It was not just the size of the Walrond herd that was affected by the bad weather. The carcass weights of the cattle the ranch delivered to market also declined dramatically. Historians seldom take this into account. During the winter the grasses growing naturally in the foothills region were badly stunted by the severe weather and covered with snow, making it impossible for the cattle that managed to survive to get enough to eat. Therefore they lost a great deal of weight. When the inclement weather returned after the brief respite in the spring Bell reported that "up to a few days ago it snowed almost half of the time and the ground" was seldom "clear of snow ... and when the ground was clear it was so cold that every thing was kept back.... At the first part of this week the grass was no further advanced than at the first of the month." As a consequence, he explained, "the weather has had its effect on the beef." He estimated that "this month will show the lightest [carcass] weights yet."[24]

The contracts with the Indian agencies called on the ranch to supply an agreed-upon total number of pounds of beef at each monthly delivery. In other words the ranch had to supply a certain "dressed" weight of beef no matter how many cattle it took to make it up. It was, therefore, important to get the animals good and heavy for each delivery in order to deplete the cattle inventory as little as possible. Grass-fed steers were considered well finished when their live weight was 1400 to 1800 pounds and their carcasses around 800 to 1,040 pounds.[25] If a contract were to call for 20,000 pounds a month it took 20,000 divided by, say, 900 pounds, or just over twenty-two cattle, to fulfill it. During a long cold winter a steer would tend to continue to grow but it would not put on much flesh. Thus it would have a relatively large frame with little meat on its bones and its carcass might well weigh as little as 600 pounds. In that case it would take 20,000 divided by 600, or thirty-three animals, to supply the necessary meat. The ranch was using a lot of cows to make up the deliveries at this time. A fat cow might have a carcass weight of 720 pounds. 20,000 divided by 720 is 27.7. A skinny cow, on the other hand, might have only 480 pounds of meat. 20,000 divided by 480 is approximately 40.4.

It is evident, then, that the Walrond experienced a considerable fall in herd size simply as a consequence of poor conditioning. It should be noted, moreover, that the profits on the cattle the ranch did send to market were also severely affected. The going per pound price for dressed beef at this time was about 8 cents. At that figure a large steer might bring in 8 cents times 900 pounds, or $72.00. During this particular winter and spring the same steer would have brought in only 600 times 8 or about $48.00. A good fat cow was worth over $57.00 while a poor, thin one might bring only $38.40. What also hurt the ranch for the future is that in an attempt to hold back some of its young steers to give them the chance to fatten properly on better summer grasses, the men sent a lot of good breeding cows to slaughter along with the culls. It is common practice for all ranchers today to market cows that are unable regularly to produce high quality calves under ideal conditions. Something is wrong with them and any feed the owner puts into them once they are fat is simply going to waste. However, many of the cows the Walrond killed during the 1886/87 winter and spring were dry simply because their calves had been unable to withstand the severe storms. These animals undoubtedly looked emaciated but there was nothing wrong with them that a few weeks on better feed would not have cured. McEachran worried about overselling the breeding stock and Bell tried to reassure him that the vast majority he had marketed were substandard. "I have no doubt we killed a few ... that you would not want killed" but most had various flaws including "big bags," or "big jaws" or were "non breeders," "cripples" or "cows as old as to be toothless and consequently almost certain to die within the next year or two." He also used the dubious argument that the Walrond herd was generally of poorer quality than that of their well-known neighbour. "I may tell you," he later wrote, that "the Cochrane Coy had killed about as many if not more cows than we had as during the ten months" of the year "they had only killed 350 steers and they supplied about three fourths as much beef as we did and besides they had no old cows at all compared to what we had." The blizzards of 1882/83 had "cleaned up" the Cochrane herd by killing all the older, poorer animals. This had left the ranch with "nothing but healthy young stock."[26]

The Walrond's heavy sell-off of cows at this time did not go unnoticed. A government "Inspector of Agencies" named McGibbon arrived at the Peigan and Blood reserves in October and complained that the ranch was going too far. He "is making a big kick about the number of cows killed and promises to have it fixed so that in the next contracts either no cows will be allowed to be killed or if any will be taken it will be at lower figures," Bell wrote. He considered this simple bloody-mindedness, since the Indians could hardly be expected to know the difference. Indeed, he said, sardonically, they "prefer cows and consider themselves badly treated if a month passes without their getting any."[27] The ranch was forced to negotiate with the department and eventually contracted to kill fewer cows. But that contract was eventually scrapped. In 1888 an agreement was hammered out between the Indian department and the ranch stipulating that if the ranch would stop including rough "stag" and bull meat in the deliveries the department would "waive the condition expressed in the contract" limiting cows to "10 percent of the number of steers."[28] This satisfied the personnel of the Department of Indian Affairs that they were doing their job, but it was hardly a proper compensation for the quality of the meat.[29]

McEachran made sure that Bell's optimistic interpretation of the heavy cow kill was reported to his shareholders. With all the old ones and the "non breeders, and poor milkers which starve their calves, all out of the herd," he told them, "I look for a more encouraging calf crop next year and as most of the cattle men remark if we have fewer they are worth so much more."[30] Indications are that McEachran was still largely blind to the fact that the natural grasses he and many others had earlier praised to the skies were being overgrazed by his own stock. The Walrond pastures appear by this time to have been losing some of their original stature, and this must have affected animal health as it made it more difficult for the cattle to get enough to eat, particularly when the snow deepened. However, McEachran rationalized that this was a temporary situation, for which his neighbours were to blame. "There is no doubt that one half at least of our losses are referable to" an influx of "cattle from the north of us on to our range during winter," he explained to the shareholders. "Mr. Pinhorne Manager of [the] Oxley [ranch] agrees with me that if the High River ranchers to the north and Mosquito creek ranchmen do not carry out their promise to herd their cattle to keep them off our ranges we must do so and I have agreed to join him in doing so."[31] McEachran's failure to grasp the limitations of the Walrond grasslands would allow him in the future to continue to run more cattle than he should have. This would help to keep carcass and, therefore, total company revenues low and herd sell-off rates high. And that would ultimately threaten the financial viability of the operation.

It is indicative of McEachran's proclivity to both dream and colour the truth that after all the losses of the 1886/87 winter he remained true to his policy of paying at least a 5 per cent annual dividend to the shareholders. It seems clear that the dividend was a cost the Walrond operation could ill afford. Therefore, McEachran's insistence on paying it requires a thorough explanation. The pressure on managers and directors of the early North American cattle ranching corporations to provide dividends was hard to resist for one basic reason. The monies with which the shareholders had purchased their holdings in the company were the only operational capital the company had. In many cases the shareholders had been induced to invest their capital on the promise of great financial rewards. Should the company appear to be unable to live up to expectations, the shareholders might well decide that it was not a good risk and thus liquidate their holdings. Obviously, should a large percentage of them make that decision they could put the company out of business altogether. That would mean not just the end of the business but a significant decline in the reputation of the man employed to manage it, possibly the termination of his career as a cattle executive, and if he himself had a high stake in the venture, the loss of his fortune. What often happened, therefore, is that the manager would declare a dividend to substantiate and underscore profits irrespective of how well he thought the company had performed.

To illustrate this it is instructive to focus on the Powder River Ranch in northwestern Wyoming and southeastern Montana as McEachran's counterpart there, Moreton Frewen, gave very direct indications of the pressures he was under to provide dividend payments in letters he wrote to people with whom he felt he could speak in confidence. Frewen, a Sussex-born gentleman, appeared in Wyoming Territory in 1878 and began immediately to fantasize about making immense profits in the western plains ranching industry. Within a few years he managed to sell his vision to a British syndicate and then formed the massive Powder River Land and Cattle Company.[32] During the short interval between 1882, when the ranch commenced operating on a large scale, and 1886, when Frewen's board forced him to step down from his position as manager, his experience was like a "crash course" on open range ranching.[33] The last lesson he learned was that cattle cannot be hurried to market prematurely simply because he needed cash to pay dividends to keep his stockholders happy.[34] After the 1883 fall roundup Frewen gathered the older steers that had been in his herds at purchase, but was disappointed to discover that considerably fewer were ready to slaughter than he had hoped. "Markets hold up pretty well, but still shareholders must be content with a moderate dividend as a great deal of the beef was not fat enough to market."[35] When he went to Chicago with what was left after cutting out the poorest of these cattle, he was even more disappointed. "We had a thousand head on the worst market of the year … but it was useless to think of selling more. The fact is the cattle are not half fat, they must wait till next year.… Our sales will barely reach 4,000 head instead of some 7,000 as I had intended."[36]

The next year Frewen was disappointed again as the stock he expected to be in great shape were "not half fat," and he could "get no offer at all reasonable for them."[37] At this point he decided that grass finishing was not a realistic proposition. Grazing was just not an intensive enough system to get the cattle ready for market at a fast enough rate. Therefore he turned to hand feeding of roughage and grain. Again his main preoccupation was to provide shareholder returns. The "cattle [are] looking, blooming," he wrote. "We shall have no difficulty in paying a ten per cent dividend on the six months ending last July and another ten per cent up to December during next April out of sales of cattle we are feeding and again … ten per cent up to June next.… Dividends twice a year will make us popular and I want very much to get support of a fresh issue of capital."[38] Unfortunately for Frewen this experiment also failed, because in his desperation for cash he just did not give the animals enough time to finish properly.

Much of Frewen's anxiety about dividends was self-induced in that he had initially raised great optimism among his investors about the rewards that were likely to be forthcoming.[39] Once he got the Powder River operation started he knew he had better find a way to demonstrate it was living up to the glowing picture he had painted. At no time did he ever attempt to measure actual profits. His concern was just to get his hands on as much money as he could as quickly as possible in order to issue the returns and let the shareholders come to their own conclusions. McEachran found himself in the same position. We do not know exactly what he told the interested parties when he first put together the financing for the Walrond operation, but we do know that in 1883 he painted a very positive picture of the potential of both the Cochrane and the Walrond outfits when trying to draw T.C. Power into his list of shareholders and that in later years he was also prepared to be very imaginative to make his operation look as attractive as possible.[40] The fact that he was capable of such inventiveness and that he almost certainly had himself read all the promotional literature strongly suggests that he, like Frewen, used superlative language to recruit Sir John Walrond and the initial small core of shareholders. We know too that after the Walrond met with early reversals, some of the shareholders expressed the desire to pull out because "the returns for the years past" had not "been what was expected."[41] Under that kind of threat – the possibility that part or all of his operating capital could be withdrawn – McEachran too felt compelled to show signs of prosperity and thus to produce dividends year after year.[42]

In short, dividends were a means of attracting and keeping the funds of the investors whose high expectations these men had helped to arouse. Because in reality they considered them compulsory rather than a share of profits, dividends could, indeed probably should, be viewed as interest payments on borrowed money. Despite James Brisbin's assertions, charges for capital were a major obstacle to the success of many frontier ranches. The short life of the Powder River outfit illustrates the absurdity of any money Frewen managed to return to his shareholders. George Lane, who borrowed heavily to buy the Bar U Ranch along with a number of other holdings in southern Alberta, died penniless in 1925.[43] It should not be suggested that borrowing *inevitably* doomed a particular operation. Obviously the amount borrowed relative to assets was a determining factor, as was operational efficiency and the owners' management practices. With respect to the latter, men like McEachran were woefully deficient in comparison to someone like James Fergus, who was able to pay a lot more attention to the details of day-to-day operations.

For a promoter like McEachran the open range system provided too much freedom when it came to estimating profits. This was mainly because it was impossible for him, or any managers on big spreads with thousands of cattle roaming hundreds of thousands of acres, to know for sure how well their company had performed financially at any one time. Most years, McEachran, again like many other managers, relied on the "book count" approach to estimate the value of his cattle inventory. That is, he would take the number originally in the herd, add the calves born each year and figure in the animals that were purchased and sold. He would then arbitrarily assume a death loss of 5 per cent.[44] This was common practice but there were a couple of things wrong with it. Firstly, the number of cattle assumed to be in the original large herds purchased in Montana and elsewhere might not be correct. As silly as it perhaps seems, the big ranchers often simply accepted previous owners' book counts when calculating how many cattle they had initially purchased.[45] Based on their rather extensive correspondence on the subject it would appear that McEachran probably had a fairly close estimate of the numbers he obtained from T.C. Power in 1883. There were supposed to be 3,900, and after McEachran took possession of and paid for the cattle, Power reimbursed him $4,000 for non-delivery of 775 head.[46] The rest of the cattle McEachran bought that year came in much smaller groups and, therefore, may well have been properly counted. However, because the cattle were almost immediately turned loose on the Canadian ranges and because in the frontier setting there were no fences to keep them from straying, many instinctively headed back towards the home from which they had come on the other side of the border. Indeed, it was necessary for McEachran to send a man back down to Montana the next summer to claim and gather all the returnees he could find. In this he needed the cooperation of Power and other middlemen to identify their former cattle. "Charles Raymond is now in Montana looking for our strays," McEachran told Power. He "reports quite a number on your range at Warm Spring. Will you please instruct" your hired men "to deliver all cattle branded WR to Raymond? He says Mr. Brooks claims six cattle" of ours "which he says were crippled" and therefore dropped out of the drive north and were never branded. Brooks "has no right to do so. At the time I did object to a few cripples" among the cattle originally purchased "but he would not let us" reject them "and they were driven out into the herds" for the trek north. Some could not keep up and therefore "fell out" and were left along the way to be gathered later. "I would be sorry if Mr Brooks would give us any trouble, in the face of the fact that I paid you for two of your cattle, which we found in the herd after reaching here" last summer.[47] There was, of course, no guarantee that co-operation would be forthcoming, particularly in the case of someone like Power, since there had been bad feelings on both sides over their last transaction. There was also no way to know how many cattle had died on the return trip south or were stolen by one of a number of rustlers operating in the volatile borderlands regions between the Walrond and Warm Springs.[48]

Therefore, whether he knew precisely how many animals he bought from Power and others in 1883, McEachran could not have known exactly how many he had actually been able to keep on the Canadian plains. And since the men seldom if ever got an accurate count he could not know how many died or were stolen each year. Animals, particularly among the very young and the old, took sick during inclement weather and died in heavily wooded thickets or in deep canyons or in heavy underbrush and were never seen again.[49] Moreover, a large proportion of the dead cattle that were eventually found were not discovered until their hides had decomposed so badly that the brands were totally obscured. Auditors today count the cattle a particular beef producer has, normally after they have been hand fed for days in corrals and/or small fenced in pastures. That way they are tame enough to be run relatively slowly through a chute. Ideally, moreover, the cattle are weighed so that the auditors can judge how much they would be worth on the market if they were to be sold by the pound. The auditors figure out an average per head value, multiply by the number of cattle and get a relatively precise estimate of the overall value. If the difference between the value of the inventory and the capital owed against it is higher at the end of the year than it was at the end of the previous year then the operation has made money. If the opposite is true it has lost money. This system is not perfect as it cannot take into consideration the quality of each and every animal. However, it provides far more accuracy than the big cattlemen could ever achieve during the open range period.

Unfortunately for the Walrond investors, uncertainty allowed McEachran to declare dividends more or less at will. What he did was optimistically calculate his book count, assume the per head value was constant, and show the Walrond numbers rising in the long term. This enabled him to return 5 per cent even in years when losses were clearly much higher than average. "Yes" he could rationalize when disaster struck, "we may have lost money this year but we have to keep a long-term perspective. If we make less than five percent in our worst years we also do better than that in our best ones." This sort of reasoning was endemic on the northern Great Plains corporation ranches.[50] It was also obviously very dangerous. McEachran may or may not have recognized that the cash he had on hand to issue dividends prior to 1888 was available in part because of the growing list of investors he and Sir John Walrond had been able to persuade to join their venture. In the future that list would lose its elasticity and the dividends would become more and more difficult for the ranch to afford.

The 1886/87 winter killed more of the Walrond cattle than any previous one had. One should keep in mind, however, that throughout this early period the calf crop and very likely the overall numbers declined every year. Because of this McEachran, himself, realized by 1887 that some serious adaptations to the environment would be necessary if the Walrond ranch was going to live up to its potential. He could see at least that he was going to have to incur more expense to provide more feed for his younger calves and older gestating or suckling cows in the wintertime. However, a much more intensive agricultural approach than that was not an option. Like most big cattlemen he had stated the case for the open range system, based on widespread grazing and very low operational costs. That meant, among other things, a small workforce and little infrastructure to control herd movements. The Walrond cowboys would continue to build more corrals and to fence in small pasture areas at the various ranches for holding delicate livestock in the wintertime and for branding cattle when first brought to the ranch. They would also construct more barbed wire fences in strategic areas in a largely unsuccessful attempt to keep out roaming bulls and the diseased animals from neighbouring herds. However, McEachran never considered hiring enough men to put up enough feed to carry anything like all the cattle through every winter. Nor did he consider taking on the enormous task of building the huge networks of fences necessary to divide the Walrond rangeland into a multiplicity of small pastures as later cattlemen were to do. Consequently, he was never to be in a position to feed anything like all the cattle through long cold spells, nor to thoroughly control breeding patterns, nor to provide a great deal more supervision of birthing. As will be illustrated, he would also never be able to develop an efficient and sophisticated system of grasslands management in order to get the very best out of his pastures. The overall impact of the changes he was to make, therefore, would be to subject the operation to higher costs without a commensurate improvement in productivity.

5

THE SECOND WALROND RANCH, 1888–1898: A NEW STRATEGY

Over and above the need to increase input costs after the 1886/87 winter, McEachran's main concern was to take some of the pressure off his business partners who had already been compelled to underwrite greater cash outlays than they were comfortable with. Together his British shareholders had committed to a grand total of thirty-eight shares at £2,500 apiece. The overall value of these along with the ten shares reserved for McEachran for managing the company amounted to exactly £100,000 pounds or $500,000.[1] Initially only £1,000, or less than half the price of each share, had been "called up," and it is likely that McEachran had indicated to the Walrond investors that their operation would be so profitable that they would never be called on to pay the full monetary value of their shares. This had been the case for the Cochrane shareholders while he had been part of that company, and one wants to remember the optimism he had expressed about ranching in general at that time. By 1887, however, further calls had raised the per share commitment to £1,550.[2] Sir John, had raised his stake to five shares, and his wife, each of his two sons and his son-in-law (Lord Clinton) had increased their holdings from one to one and a half shares, as had Walter Henry Holbech and Julia Neville Grenville. Thomas Henry Goodwin Newton, like Sir John, now also had five shares. Thus the two largest stakeholders were responsible for £12,500[3] each ($62,500) and, based on the calls, they were actually out of pocket £7,750 ($38,750).[4] The other two of Sir John's relatives who had been with the company from 1883/84 had paid out £4,650 for their three shares ($23,250) and were committed to a total of £7,500 ($37,500).[5] These were sizeable amounts of money based on late-nineteenth-century currencies.[6]

The prospect loomed that should the ranch require any more cash the investors would have to dig substantially further into their pockets. Even at this stage, the only reason that further calls had not been necessary was that McEachran and Walrond had recruited a small core of new investors. Between 1884 and 1888 the number of shareholders rose from nineteen to twenty-five. Lionel Boyle dropped out and was replaced by seven new men. Five were residents of England. C.A.W. Troyte, another of Sir John Walrond's sons-in-law, bought 77 of a new issue of £10 shares.[7] All the rest bought 155. Francis John Mills Mason was a retired "Major" from St. Mary, Warwickshire;[8] Henry Aubrey Cartwright was a retired "Colonel" from Eydon Hall, Byfield, Northamptonshire;[9] Salusbury K. Mainwaring was a Justice of the Peace from Shrewsbury;[10] and Sir Albert Osliff Rutson was a "Gentleman" living in Newby Wiske, Yorkshire.[11] The other two were Canadian. They each also bought 155 of the new shares. James Ponley Dawes was a brewer from Lachine, Quebec, and William Miller Ramsay was an "Insurance Manager" from Montreal. At £10 or $50 per share the new investors had thus put another £7,570 net ($37,850) into the operation.[12]

In part to negate the need for them to underwrite the company further, the directors decided to terminate the Walrond Cattle Ranche Limited at the end of 1887 and start 1888 with a new corporation, the Walrond Ranche Company Limited.[13] Initially, the force behind this move was Sir John Walrond himself, but there can be little doubt that McEachran supported it, as the protection of the Walrond family money seems always to have been important to him.[14] Sir John's main concern was to prevent the ranch from detracting from the value of the portion of his estate that he intended to pass along to his youngest son Arthur. Soon after the original ranch was started in 1883 Sir John, then only six years from his death, agonized over the question of how to pass his interest in the ranch on to both his sons. His first reaction was simply to compose a "codicil" to his will leaving three shares to William and the other two to Arthur.[15] In keeping with the long-standing British convention known as primogeniture, William as the oldest son was to get the bulk of the Walrond estate. Sir John seems to have believed that he would thus be well looked after. However, Arthur as the second son would be less secure, and Sir John was concerned that he might be called upon to put more cash into the frontier operation.[16] In the codicil, therefore, Sir John described one of the two shares willed to Arthur as "fully paid up" and he charged his personal estate with providing any amount on the other share, which at his death should remain unpaid. Then in 1887, presumably sensing that he could not simply call the one share fully paid up unless it actually was, he directed that it should "not be transferred as a fully paid up share" but should be "subject to payment of any sum" left unpaid.[17] The problem with this, of course, was that it would leave Arthur responsible for up to £950 from further calls. There was one solution – to dissolve the old corporation and form another in which all shareholders received 155 *fully paid* shares worth £10 apiece (£1,550 in total) for each of their original £2,500 partially paid up shares. Once this was done, Sir John composed another codicil to his will leaving 205 of the shares to Arthur and the rest to William.[18] This freed both sons from having to pay any more towards the full value of the original shares, and it brought the added advantage of protecting all the original investors, including all the other members of the Walrond family. At the same time it made the company somewhat more attractive to prospective investors who could now join the list of shareholders for any multiple of £10.

If McEachran and the rest of the Walrond directors really did expect a significant influx of investors in early 1888 they must have been disappointed. After the formation of the new company the number of shareholders rose by just three, and the new men put a relatively small amount of money into the organization. Aurelius Bruce Mitchell, of the pen-making family with that surname, and William Maschwitz, both of whom lived in Edgbaston Birmingham,[19] each bought fifty shares worth £500 or $2,500; and James G. Ross, an accountant from Montreal who now became the company secretary-treasurer, bought ten shares worth a £100 or $500.[20] Ross was a descendant of P.S. Ross, who had opened an accounting office in Montreal in 1858. James was to become paymaster of that business in 1912 and eventually merge with G.A. Touche and Company, which opened its first office in Toronto in 1909, and Deloitte and Company, which had started up in London in 1845. The triumvirate was destined to become the multinational accounting firm known today as Deloitte Touche Tohmatsu.[21]

The shares McEachran himself had been allotted by the Walrond Cattle ranch had been worth £500 each for a total of £5,000. They were now converted into 500 shares worth £10 a piece. At this point McEachran negotiated a new agreement with the company that left him as vice president and managing director with a share value that would continue to rise with time.[22] On 15 November 1888 he was to get 30 shares, on 15 May in years 1889 through 1891 he was to get another 30 and on 15 May 1892 he was to get another 35. This would bring his total to 665 shares and make him the second largest shareholder in the company – next only to Sir William Walrond, who inherited most of his father's holdings when Sir John died in 1889.[23] Though not in the 1888 agreement, documents indicate that McEachran was granted another 30 shares in 1893 bringing his total to 695.[24] The same annual increment must have been repeated each year until the ranch was reorganized in 1898. This would have given him another 120 shares for a total of 815 worth £8,150 pounds or $40,750. Interestingly, with the approval of the directorate McEachran also now took an annual salary of $3,000. This has to be viewed in the light of the difficulties the ranch had experienced over the previous four years, particularly in 1886/87. Suddenly the long-term viability of the organization was not looking as secure as before, and he elected to take a salary in order to avoid the possibility that he could end up with nothing from the ranch should its shares eventually prove worthless. McEachran was also again eligible for all the 5 per cent annual dividends paid out to the other shareholders. He had 510 shares when the company started and 815 when it ended in 1898, and, therefore, his average number over the life of the ranch was 662 1/2 worth $33,125.00. His approximate average annual cash take from the dividend was 5 per cent of that, or $1,656.25. During the ten years of the Walrond Ranche Company then McEachran was getting just over $4,600.00 annually in wages and dividend payments while compiling a paper fortune in stocks.

The total number of all the fully paid up shares in the Walrond Cattle Ranche rose by late 1893 to 7,170. The total capital at that point was thus £71,700 pounds sterling ($358,750.00). Less McEachran's *free* shares, the total amount of capital the company actually took in was £64,750 pounds ($323,750.00).[25] Since the amount of new capital raised was so small and since no more shareholders would be brought in during the rest of the Walrond Ranche Company's history, the operation had for the first time to generate enough profit from livestock sales to cover the cost of operating. Otherwise it was heading down the road to insolvency. This chapter strongly suggests that it was doing precisely that.

In the period from 1888 through to 1896, when the Canadian government would rescind the leases on all the great ranches, there were three annual costs on the Walrond that might be termed "fixed" because under McEachran's direction they had to be paid no matter how well the ranch was doing. These costs were not operational in that they had nothing to do with the nurturing or marketing of livestock. It seems clear, however, that they put the company under considerable financial pressure. First there was the $2,756.40 that had to be paid out to the government for the lease of its 275,640 acres of land. True, at a cent an acre per year, this was considered a very good deal. On the other hand, as will be seen, when viewed against the other costs the lease payment was far from inconsequential. The second fixed cost was McEachran's $3,000.00 salary. Finally, there were the dividend payments. At 5 per cent they cost the company between $16,187.50 and $18,237.50 each year depending on how many stocks McEachran held at any stage. So the average was just over $17,000.00.[26]

In total, therefore, the ranch spent circa $23,000.00 annually that did not contribute towards paying its ranch hands, butchering its fat cattle, building infrastructure or putting up feed. To illuminate the impact these charges had on the viability of the ranch as a whole, they can be measured against the most significant operating expenses. During the Walrond Ranche Company years the latter rose considerably. This was firstly because in the wake of the 1886/87 winter, McEachran and his

SOMEBODY ELSE'S MONEY

A FARM NEAR THE
SOUTH END OF
BEAVER CREEK IN
2008. PHOTO BY
THE AUTHOR.

managers realized they were going have to do more feeding during the wintertime and shelter more of their most delicate animals from winter storms. This required extra capital for equipment to put up and stack various forms of roughage. Hay was cut and stacked at all five of the ranch sites and, on the lower ranch (or "farm"), where soils were deeper and the frost free period relatively long compared to the sites higher into or on the west side of the Porcupine Hills, various field crops were grown.[27] "We started yesterday to cut the oats and if the present fair weather continues we will get pretty well on with them before the men have to go to round up on the other side of the river," Bell told McEachran. "There will be considerable [green] feed from it."[28] At the same time he experimented with a more exotic crop – field peas – although these were reported to be a "complete failure," presumably because of early frosts.[29]

The main supply of feed continued to be hay. From 1887 on a crew of men was kept busy in the summertime mowing and raking in meadows where the natural grasses grew the highest and then hauling and stacking it in strategic places.[30] In order to overcome the difficulty of finding enough hired hands for the job the ranch also began to buy hay from small entrepreneurs, who would sign a contract to put up a certain amount at a particular price per ton.[31] This hay might be produced on or off lands that were part of the Walrond lease. On 20 July 1887 a contract was signed with one William Farmer "to put up 8 to 10 tons of hay … in the hay corral at the camp on Jones Creek." The price was five dollars a ton and a system was worked out to determine how to measure the amount of feed in each stack.[32] Obtaining large amounts of roughage for the stock, whether by its own crews or by contractors, required the fencing in of more pastures in order to keep more animals close to the feed in sheltered areas. Extra men were also needed to dole the roughage out to the cattle during inclement weather. The Walrond also required men to build additional "feeding corrals." These were small log enclosures around stacks that had a gap between the horizontal rails through which the cattle could eat as the hay was forked to them but which restrained them from actually trampling on it. "We are going to build a small feeding corral at the cabin on Jones creek and do some feeding there if necessary," Bell wrote on 6 November 1887. "The extra hay …

        SOMEBODY ELSE'S MONEY

is likely to be needed as the prairie ... has been burnt off," by fires "and feed will be scarce."[33]

During this period as in the past, the ranch had at least four men killing and butchering cattle for the two reserves, and it seems to have employed one extra man for the cattle going to each reserve to feed the animals for several days in the holding pens before they were killed.[34] This was probably only in the wintertime when carcass weights were the most difficult to maintain. The horse breeding business was also expanded. In July 1887 McEachran reported to the head office in London that "the mares and foals are doing well ... and I am of the opinion agreed universally here that this Callum Creek range is the best horse range in Alberta or anywhere else.[35] I hope arrangements will be made for 200 or 300 fillies with stallions for next spring as they are not only immensely profitable but are nearly without such as stock breeding can be."[36] By the early 1890s enough Clydesdales and Shires had been brought to the ranch to require a small work force of about four to six to watch them year round, defend them from wolves and rustlers, and to castrate, brand, break, and train the younger ones. McEachran's first horse manager was Lew Murray.[37] David Warnock took over from Murray in 1893.

What we know about the nationality of the workers as a whole suggests that while this version of the Walrond ranch got most of its hired men from eastern Canada and the British Isles the American representation actually increased with time. The census reports for 1881 and 1891 do not give nationality, but the 1901 report does, and in the winter when labour costs were lowest, there were five Canadians (one from Cape Breton and four from Ontario) at the Callum Creek headquarters along with one man from Ireland, one from England, and an English domestic named Bessie Haimur. There were also four Americans. James Mollsion replaced Patterson as cattle foreman from 1887 to 1890, at which time John Lamar took the position. Lamar and three fellow Americans were on the ranch at the time the 1901 census was taken.[38] Total labour costs rose substantially after the spring of 1887. In 1888 the ranch was employing twenty men for six to eight months – so say seven months. The pay, including that for wives and foremen as well as for the regular cowhands, averaged about $40 a month for a total annual cost of $5,600.

For approximately five months the ranch employed about twelve men costing a total of $2,400. If Bell and David Warnock were each getting $100 a month they were costing the ranch $2,400 a year. Doc Frields quit as onsite manager in 1885. Jerry Paisley replaced him from 1885 to 1890 and James F. Scott did the job from 1890 to 1893.[39] Ostensibly they got about $150 a month or $1,800 a year.[40] Thus the total annual labour cost was something like $12,200.[41]

Feeding expenses also soared in these years. In the 1890s the Walrond accumulated an average of 550 tons of hay a year. The cost for the contracted portion, which made up the bulk of it, ran from $3.75 to $6.00 a ton.[42] The cost was about the same for the hay the Walrond's men put up, since it too required paying for both labour and equipment. The total cost would thus have been around $2,750.00.[43] The ranch began "wintering out" some particularly delicate stock to small neighbouring ranchers in this period, who put them in corrals and hand fed them. The contractors charged $3.00 per head per month for the biggest animals and proportionately less for calves and smaller yearlings.[44] By the mid-1890s the ranch was sending about 1,150 to custom feed lots. Figuring out an average per animal is difficult because it depended on the severity of the weather in a given fall, winter, and spring and the consequent time the service was needed. However, just after the turn of the century David Warnock would report "approximately $2,600.00 will be paid out to feeding contractors by the 10th of April."[45] The 1900/1901 winter was not a particularly severe one so it would seem reasonable to assume that about that much money went to the feeding contractors each year.[46]

The major operational expenses, then, for labour, hay accumulated on the ranch, and custom feeding was $17,550. In late-nineteenth-century terms that was a lot of money, but what seems more remarkable is the fact that McEachran's salary plus the annual total dividend paid to all the shareholders including McEachran surpassed it. The most financially successful and respected joint-stock companies today are those that put company profits ahead of personal rewards to the directors and executive officers. By that measuring stick the Walrond was anything but a good company. Indeed, there is no escaping the conclusion that it was a veritable "cash cow" for McEachran in particular. He had talked his board into believing that he had organized a great money-making scheme for them and should be proportionately compensated. In this period it took even more out of the company's cash supply than it had previously to channel money back to him. At the same time that he began taking a substantial salary the number and total value of his shares continued to rise and, consequently, so did the real cost of his 5 per cent annual dividend. In a few words, he was a very expensive manager – and, considering that he was onsite for only a few weeks a year – one who did not shoulder an incredible workload.

All the feeding done on or for the Walrond in this period clearly increased costs quite a lot. The reason that investing more in hay and green feed did not get the ranch to the point where it was feeding anything like all its livestock for any substantial part of the year was the daunting nature of the task. To ensure that none of the cattle would ever go hungry in the wintertime, the amount required for feeding would have had to be multiplied many times over. Gestating and/or nursing cows, the bulls that service them, and growing or fattening steers require about a ton and a half of hay apiece to be more or less assured of coming through a long winter on the northern plains in good condition.[47] The Walrond owned on average in this period about 8,500 head in its beef herd, excluding newborn calves. About 5,200 were classified as cows, 300 were bulls and 3,000 were steers.[48] These cattle would have needed 12,750 tons of hay to keep them all sufficiently satisfied during the hundred or so most inclement days each winter.[49] About 1,000 of the ranch's 1,400 or so calves would also have been mature enough to require feed when pastures were covered with snow. To keep them growing and healthy would have taken about a ton of hay per head, or another 1,000 tons. In total, therefore, the ranch would have required at least 13,600 tons of hay. The cost to procure it would have been $68,000 in total[50] – an increase of circa 2,500 per cent.[51] To men who had been promised, or who had themselves made promises, that costs could be kept down almost to nothing, this was unthinkable.

It scarcely needs to be added that costs were not the only inhibiting factor. To gather 13,600 tons of hay with horse-drawn equipment from natural hay lands scattered over thousands of acres of land in rough and hilly country would have taken an army of at least three hundred men and then another one perhaps half that size to haul the hay and fork it to the cattle in the wintertime.[52] There were surpluses of labour between the roundups when some of the cowboys were laid off, but in this early frontier period the population base was still very sparse in the prairie West. By the turn of the century there were only about 100,000 people in an area from Calgary to the American border and from the Rockies to the eastern boundary of Assiniboia.[53] Therefore, manpower of that magnitude was simply unavailable. Regular winter feeding of all the cattle would also have involved hiring extra men to build all the corrals required to protect the many stacks of hay and to provide all the extra fences to enclose the cattle near them during bad weather.

The most cattle ever mentioned in the correspondence between McEachran and his hired men as being on feed in the winter time was 2,300, consisting of cows suckling calves that were too small to be weaned, cows that were heavy in calf, breeding bulls and semi-domesticated and therefore poorly acclimatized doggies or young steers brought in from Manitoba and/or Ontario. The rest continued to be subjected to the vicissitudes of the weather summer and winter. Moreover, nature's powers of destruction did not subside in this period. The ferocious winter of 1886/87 is the most celebrated of the natural disasters on the northern Great Plains in the late nineteenth century but it was certainly not the only one. Numerous cattle were lost on many of the foothills operations in the winters of the early 1890s as well.[54] Moreover, at about the same time, wolves began to prey much more heavily than previously on the younger calves and colts.[55] Prior to the rise of cattle, sheep, and horse ranching, the plains had been all but divested of wolves, primarily due to excessive killing for the fur trade and the depletion of the buffalo herds, which traditionally supplied much of their food staple.[56] When the ranchers turned their first herds loose, however, the beasts gained a new food source that was much easier to prey on than the wild, wary, and relatively powerful buffalo had been. By the mid- to late 1890s wolves had thus become one of the stockmen's most formidable enemies.[57] It was in 1894 that the Walrond managers suddenly became aware of this fact. The beasts "have been giving us a hard deal during the last two weeks," Warnock told McEachran in July. In just "a few nights they killed ten head of yearling colts besides a number of yearling cattle and calves.... We found several of the carcasses freshly killed in fact warm and poisoned some of these but the wolves did not touch the bait. We have been doing our best to kill them with the dogs but so far, have only succeeded in killing two full grown ones. The dogs are too light and get a terrible mauling every time they tackle" one.[58] In an attempt to explain why the numbers of cattle came up far short of their expectations in 1897 Warnock was to suggest that wolves more than anything else explained the deficiency. "Take for instance, the damage" they did "amongst horses," he said. "In 1894 ... [they] killed in less than six months some forty odd head of one and 2 years old colts belonging to the Coy."[59] This at that time was about a twelfth of all the Clydesdales and Shires the ranch owned, and Warnock was intimating that similar damage must have been inflicted on the cattle.[60]

It is evident that losses to wolves were at this time being augmented significantly by abusive grazing techniques. If the Walrond grasslands had been showing signs of deterioration in the 1880s there can be little doubt that by the mid-1890s it had become a serious problem. Influenced by the promotional literature and driven by their own well-stimulated imaginations, virtually all the big frontier cattlemen over-estimated the grazing capacity of their natural pastures. What they failed to understand was that to be really productive, grazing areas on the Great Plains require close management. Above all it is crucial to keep the number of cattle feeding on them proportionate. The Canadian government initially decreed that the leaseholders should stock their operations at the rate of one animal for every ten acres. Few of them brought enough stock to their lands to achieve that ratio, and in 1888 the government agreed to allow one animal for every twenty acres.[61] However, in many areas even that ratio was far too high.

McEachran was justified in describing much of his land as excellent for grazing. The region not only gets enough precipitation but it has large areas that are flat enough to give the rains a chance to seep into the soil and thus replenish the natural foliage rather than immediately running off. Drought can still be a problem as the Chinooks that regularly

FISHING BELOW McLACHLAN FALLS, CALLUM CREEK, UPPER WALROND RANCH, ALTA.

TWO MEN FISH-
ING BELOW
McEACHRAN
FALLS, CALLUM
CREEK. GLEN-
BOW ARCHIVES
NA-237-39.

feed into the area have a drying effect. However, most years many of the creeks flow summer and winter, as does the Oldman River, and there is usually sufficient drinking water for any number of livestock. Moreover, the native rough fescue and other mixed grasses cure well in the summer and fall and thus retain high levels of digestible carbohydrates and crude protein after the growth season.[62] Along the Oldman River, and Beaver, Tennessee and Olsen Creeks on the lower block,[63] and in the massive rolling plain surrounding Callum Creek and its several tributaries, the grazing potential is second to none.[64] Unfortunately, these sections were also the most subject to abuse under the open range system. If left on their own cattle and horses will inhabit almost exclusively the "riparian" areas in the warmer months – that is, those areas in close proximity to a water source. Here the stock finds the most lush and longest grasses and, when thirsty, can readily access water. The problem is that the grasses soon become badly diminished by overgrazing and trampling and from the cumulative effects of subjection to substantial amounts of livestock urine. Once the grass in one riparian area is depleted to the point where grazing becomes impossible the animals move on to another area, inflicting similar damage on it. Eventually all the best grasslands on a particular ranch may be affected. If after time the animals can no longer find good grazing by a water source they will graze some distance away from one, making the trek back to it when the urge to drink strikes. This will cause them to "walk off" much of the nutrition they take on from grazing and, therefore, to fail to gain weight properly.

What modern cattlemen do to protect their grasslands is fence them into relatively small sections and then use a system of "rest rotational grazing." They move the cattle into a given section that has a water source and then, after several days rather than months, "rotate" them into another section before the leafy matter on the plants is eaten off by more than about two-thirds. This is important.[65] "Grazing or browsing too much of the leafy material, the collector of solar energy, will wear the plant down and reduce its ability to store energy in its roots."[66] Cattlemen have noted, moreover, that when the hooves of heavy herbivores impact the land for short periods they actually have a positive "ground-disturbing" effect, which promotes seed germination and thus enhances plant growth.[67]

In the early ranching period the drinking water source for livestock was almost always a stream, lake or slough; more recently it might be a man-made well that uses wind power or electricity to pump water to a trough. Some modern ranchers also place a tank some distance from the natural water source and pump the water to the tank for the cattle to drink. Usually cattle prefer to use such a facility rather than wading into a stream, lake or slough. The advantage is that the trough can be moved from time to time to prevent the kind of really severe damage to the vegetation that occurs at the edge of a stationary source.

Under the rest rotational system each fenced-in pasture is given short rest periods over the course of any one grazing season and then is also allowed to replenish for an entire year every several seasons. Besides keeping the grasses healthy this provides for the growth and development of small trees and shrubs, which otherwise would be held back and even destroyed by the stock. Wood vegetation is necessary to maintain channel and bank stability on streams and rivers and to enhance ground porosity and thus moisture levels in other areas.[68] The above photograph shows Callum Creek in 1893 after livestock had been allowed free access to it for ten years. The small wood vegetation had all but disappeared and even the bigger trees had been killed.

Another important management system is known as "time-controlled grazing." On many foothills ranches, lowland fields are grazed early in the growing season (early June to late July) since the native wheat grass matures early and loses its nutritional value if not eaten down at that time. The drier upland ranges are kept free of livestock until the dormant period from August on when native rough fescue can be used to best advantage. These practices allow the regrowth that plants require for rebuilding roots and energy supplies.[69] The photograph below and the two taken from a recent publication on grasslands management allow us to view the bionetwork on the Walrond ranch after it had been in operation for twenty years against that achieved in the 1980s when greater attention was paid to cattle numbers and in 1997 after a fully sophisticated system of rest rotational grazing had been implemented.

W.R. ROUNDUP RIDE.

SOMEBODY ELSE'S MONEY

WALROND ROUND-UP RIDERS, 1903. THE GRASS IS VERY SHORT IN COMPARISON TO ITS PRESENT STATURE (ILLUSTRATED IN THE TWO PHOTOGRAPHS BELOW). GLENBOW ARCHIVES NA-102-21.

CALLUM CREEK FIELD UNDER CONTINUOUS GRAZING IN THE 1980S.

L. Fitch, B. Adams, P. Ag, K. O'Shaughnessy, *Caring for the Green Zone; Riparian Areas and Grazing Management*, 3rd ed., 23, online: www.cowsandfish.org/riparian/caring. html

CALLUM CREEK UNDER A SYSTEM OF ROTATIONAL GRAZING IN 1997.

L. Fitch, B. Adams, P. Ag, K. O'Shaughnessy, *Caring for the Green Zone; Riparian Areas and Grazing Management*, 3rd ed., 23, online: www.cowsandfish.org/riparian/caring. html

In the earlier period the taller rough fescue and wheatgrass, called "de-creasers" because cattle like them the most and therefore eat them down first, had been replaced by shorter "increasers," including blue grama and porcupine grass, which cattle find less desirable. It was the decreasers that McEachran had unknowingly referred to in 1881 when he had said that "in some places" the grass "was so thick and so long as to impede the progress" of horse-drawn wagons.[70] Control of cattle numbers brought back a percentage of these plants in the 1980s, and then a more sophisti-cated approach fully restored them by 1997.[71]

The key to grassland management is constant monitoring. It is es-sential for the livestock producer to watch his pastures closely so that he is ready to move the animals when necessary. Variations in the produc-tive capability of his grazing lands can be incredible. At minimum three times as much feed can be got out of lands that are properly managed than from those that are not. Or, to put it another way, three times as many cattle can be pastured on grass that is nurtured than on grass that is abused. The number of acres required to pasture a dry cow or a cow/calf pair year round on the better pastures when McEachran's riders drove the first cattle to them in 1883 was about twenty.[72] After several years of allowing the cattle to access them at will, however, it would have taken about three times that many. Moreover, much of the leased land away from the river and many creeks was not of the best quality (see aerial photos below).

On the steeper slopes in the Livingstone Range and the Porcu-pine Hills the soil is thin and drought is problematic as rainwater drains off very quickly. In both regions there are also thick coniferous forests, which in the Livingstone Range are supplemented by heavy poplar and willow growth. While some trees and bushes can augment most pastures, very thick groves of either will do just the opposite by blocking out the sun and using up most of the soil nutrients and moisture.[73] The carrying capacity in such areas is extremely low.

Very roughly, under the extensive techniques employed by the first ranchers the average amount of good and poor grazing land combined

SOMEBODY ELSE'S MONEY

SPRINGFIELD RANCH, BEYNON, ALBERTA CIRCA 1900. THE GRASS HAS BEEN TRAMPLED ALONG THIS RIPARIAN AREA TO THE POINT WHERE IT IS VIRTUALLY NONEXISTENT. GLENBOW ARCHIVES NA-43-196.

SOMEBODY ELSE'S MONEY

Longhorn cattle on range, southern Alberta. Clearly this pasture is badly overgrazed. Glenbow Archives NA-4035-199.

SOMEBODY ELSE'S MONEY

THIS PHOTO-
GRAPH SHOWS
WALROND PAS-
TURELAND ALONG
CALLUM CREEK
IN 2008. NOTE
THE LENGTH OF
THE GRASS STICK-
ING THROUGH
THE SNOW.

THE LIVINGSTONE
RANGE FROM THE
EAST. PHOTO BY
THE AUTHOR.

SOMEBODY ELSE'S MONEY

Somebody Else's Money

that was required to pasture a cow or cow/calf unit year round would have been at least 70 acres.[74] Thus the Walrond's 275,640 acres were capable of carrying no more than 4,000 head.[75] As we will see, Walrond cattle were able to stray off the company lease along the Oldman River and east of Beaver Creek (though any relief to the home pastures was largely offset by neighbouring cattle that strayed onto the lease).[76] Ostensibly as well from 1887 on, 1,500 to 2,000 were commonly fed or custom fed for about a hundred days over the winter. This gave the operation the capacity to handle something like 1,600 more, or 5,600 in total.[77] Still it is clear that both the Walrond Cattle Ranche Company and the Walrond Ranche Company overgrazed by a considerable degree, as they normally kept over 5,000 cows plus 300 breeding bulls and at least 3,000 steers. The first ranch also had around 100 saddle and workhorses and 40 to 50 Clydesdales and Shires and the second ranch some 700 horses all told once McEachran expanded the breeding business.[78] Through years of overgrazing, moreover, grasslands become *progressively* less productive.

On the Great Plains generally the Walrond was far from alone in abusing the ecosystem. By the late nineteenth and early twentieth centuries it had become a major problem on every ranching frontier from Texas to Montana.[79] One of the major reasons for this, over and above the promotional and romantic literature and the tendency of men like McEachran to take it seriously, was recognition that in the pre-settlement era the plains and foothills had been heavily stocked with buffalo. If the wonderful natural pastures were capable of feeding literally millions of these large indigenous animals, pundits reasoned, surely the same pastures could carry any number of cattle, sheep, or horses. What they failed to consider is that the buffalo balanced their own needs with those of their grasslands by routinely migrating from one feeding ground to the other, giving each at least one long interval every year in which to replenish. Their normal habit was to graze down on the open plains in the warmer months and then to take shelter from the cold northwest winds by moving to the hills and woods of the high country near the Rockies in the wintertime. This way they allowed the plains a long period to rejuvenate in the winter months and gave the uplands the same during the rest of the year. Moreover, the buffalo tended to move around constantly during either season rather than staying on a particularly fertile natural pasture until it was badly eaten and trampled down. They would graze in one spot for a few days and then move on.[80]

Unfortunately for the early ranchers, left on their own, cattle do not have the same inclinations as buffalo. Not only do they congregate in a specific riparian area until it is damaged almost beyond repair, but they also do not adopt regular seasonal migration patterns. Many ranchers drove their cattle down onto the plains in the spring and then back up into the hills as winter was setting in. However, cattle lack the heavy fur around the head that the buffalo are endowed with, and thus when the colder winds started to blow out of the northwest they would instinctively turn their backs to it and then move in the direction it was blowing. Before the range was fenced, therefore, a large percentage of them would end up on the plains in winter. During the summertime, on the other hand, as riparian areas on the lower pastures became exhausted some of the cattle would roam back up into the high country seeking better pickings around the streams, sloughs, and lakes there. The net result was that throughout virtually any year domestic animals could be found grazing high and low, and none of the grasslands was afforded time to recoup.

The deterioration of the Walrond pastures must have been most pronounced on Beaver Creek, to which the cattle were driven when they first came in from Montana. The cattle would have crowded in along the creek and then slowly damaged greater and greater areas on both sides of it. Eventually this forced them to search for better pastures further afield. Some of them found what they were looking for relatively close to the lease. But as these pastures were damaged it was only by pushing on into regions well beyond the lease that any of them managed to find similarly fruitful rewards. The more mature steers that had been born and raised on the frontier and were familiar with the environment were relatively mobile compared to gestating or nursing cows or the bulls that for obvious reasons stayed close to them.[81] From the lower block steers and, presumably, only some of the younger healthier "she stock" would leave the Porcupine Hills for ideal grazing in the valleys of Willow Creek and its tributaries to the east, which they could then follow south to the Oldman River and then east again from there. The same sorts of animals from the upper block would simply follow the Oldman River east. The cattle would move along the valleys as they ate down the grass. At the end of the summer the Walrond cowboys would conduct roundups in the outside regions, and they always found quite a number of cattle.[82] These cattle were generally in better condition than the rest and a significant percentage of them were sent to slaughter in the fall. Many other cattle did not do as well. When the colder months of the year began they often were a little on the thin side if not downright gaunt. As winter proceeded they found the pickings on the range rather slim as much of the taller rough fescue and wheat grass that in earlier times would have stuck through even rather deep coverings of snow had been so badly eaten down. Most of the nutriments these animals were able to imbibe from grazing were thus used up on energy their bodies required to fight the cold. The evidence of overgrazing in the 1890s is detectable in the dressed weights of the animals delivered to the Indian bands between November and April. We do not have all the figures from beginning to end but we do have a considerable number of them for the period from 1894 through 1898.[83] What they demonstrate is that the net carcass weights were consistently low, that the drop in the wintertime was always great, and that the net average yield per animal worsened with time.

In part to bolster his supply of beef McEachran began a practice in 1895, that then became annual, of purchasing "doggies," or yearling steers and heifers, from the East to put out on the pastures in the spring and hopefully get ready for market in two or three years rather than three to five years as was the case with the calves born on the ranch. The doggies were both steers and heifers – the latter were neutered on the ranch to prevent them from breeding and then listed by Warnock as "s" (for spayed) cows once they were sold. The influx of the doggies not only meant more cattle competing for the Walrond's now badly grazed-down pastures, it must also have helped to speed up an invasion of destructive weed species. Seeds of sow thistle, leafy spurge, and Canada thistle, which were well known to Ontario farmers and grazers, migrated west in the intestines or in the fur of eastern stock.[84] Healthy prairie grasses will compete well with most weeds. However, particularly in the Walrond's riparian areas the native flora were in relatively bad shape. Therefore, the seeds flourished and spread rapidly like European diseases among Native peoples. This suggests infestations like that described by the South Dakota rancher who had been so outspoken in decrying the limitations of western grasslands in the 1870s.[85]

The first of the Walrond doggies were killed in 1897. However, they did little to stem the decline in overall carcass yields. The net dressed weights of all the animals delivered to the Blood reserve in 1894 and 1895 and the Peigan reserve in 1896 to 1897 and the Bloods from 1897 to 1898 were calculated monthly by Warnock and sent to McEachran in Montreal. Onionskin copies are in the archives. A fully finished grass-fed steer carcass could, as we have noted, be expected to yield over 900 pounds. In the fall of 1894 the August steers at the Blood agency weighed 744 pounds, those for October weighed 808 pounds, those for February 672 pounds, and April 600 pounds. In the same period the cow carcass weights, which one would expect to be around 720 pounds, dropped from 672 pounds to 518 pounds. In November 1896 Warnock told McEachran that "after working over the range John thinks we will need all the beef" we have "to fill the Piegan [sic] contract. A great many of the cows are not fat enough to make beef in January and February and numbers of them will not hold their condition this winter. Stags [i.e. very rough steers] too are not in the condition they ought to be."[86] In April 1897, at which point the long winter season was coming to an end and spring about to set in, his prediction proved out. The animals "are very light now, and it seems a pity to sacrifice them in that way. They could bring far more money three or four months hence."[87] At that time the dressed weights of the steers had dropped from 764 pounds net the previous November to 583 pounds; and the weight of the cows had declined from 647 pounds to 472 pounds. The following winter the Blood weights declined precipitously once again. In September 1897 the steers weighed 647 pounds and in April 498 pounds and the cows dropped from 575 pounds to 425 pounds.[88]

It is worth illustrating one more time just how much small carcasses reduced total ranch income. At six cents per pound, steers averaging 900 pounds net were worth $54.00. If the ranch sold a thousand properly finished steers a year it could expect to bring in a total of $54,000.00.[89] However, poorly or unfinished steers such as those sold in April 1898 were worth only $29.88. The difference was over $24.00 a head. The overall difference for the ranch in any given year might be as high as $24,000.00 on steers alone. The fact that the numbers consistently show carcass weights for both genders clearly trending downward over a period of years suggests that the Walrond operation was slowly (or perhaps not so slowly) going bankrupt certainly by the late 1890s. The margin between what McEachran had paid for the cattle and what he was being paid was eroding at a very alarming rate.

McEachran's two major business mistakes then were to incur overly onerous expenses and to place too many cattle on his pastures. What he should have done when he discovered the carcass weights falling was dramatically pare costs, firstly by eliminating the dividend. He should then have dramatically cut down on the size of his herd. This he could have accomplished by selling the poorest of his cows and steers, which would have left him with a totally cleaned up and, therefore, much improved remnant. With the capital attained from both sources he would then have been able to keep the ranch going while holding back the rest of his cattle until they were good and fat. At that stage his take per head and, therefore, his cash flows would have improved.[90] Instead he did the opposite. He began actually supplementing his core herd by bringing in doggies from the East. The decision to purchase yearling and two-year-old stock was one that many of his fellow Great Plains ranchers made. It is sometimes seen as an intelligent move by cattlemen to stock that were young, hardy, and mobile enough to resist both drought and the harsh winters on the prairies.[91] In the Walrond case, however, and, indeed, in that of Moreton Frewen and presumably numerous others, it might well be seen as a product of a largely self-induced cash shortage. Under extreme pressure to cover expenses that he himself had driven up through dividend payments (and his own salary), McEachran started purchasing cattle that he believed he could market more quickly. In other words, in order to keep his marketing high enough to bring in the necessary money to cover costs that he could easily have eliminated, he made outlays to purchase more cattle, which put new strains both on his liquid resources and his deteriorating grasslands.

6

ELEGANT HORSES
IN A RUGGED SETTING

When examining the northern ranching frontier of the late nineteenth century, historians have directed our attention almost exclusively to beef production.[1] Many of the first ranchers in the northwestern states and in western Canada kept herds of sheep or fine horses.[2] In the 1880s the Walrond ranch followed through on McEachran's desire to get into the equine business in a relatively big way. The venture encountered a plethora of difficulties. Most of the Walrond horses, like most of the cattle, were allowed to graze year round in the harsh Great Plains environment with a minimum of human intervention. This saved the ranch from major expenditures on labour and feed and on the construction of some fences, corrals, and outbuildings. However, it also made it impossible to insulate the horses from the elements or to effectively control bloodlines. That, more than anything else, explains why the business ultimately failed.[3]

After suggesting that the ranch should increase the number of Shire and Clydesdale horses, in 1887 McEachran quickly began to amplify the Walrond's commitment. In 1893, by which time David Warnock had taken over from Lew Murray as horse manager, the herd rose to 448 animals and by 1894 it stood at 546.[4] The ranch usually ran between 130 and 170 geldings, which were supposed to be marketed in Canada and Great Britain as workhorses, and 315 to 375 mares and fillies, the most productive of which were used for breeding and the rest of which were sold along with the geldings. The ranch also maintained several stallions and each year the mares produced well over a hundred foals. The methods gradually developed for nurturing the animals brought modest refinement to the open range system. By the mid-1890s steps were being taken to give close attention to some when environmental circumstances were severe. "I have come to the conclusion" that we should "wean all the big strong foals," wrote Warnock in the fall of 1894. "The weanlings could be put in the stubble field at the back of the stud stable where there is excellent feed, and, if necessary fed some green feed every day. A few of the weaker and younger foals with their dams could be accommodated in the saddle horse pasture for another month.... A number of the 4 years old mares and some of the older ones are very thin.... As it is a number of the mares are giving very little milk and their foals are almost self-supporting. If weaned and given a little oat hay daily, they ought to grow and do well."[5]

McEachran agreed and measures such as Warnock suggested were undertaken. However, as these measures affected only a small percentage of the stock, problems that had afflicted the business in the past continued to do so. Of these problems, resurgent wolf populations were probably the worst. In the fall of 1894 after all the horses had been rounded up, Warnock reported with obvious incredulity that "we have only gathered forty-nine yearlings out of one hundred and one turned out in May last.... [We] have thoroughly ridden all the surrounding country within a radius of 20 miles from the ranche and are satisfied that we have found all that are alive.... The number of wolves in this part of the range at present is I think unprecedented."[6] Even when a portion of the stock was penned up the wolves would slip through the fences at night and take them one at a time. After informing McEachran of the need to modify their approach, Warnock gathered and enclosed the mares with young offspring. Shortly later he reported that "we have lost four [foals] ... by wolves and one from natural causes. We have been very fortunate in not losing more and nothing but hard and constant riding" prevented the beasts from "destroying a large number of foals."[7] Warnock also indicated that the horses with high bloodlines were the least well equipped by nature to defend themselves. All the Shires and Clydesdales, he felt, were "entirely devoid of the instinct of self-preservation."[8] The ordinary riding horses that were kept for working the herds on the range and which for generations had been bred and raised in the West, were faring much better. The "cayuse[s] … are afraid of wolves," and "will fight when cornered." They "seldom get bitten."[9] The ranch kept Native "wolfers" at work poisoning and trapping, but in 1896 when McEachran made the decision to quit the horse business, significant eradication had still not been achieved.[10]

Another major challenge confronting the business was the difficulty of producing animals on western ranges that showed well to discriminating buyers. The main objective was to market heavy draught or "work" horses of the highest quality. Buyers of that type were always favourably impressed by a large, powerful-looking body and a smooth, well-groomed appearance. The Walrond animals repeatedly fell well short of their expectations. From a strictly cosmetic point of view a great impediment was simply the brands on their hides. Branding was necessary under the open range system for reasons over and above the need to cut down on rustling. Because livestock wandered, mixed, and mingled over vast areas, owners could easily lose track of and find themselves unable to identify their own animals or even to classify them according to sex and lineage. Branding was a means of indicating which horses belonged to which ranches and distinguishing age and ancestry. The animals were often marked on the flank, the shoulder, the cheek and under the mane. Eastern buyers viewed this as a form of disfigurement and reacted accordingly. On 16 May 1894, Warnock informed J.G. Ross that "we have found and marked all the horses with the exception of three geldings 3 years old.… It is a great pity to number and disfigure the young stock with so many brands. Some of the best fillies and geldings are branded in no less than four different places – in fact they are covered with brands like a bunch of Texas steers – and their value in the best markets much depreciated in consequence."[11]

Another barrier to the production of animals on the plains that looked to be of the highest quality was the combination of overstretched grasslands and severe weather. The damage these animals often did to the natural grasses in riparian areas was severe. In the warm weather they too would try to stay as close as possible to a stream, slough, or lake in order to drink several times every day. And they would help the cattle to deplete the grass to such a distance around the water source that it would become necessary for them to travel almost constantly to satisfy both thirst and hunger. They thus also could reach the point where they were walking off more energy than they were able to take on. The young growing and the mature nursing animals were affected the most. "Although the wolves have not bothered any of them lately the mares and foals are not as fat as they should be," J.W. Mathison, who replaced Bell as ranch clerk in 1888, wrote in the summer of 1892, "some of the foals are getting footsore with traveling. The days are getting shorter now and the mares do not get as much feed as they should."[12] When the animals went into winter in a poor state the cold weather was bound to cause a higher death rate than would have occurred were they corralled, stabled, and fed as in the East and Europe. The ones that were most at risk on the plains were those that were imported from the latter places to improve herd quality and then in short order left to their own resources. Thus, for instance, a ranch administrator recorded in 1888 that "one of the last shipment of ... fillies" had been lost. "She stopped feeding" due to "exposure to the cold, she was stiff in her front limbs and swollen in her fronts. Bringing her home about 8 miles did not help her. She was blanketed ... [and] given a dose of linseed oil" but to no avail.[13]

The losses to cold weather, though relatively severe, do not seem to have approached those resulting from predation. Compared to cattle, horses are relatively hardy. When given enough time to properly acclimatize they grow a thick coat of fur when temperatures dip for prolonged periods, and they are adept at scavenging for food. Unlike cattle, they have the sense to "paw" through deep coverings of snow to feed on even the short grasses below, and thus most of them managed to get enough to eat on the open range to survive. On the other hand, after going into the winter in less than fit form they certainly were unlikely to improve. Their digestive systems were not capable of extracting enough energy from grazed-over and nutritionally depleted winter grasses to keep them looking rounded and healthy. Consequently, when they were brought in from the pastures in the spring, their coats were usually dull and their bodies a little on the scrawny side.

This problem was compounded by the fact that before wells and pumps were utilized the natural water supply was usually not ample in the wintertime. "The majority" of the horses "are now on Callum Creek" Warnock told McEachran in January 1894. While "there is good footing ... the creek is giving a lot of trouble again and today three of us are all ... chopping a hole for the calves and foals to drink.... We had to open a new hole and had to cut through ice fully three feet thick to strike water and then cut grades on both sides to allow the animals to reach water. In spite of all the time and labour spent the stock do not get sufficient water. It requires some one to watch the ... holes continually as calves and foals are constantly falling in and if not immediately rescued would drown." Warnock longed for better facilities: "a good well with a force pump or small windmill would amply repay the outlay in one winter."[14] Horses, like cattle, can get by without water in winter by eating snow. However, this is not ideal, and in combination with a substandard food supply it can severely affect how they look. "The 5 years old geldings ... are rough in their coats, and would not compare favorably with Eastern horses. If they only had three weeks of green grass they would have quite a different appearance," the men would typically warn McEachran in the spring.[15] Oscillating temperatures sometimes proved tough for the horses to adjust to as well. "Up till the last night or two, very hard frost has prevailed," Warnock reported in 1895, "the changeable weather has been extremely trying to stock, of every description.... I find that our horses are nearly all coughing, and not looking well." A "bad form" of the disease known as "strangles ... has broken out amongst the yearlings, and I am afraid we will lose several of the weaker ones."[16]

Poor conditioning and/or hide disfigurement consistently lowered the value of the Walrond animals. Time and again McEachran and Warnock offered the best of their Clydes and Shires for sale, and in nearly every case discussed in their papers either they or their clients were disappointed with the results. In April 1894 McEachran concluded an agreement with Major James Bell to supply the North West Mounted Police establishment at Indian Head in the Assiniboia region, with sixteen head of Clydesdale mares.[17] Warnock selected "the pick of the not-in-foal mares" for the deal. Later both he and McEachran received a letter from Bell complaining about quality. The "mares were too light," Bell informed them, and just "not the class he expected." He also said he had been "told that some of them would weigh up to 1600 lbs." Warnock was astonished: "coming off the grass after wintering out as they did, there is not a mare in the bunch that will weigh 1600 lbs, indeed I doubt very much whether the heaviest mare will weigh over 1400 lbs." Major Bell, he said, should "take into consideration the fact that these mares had just come through a hard winter. By the middle of June they would have averaged 150 to 200 lbs heavier and would have had altogether a different appearance."[18]

On a number of occasions the Walrond managers also put some of their finest animals through sales rings in eastern Canada or Great Britain where brokers were able to bid on them. Each time they were frustrated with the prices they received. In November 1893 they tried Glasgow. Warnock believed the shipment was likely to "prove a good advertisement," and might even "help to remove the prejudice against branded horses."[19] A few months later, however, he was "disappointed to hear" that they had "received such small figures."[20] In the autumn of 1894 he again sent geldings to Britain and again he was "very much disappointed to learn that … [they] sold badly."[21] Warnock estimated that at the prices received for them "some old country farmer" had probably bought them and would now get them into shape through lots of "work and feed." Doubtless he would then "nearly double his money" by reselling them. Warnock made some profitable small sales of the finest horses he had sometime early the next year. We have "about 22 head of 5 years old geldings … and 52 head of geldings 4 years old," he told a prospective buyer in May. "We have also a lot of mares, ranging from 4 to 8 years old. The geldings we hold at $100.00 … cash, delivered at Macleod, but, if you took some mares we would let you have them cheaper. We will sell mares as low as $80.00 per head. There are some fine animals in the bunch." He advised the same person that he could "see a sample of our horses in the stables of the Sheddens Cartage Coy. Winnipeg, and … at the farm in connection with Stony Mountain Penitentiary." He also mentioned that "two weeks ago the Ogilvie Milling Coy. of Montreal, and the Grand Trunk [Railway] purchased a carload (about 15) of our horses at prices ranging from $225 to $275 per team."[22]

However, the auction sales in the East continued to be disappointing. In the fall McEachran tried the Montreal market with "a very nice lot" that were "well broken," and "fit to go into hard work."[23] He held the horses in Montreal for several months to feed and groom them before offering them.[24] Again, however, both men were "extremely disappointed that the horses ... met with such a poor demand." Bitterly, Warnock told McEachran that the Montreal dealers were bribing the stablemen to 'Boycott' the horses.[25] By this time Warnock was convinced that the best approach would be to offer the horses for sale at the ranch rather than shipping them the long distances to the East and overseas. "Henceforth, I think there will be no necessity for shipping," he told McEachran, "We can sell all our horses here without expense or risk."[26] This enthusiasm seems to have been based on contact with a dealer from Belgium who agreed to take nine geldings and four mares at $70.00 apiece – a decent price considering there were no transportation or other costs to get the animals to distant sales rings. It was also based on the Belgian's expressed interest in future purchases. "He says the market is going to become steadily better and that" his home market "can take all the horses we can raise.... He intends to buy from us about every two months, and ship direct to Belgium."[27] This enthusiasm proved misguided. Perhaps the buyer's own customers were as disappointed with the stock as others had been. Whatever the case, there is no mention of any further contact with him in the ranch correspondence.

Thus, at very most the ranch made only one or two very small rewarding sales of their finest horses in the 1890s. It is clear, moreover, that attempts to market the second and third best animals proved every bit as discouraging. The Walrond, like any other frontier breeding operation, always had quite a number in its inventory that could be described generally as "old, small, unsound or bad doers."[28] This was in part at least because of the difficulty on the open range of preventing the indiscriminate mixing of herds. Stallions can sense when mares and fillies are in heat, and unless kept in a barn or a corral with a very strong and high fence they are almost impossible to keep away. Thus outside stallions, often of dubious quality, that lived on the open range managed to mingle undetected with the Walrond herd. Ranch employees attempted to watch the horses more closely than most of the cattle in order to keep them isolated.[29] However, the Walrond animals strayed as well. "Six young horses" went missing, Mathison wrote in a memo on 27 April 1889, "some of these we found several miles to the west of the lower ranch on Willow Creek."[30] On 15 June 1893, one of the men told Ross that we have been "counting the young horses and find that there are several head out yet." As time went on, the ranch constructed special fences to help solve the problem. However, with such a limited work force basic maintenance requirements were sometimes not met. "The horses at Five Mile have been giving a lot of trouble lately. The wind keeps blowing down the fence almost daily, and the horses get out."[31]

The inferior horses needed to be marketed as they matured to keep the costs of maintaining them as low as possible. Relatively speaking, expenses were high. By the early 1890s the ranch had a total of six employees dedicated to the horse operation alone. Five men were necessary to herd the animals and to both break and train them for prospective buyers, and the wife of one of the men was employed to clean and prepare meals for the crew.[32] There was no point in looking for sales for the poorer animals among consumers in the East and overseas: the traders in those markets were resisting the best western horses and were thus likely to refuse to even consider the second and third grades; and the cost of shipping these animals great distances might very well eat up most of their low value. They had to be marketed in the West and local demand in general was very soft. In February 1894 Warnock told McEachran of a man named John Turner from the Sheep Creek region who commonly imported Clydesdale stallions from Ontario to sell in Alberta. These, he said, always met "a ready market," bringing in "from five to eight hundred dollars" a piece. Warnock was hopeful that he could compete with Turner by showing some of the Walrond stock in Calgary in April.[33] When he went down to the city to investigate, however, he discovered that there was "absolutely no enquiry for heavy draught stallions in Alberta." Money, he opined, was "extremely scarce" and "everybody wants to sell." He felt it would be possible to get rid of "a few" but only on credit and then, of course, "the difficulty is to get the money."[34]

Nonetheless Warnock had eventually to search for customers and, as he expected, he was forced to offer credit in the form of notes (rather than cash) allowing payment at a later date. This enabled the buyers to sell the animals before actually having to part with their money. Warnock made two deals, both in Edmonton. Seventeen head went to R.A. Essery from a company named Allen and Essery. Another dozen went to a man named J. Dimmer. One or more of the notes that each man gave Warnock later defaulted and he was forced to repossess some of the animals from both deals.[35] He was unable to find anyone to pay him cash for these and ended up trading most of them for cattle. It would take him until November 1902 to settle the debt owed by Allan and Essery for horses they managed to market before they could be seized.[36] As bad as this experience was, it fell far short of getting rid of the substandard horses. "There are another thirty or forty head that ought to be culled out," Warnock confided in April 1895, "but I am afraid there will be no market for these" at present.[37]

It is not surprising that McEachran became discouraged with the horse business and decided to get out. In pursuing that decision Warnock undertook several small local sales in 1896 and kept the price low enough to stir some interest. Seventy-one head brought an average price of $55.[38] He tried another sale of twenty-three in London, but the result is not discussed in the correspondence. Overall the demand continued to be weak, and in the following year McEachran unloaded the bulk of what was left – some three hundred head – to local buyers W.H. Fares and Patrick Burns for $50 each.[39] This was just $10 per head more than ranchers were paying for grade saddle horses of mixed ancestry to work their livestock herds.[40]

Ultimately the Walrond venture into the high-bred horse business was little short of disastrous. Losses to predation and the weather reduced the numbers the ranch was able to market in any given year, and the stock that was offered for sale normally brought low returns as a result of markings on the hides, poor conditioning, or dubious bloodlines. How typical the Walrond experience was is not easy to estimate. There can be little doubt that some of the other big frontier ranches like the Bar U, the Quorn, and the Bow River Horse Ranch in western Canada or the Cross S, Eureka, and Green Mountain outfits in Montana faced many of the same impediments.[41] There is evidence, however, that a few of the ranchers raised horses successfully. As noted above, A.E. Cross in Alberta claimed after the turn of the twentieth century that it was that side of his operation that had been successful enough in the early days to more than make up for calamity on the beef side. After the disastrous winter of 1886/87, he said, the horse sales "paid the total capital invested in three years besides 50 head to the good."[42]

One secret to understanding the disparity in success rates between the Cross and Walrond operations is to grasp the difference between extensive and intensive agriculture. At first Cross also allowed the bulk of his horses to fend for themselves year round on the open range. After taking the early cattle losses, however, he quickly changed his approach. His operation at Nanton was much smaller than the Walrond. Cross had a quarter as many horses and a tenth as many cattle, and he was able to fence in enough small pastures at his home place, build large enough networks of corrals, and accumulate enough feed to keep all his stock well supplied and protected through severe weather.[43] While he would not have managed his pastures as closely as many modern ranchers do, he also did not significantly over-graze. He was thus one of the few westerners who year after year got his mature cattle fat enough to satisfy the discriminating buyers of Europe.[44] "Nearly all my steers go as exports to England," he boasted, "leaving very few rough ones for the local market."[45] For handling the horses Cross saw that his men had the facilities they needed to treat the animals with the greatest of care. He kept his best specimens close to home, pampered, well-fed and show-ring worthy at all times and almost certainly stabled them when necessary.[46] He too lost some horses to wolves and weather, but percentage wise, his death rate seems to have been relatively low.[47] He almost certainly branded his horses once, but because his numbers were manageable and his herds watched closely it would not have been too difficult for him to keep track of age and ancestry without unduly marking up the hides. For these reasons Cross's animals showed much better than average. "I did very well by always watching the local demand and having my horses ready for any purchaser that might come along, and never lost an opportunity of making a sale if any fair price was offered."[48] Horses "do well in almost every part of this district but require careful management and plenty of experience with a natural gift of looking after them, in order to make them a success."[49]

Evidently, then, both frontier and natural environmental factors that plagued the Walrond's high-bred horse business could to some degree be overcome by adopting a considerably more intensive approach than McEachran instigated in the 1880s and 1890s. When predation was severe it was necessary to handle horses in smaller numbers and in smaller properly fenced pastures or even corrals so that they could be guarded closely day and night. In recent times northern Great Plains ranchers have had considerable success in keeping wolves at bay during the birthing season by camping out among their stock. After the re-introduction of the gray wolf to Montana and Idaho in the 1990s one rancher "had a steady stream of volunteers camping with him ... each tasked with the job of observing the wolf den and discouraging the animals ... from approaching." It apparently worked; "not a single animal" was taken.[50] Modern horsemen have the facilities not just to keep their animals in protected areas but also to ensure that they are separated from outside herds so that branding is unnecessary, bloodlines are maintained, and the spread of diseases kept to a minimum. And, like A.E. Cross, they know better than to leave prized animals on their own to deal with extreme weather and snow-covered grasslands. McEachran seems to have learned some things through experience. In 1903 he would make the decision to go back into the commercial horse business in order to feed what he described as a "very large local demand."[51] This time he kept his numbers much lower than before – around seventy head – and presumably, he made sure that his stock was somewhat more closely nurtured and controlled.[52] Unfortunately returns must still have been modest. The horse market in the first few years of the new century was bolstered by the British need for mounts in the Boer War in South Africa. Once that outlet was filled, Canadian producers were forced to compete with steam and then gasoline power for the settler market and prices declined significantly.[53]

7

FIGURES DON'T LIE: THE BIRTH
OF THE THIRD WALROND RANCH

In early 1898 Duncan McEachran reorganized the Walrond Ranche Company by forming and selling stocks in the New Walrond Ranche Company and buying out his original investors.[1] He did this, one presumes, in co-operation with William and Arthur Walrond, who had assumed their father's interest after the latter's death in 1889.[2] The move was prompted by two factors: the cancellation of the company's lease by the federal government in 1896,[3] and the desire of a number of the British investors who had been dissatisfied with their returns over the previous fifteen years to redeem their shares.[4] The extremely important question this chapter will try to answer is: why did McEachran not keep to his original plan, which was to shut the ranch down, liquidate its resources, and pay off all the shareholders?[5] As will be underscored here, he could not have been at all pleased with the company's performance.[6] Yet, after adopting the plan to shut down, he suddenly reversed course, put together a new board of directors, and resumed ranching as vigorously as ever before.[7]

One key to this puzzle seems to be that by the late 1890s the ranch was already in a poor financial state. In 1907, McEachran would sell the Walrond's cattle and all its other liquid resources and yet manage to secure only enough capital to redeem a small fraction of the book value of its shares.[8] The stockholders were to be out of pocket over $200,000, and the assets the company had left would be worth far less than that.[9] It is tempting to suggest that this was largely the result of losses sustained over the killing winter of 1906/07, when so many of the cattle on the open range died.[10] If that were the case it might persuade some to argue that to that point the ranching industry had been reasonably profitable.[11] An investigation of the ranch's position in the late 1890s, however, suggests that the blizzards of 1906/07 were merely the final blow in a long series of ailments.

There are two possible explanations for what McEachran did in 1898. The first is that he could not bring himself to come to grips with the lamentable state the company was in. To close down the operation would have necessitated selling everything, and it is possible that McEachran was reluctant to admit that the Walrond's assets were worth significantly less than he had been leading his shareholders to believe. The second factor might have been that he felt the ranch could do much better in the future than it had in the past. Fifteen years of experience on the western frontier had taught him and his onsite managers to alter their practices, and it could be that this influenced him to believe that prospects were much improved. This chapter will argue that both explanations are relevant. To put it as simply as possible, McEachran could see that the financial position was less than ideal by early 1898, but he felt that along with other factors, enhanced ranching techniques might enable him to see that all the shareholders could be properly compensated. This would save the ranch, his own reputation and, along with it, his rather lucrative earnings.

McEachran told his shareholders that the gross worth of the company was $240,000.00 in 1898.[12] When one itemizes and evaluates all its assets, however, this would seem far too high. The ranch owned just 160 acres of land at the Beaver Creek thoroughbred ranch.[13] The quarter section was worth about $1.25 an acre, or $200.00 all told.[14] The company also owned a number of houses, barns, sheds, corrals, and field implements, but these would have brought very little return had they been sold in the unsettled and sparsely populated foothills at the turn of the century.[15] Since the company had sold out of the purebred horse business by this time, its net worth was primarily contained in its cattle inventory. The value of that is, of course, problematic, but it can be estimated somewhat satisfactorily through a scrutiny of the correspondence and memos in the company papers. One of the first and most obvious challenges is to figure out the number of cattle the operation had. This was something about which McEachran and David Warnock were as usual unsure. While still contemplating liquidation, McEachran tried to assess his inventory in the early winter of 1897/98. By that time the roundups were finished, no count had been taken for six or seven years, and most of the cattle were widely scattered on winter pastures.[16] Therefore, he had only two rather dubious methods of determining how many animals there were. He turned first to his book count. Since the previous count, in 1891, the Walrond managers had continued to write off 5 per cent a year. On McEachran's calculations this left 12,311 animals, but he realized, and admitted, that this could be wrong.[17]

McEachran was forced to turn to the second method of calculating the numbers when someone apparently representing one of his shareholders wrote to the secretary of the company, asking him to spell out in simple terms how many cattle there really were.[18] The request was eventually passed on to Warnock. When the latter reported back to McEachran, his words must have been very worrying. "Having been with the roundups a great deal during the past summer," he said, there appeared to be a substantial "shortage of cattle." Warnock felt obliged to try to come up with an explanation. He said that he supposed it was "almost wholly attributable to the ravages of wolves in the calf crop during the past six or seven years."[19] Up to the summer of 1895 the loss amongst calves in the foothills and Porcupine Hills must have been "at least 15% annually, i.e. from the time the calves were branded in June until the following June." This he believed was now producing a dearth of "three and four years old steers and heifers."[20] He also felt that there was "undoubtedly a shortage as regards cows," which he seems to have blamed primarily on the same factor.

The cattle foreman, John Lamar, who had gone out on all the roundups in the fall with the clear instruction to get as close an estimate of the numbers as possible, offered the opinion that altogether there were only about 9,000 cattle still alive on the ranch. Warnock reported that in his judgment the foreman had not "underestimated the overall number."[21] In other words the figure of 9,000 might well be high.[22] Let us assume, however, that the figure was correct and then attempt to determine the financial position it would have put the Walrond in at the time McEachran had to decide what to do about the desire of a number of his British investors to pull out. One thing is for sure: he did not fail to realize that should he sell his livestock at that point he was not going to have an abundant supply of marketable slaughter cattle. Besides the warnings of his local manager and foreman about three- and four-year-olds and cows, he had the evidence of the dressed weights of the animals he was supplying a few at a time to the Blood and Peigan Indian reserves. They had been steadily falling over past winters, and as of February 1898 they were doing so more dramatically than ever before. McEachran must have known that the process would continue well into the spring.[23]

In the prospectus for the New Walrond Ranche Company that he composed in late February 1898, McEachran estimated that he had at least 1,200 "coming four-year-old steers" and 800 cows and spayed heifers, all of which would be sold for beef at the end of the next grazing season.[24] One immediately suspects he was exaggerating, given the shortages his foreman and manager had warned him about and considering other embellishments in the prospectus.[25] It needs to be understood that had the ranch decided at this stage to unload all its cattle it would not have been able to sell them to the Indian agencies because they could take only a handful at a time. Rather, it would have had to sell to buyers like Patrick Burns, who one way or another, could handle thousands. In the fall of 1897 the ranch had made its first big sale to Burns. It got $42.00 for the steers, $33.00 for the spayed heifers, and $30.00 for the dry cows.[26] The going rate by the pound dressed weight when McEachran contemplated selling out in late 1897 and early 1898 was about six cents.[27] In the winter of 1897/98 the average weight of the Walrond steers dropped by about 145 pounds. Had the buyers been willing to take them, they would thus have fallen in value by six cents times 145, or $8.70. This would have made them worth $33.30. Unfortunately, however, the buyers would not have been willing to take cattle at that weight and price. This points to a major advantage the ranch gained when selling to the Indian agencies – they paid the same amount per pound for light carcasses as for heavy. As anyone in the beef business would expect, the buyers who purchased for the packing plants regularly refused lighter cattle because then, as

SOMEBODY ELSE'S MONEY

now, low yielding carcasses were far less economical to process. Thus, for instance, in 1888 Bell had reported that "the cattle buyers were here a few days ago and looked through the cattle but did not think they would suit them as they said a great many of the older steers were too coarse for their purpose and the younger ones too light."[28] When American ranchers persisted in sending lightweight cattle east to be sold at auction, they were commonly discounted by at least a cent a pound live or two cents a pound dressed weight.[29] Therefore McEachran would have been getting much less than $33.30 for his steers. Each time the cowboys delivered to the Indian agencies, they presumably tried to take the bigger end of the animals that were grazing relatively close to the reserves with a few poorer ones thrown in. If McEachran had tried to sell the entire 1,200 he claimed he had as one lot in March, after writing up his prospectus in February, he would not have netted above the average weight of those delivered to the Indians throughout the winter and spring, or about 562 pounds.[30] Therefore, he would have got no more than four cents times 562, or $22.48 apiece for them. If we allow him that for his supposed 1,200 oldest steers, we get a total of $26,976.00. His "fat" cows and heifers would have been similarly discounted and thus, at the March carcass weight of about 467 pounds at four cents, they were worth $18.68 cents each or $14,944.00 for the lot.[31] This would give a net worth of $41,920.00 for all the animals that were the closest to being ready for the beef market.

The average value of the other supposed 7,000 Walrond cattle is very difficult to calculate, but since that of the "slaughter" steers and heifers combined was $20.96, estimating the remaining calves, cows, and yearlings at $17.50 seems reasonable.[32] Seventeen dollars and fifty cents times 7,000 equals $122,500.00. The ranch also had fifty bulls worth about $50.00 each[33] or $2,500.00 in total, and around a hundred riding and work horses also worth about $50.00 each or $5,000.00 in total.[34] Thus all stock can be valued at $171,920.00.[35] This figure could be rounded up to $175,000.00 in order to give the ranch a small amount for the quarter section it owned as well as the equipment and buildings and miscellaneous items like any hay or green feed it had on hand.

In his February 1898 prospectus, McEachran did not mention any cash on hand, and the fact that he stated that "the result of ... liquidation" of all the old company's assets would merely be "to return the whole of the capital" to the investors suggests that he had very little over what he needed to operate in the short term. This is further evinced by his announced intention to run the new company with money attained through the monthly beef deliveries to the Indian agencies.[36] When he made that announcement he unquestionably already knew that the net weights of the cattle he was shipping to the agencies were falling dangerously. The old Walrond was being terminated, and the new one was not legally bound to honour its commitments. If he had had any significant amount of operating capital, it would have made a lot more sense for McEachran to give up the contracts immediately in order to allow the cattle to grow and fatten properly.

The point of all this, then, is that McEachran's organization was not in nearly as good financial shape as he was implying. The value of all its assets was at very most $175,000 when he was telling his stockholders that it was $240,000. Liquidation would have made this all too clear and would, no doubt, have hurt McEachran's pride as well as his finances. There was one important positive advantage the formation of a new company provided both McEachran and the Walronds. It brought them an opportunity to significantly reduce their own exposure. Among the company papers in the Alberta Joint Stock Companies Register there is a list of shareholders compiled in 1943 – nineteen years after McEachran's death.[37] In it his estate is shown holding only 280 shares, which in 1898 had been worth just $14,000. This would seem to indicate that despite a promise in his prospectus that he was going to invest $30,000 in the new company, he actually used the reorganization to in effect cash out some 535 shares. That would have brought him a total of $26,750.[38] If McEachran himself did the math properly to determine the company's net worth he must have had severe doubts about whether on liquidation it would have the resources to pay him and all the rest of the investors dollar for dollar.[39] In that case he would come up short anyway and few of the shareholders would be very happy. And there was always the possibility they might demand that he be forced to sacrifice his holdings simply on the principle that if he had ever told them the truth past boards would never have made such generous agreements with him. Considering all these factors it was better to reinvent the company under a new name and keep it going. Also of some significance in that decision was the fact that, based on an earlier contract McEachran had negotiated with the company, he was eligible (and received) a commission of £1,550 pounds ($7,750) for selling the company.[40] Reorganization also ensured that his annual salary would not just continue in the future but also in fact rise substantially. Sir William Walrond was initially made President of the Board of the New Walrond Ranche Company, but this was only to give it credibility in the eyes of potential British shareholders. After an interim period he stepped down and McEachran himself became president and general manager. This put him in a position to pay himself as he saw fit. Ostensibly, between 1898 and 1911 he took $8,000 a year in salary rather than a smaller amount plus shares.[41]

Thus McEachran ensured that his own fortune from the entire Walrond venture was insulated from any future failures. The Walrond family members did the same by redeeming most of their shares. This was an expedient time for William in particular to cash out. It is evident from the family legal papers at the Devon Record Office in England that he had been experiencing some difficult and embarrassing financial problems. In 1892 he had bought into the banking firm in Exeter of which his brother, Arthur, was already a partner. After so doing he was short of cash, and in the course of two years he took out personal loans from the bank and from one of the partners and ran up a rather large overdraft. When they realized he was unable to pay them back the partners decided they no longer wanted Sir William as a member of their firm and more or less forced him out.[42] The following advice from his lawyer, illustrates the awkward position William was in. "I have had a long talk with your brother and he has seen Mr. Sanders" (the senior partner in the banking firm) "but he absolutely declines to alter his proposal. It is therefore for you to decide whether you will accept it.... I do not consider you have broken the partnership deed. Nor do I think they can force you to put your accounts right at once as that could only be done by an application to the Court — and so long as you remain and abide by the terms of the partnership deed you can take your share of the profits but it will be an unpleasant position. You will be much harassed to find the money" to cover both the debts and your own "present needs."[43] Sometime in the early twentieth century the Walronds were obliged to sell Bradfield Hall, which had been the family residence since the early sixteenth century. No doubt the capital Sir William was able to redeem from the shares he had bought in the Canadian ranch, and those his recently deceased father had left him, brought welcome relief. William died in 1925, and in the 1943 list of shareholders he is shown owning only fifty-two shares originally worth $2,650, and these in conjunction with his nephew, Captain John E. Acland. Of the rest of the family the largest shareholder was not really a blood relative. The twenty-first Lord Clinton was the son of Sir John Walrond's son-in-law, the twentieth Lord Clinton, and his first wife, Henrriet Williamina Hepburn-Forbes (Sir John's daughter, Margaret, was Clinton's second wife). The elder Clinton had owned $18,750 worth of shares, but in 1943 the younger one had just 150, originally worth $7,500.[44] The only other Walrond relative in the 1943 document, Arthur's daughter Nancy Bonsor, is listed as owning 270 shares, originally worth $13,500. Absent from both the 1913 and the 1943 lists are the names of Arthur and William's mother, Lady Francis Caroline, and the other Walrond son-in-law who had once held shares, C.A.W. Troyte. One way or the other, therefore, the Walrond family managed to reduce their holdings by nearly 75 per cent.[45]

McEachran undoubtedly felt some responsibility to the Walrond family. They had originally formed the company on his advice and he could not have relished the idea of the significant lowering of his stature in their eyes that might come from a considerable loss in the value of their holdings. Was McEachran purposely trying to mislead the rest of his shareholders in 1898? Yes he was. He had been paying out dividends over the years for the most part without knowing whether the value of his inventory was going up or down – in other words without knowing whether the ranch was actually profitable. Had this been discovered he could in most years have claimed ignorance about the herd count. In early 1898, however, he had been warned that his numbers were short, and he had to be aware through the Indian contracts that the value of his livestock was dwindling dangerously. He certainly kept that to himself. In reorganizing the Walrond he hoped to sell 6,000 shares in the new company at $50 to bring in $300,000.[46] In the end he must have been disappointed. The 5,041 (including his own) shares he managed to sell had a total value of just $252,050.[47] Still, that was to purchase assets worth some $70,000 less than that. It should not be forgotten, moreover, that the latter figure accepts the cattle foreman's rough estimate of total herd size and McEachran's calculation of the number of cattle that were closest to being ready for slaughter.[48] Both very likely were high.

It does seem evident, however, that McEachran did not really intend to cheat his investors. While he clearly secured a handsome monetary reward to which he had little moral right, and at the same time made sure that any future risk would be with other people's money, it is also evident that he honestly felt he could see to the regeneration of the company, based in part on operating techniques experience had taught. In so doing, he would make back everything it had lost. In the end this would be good for everyone. He would avoid coming to grips with the company's financial state, and he and all the owners, new and old, would be properly rewarded for their involvement. The advantages McEachran believed the new company would enjoy over the old one were numerous. One of the most obvious was avoidance of the horse business. "The new Company," he wrote in his prospectus, "will have no concern" with that.[49]

Another practical improvement McEachran felt the New Walrond would enjoy was the eventual solving of the wolf problem. He seems to have believed that this was not going to be enough, considering the other constraints, to make horse ranching profitable, but that it would provide crucial relief to the cattle business. When he told potential investors that "wolves, which were abundant and caused considerable losses in past years are now almost exterminated,"[50] he was exaggerating and he knew it.[51] However, he did have reason to think that western ranchers were winning the war against the predators. For one thing, they had found a new and much more efficient form of poison. "We are meeting with great success in the use of the 'Compressed Strychnine Tablets' that I secured from … Philadelphia," Warnock had told him in the autumn of 1894,[52] and since that time "wolfers," particularly from the Stoney Indian tribe to the north, had been hunting and trapping them with what appeared to be considerable success.[53] In December 1897 Warnock told McEachran that wolves "have been getting very numerous lately. During the time that the bounty was discontinued last winter and spring, the Indians stopped hunting and much of the benefit derived from their energetic warfare during the two previous years was lost." However, he also said that the bounty was now being paid again and that the Stoney Indians were once more "at work" on the problem. "Within the last ten days they have killed three full grown bitch wolves on Heath and Cabin Creeks.[54] One of the wolves is almost pure white and judging by the appearance of her teeth must be all of fifteen years old. I will warrant that she and her progeny have killed many hundreds of W.R. calves during the past years."[55]

Obviously, McEachran had also learned the importance since the first great killing winter of 1886/87 of implementing a number of intensive farming practices on his operation. This the Walrond would continue to do. Warnock was to keep reasonably large supplies of hay and green feed on hand, and he would repeatedly set his crews to work enclosing more of the ranch with barbed wire fences.[56] The ranch was also to continue the practice of farming out numerous of its most delicate animals to smaller ranchers and settlers who would custom feed them over the winter for a price of about $3.00 per head per month. Consequently the Walrond was better able to protect all the domesticated "doggies" from the East that, at any one time, had not adjusted to the wilds sufficiently to look after themselves in inclement weather and many of the other cattle that because of age or over-work were considered at risk.[57] While this was expensive it could be supposed to cut down on the death loss, and McEachran believed it would help to prevent the reoccurrence of more disasters.

Other benefits he foresaw for the future had to do with changing circumstances rather than improved techniques. The first he mentioned was that the ranch would no longer have to pay rent for its leased property. The Dominion government had cancelled the original leases in 1896, and since that time the Walrond had been operating on free range. The rent had only been one cent per acre per year, but McEachran pointed out that on 300,000 acres this amounted to $3,000.00.[58] He was exaggerating a little, as his cost must really have been $2,750.64. Still this was a reasonably significant sum. One other thing that offered reason for hope in early 1898 was that "new markets" had "been opened up with every prospect of immediate and rapid extension."[59] Foremost were those associated with the building of the railway through the Crowsnest Pass and the development of the mining industry there. Warnock was particularly optimistic about the prospects it offered. Due to the railway, he said, "the beef contractors are killing about 300 head of cattle per month and I think, expect to keep that up all winter."[60] One of our own former employees "is up in the Pass now, inspecting cattle and hides. He is going to buy cattle (beef) on commission" for the middlemen who have contracted to supply the railroad.[61] Both McEachran and Warnock were also buoyant about the "opening up of the Yukon River and Klondyke Mining Lands,"[62] which had so recently followed the discovery of gold on Bonanza Creek.[63]

On a more general plane, both McEachran and Warnock believed that the West as a whole was filling up and that this would soon bring an almost insatiable demand for beef. "There can be no doubt about there being a shortage of cattle in America, and the scarcity of beef promises to be greater every year for some time to come," Warnock wrote in March. "In the States herds of breeding cattle have been changing hands at high figures and several large Montana Cattle companies are establishing breeding ranches in Texas. In this district beef brokers Gordon and Ironsides have been snatching up all the small bunches of cattle offered for sale and have taken them to their ranche north of Calgary."[64]

Duncan McEachran, very much like Moreton Frewen in Wyoming, was an incurable optimist as well as a promoter. When he organized the New Walrond Ranche Company in early 1898 he foresaw that new approaches, which he and his managers had learned over time, along with ever-expanding markets would more than make up for losses he felt terribly reluctant either to accept or to explain to his shareholders. To him it was sensible to protect himself financially by converting most of his own holdings in the company to cash. After all this was all profit since he had paid nothing for it. Moreover, if the ranch were indeed to do better in the future than it had in the past, he would not just save face but also continue indefinitely to enjoy a very generous annual remuneration. At the same time he was able largely to protect the Walronds and to pay off the malcontents among his shareholders. In truth, from a personal perspective he had much to gain and little to lose. Perhaps the question should be, not why, but why not?

8

CONFRONTING THE FRONTIER
BUSINESS ENVIRONMENT

The New Walrond, which officially began operations in 1898, was more Canadian than any of the other versions of the company had been. The Head Office now moved from London to 1766 Notre Dame Street, Montreal. Including McEachran, who was soon to move from his position of vice president and general manager to *president* and general manager, seven out of nine of the members of the board of directors were Canadian.[1] One of the seven, William M. Ramsay, had, like McEachran, previously been a shareholder. The rest of the Canadian directors became shareholders for the first time. They included some of the richest and best-known men in the land. There was William Watson Ogilvie from Montreal, who with his brothers Alexander and John had operated W.W. and A.W. Ogilvie Company Limited (1847–1973).[2] After the death of his brothers the company had fallen into William's hands, at which time, according to a biographer, he became the "largest individual miller in the world."[3] At the turn of the century he was to add Ogilvie Flour Mills Company Limited (1900–1983) to his business empire. Ogilvie had much in common with McEachran. Besides residing in Montreal the two men shared a Scottish heritage, they both were staunch Conservatives, and they both ran large western corporations that occasionally did business with each other.[4] Moreover, they shared an affection for fine livestock. When in 1895 Warnock had told a correspondent that the Ogilvie Milling Company and the Grand Trunk Railway had purchased a carload of horses at from $225 to $275 he was unquestionably speaking of some of the top Clydesdales or Shires the Walrond ever produced.[5] In late 1897 McEachran met Ogilvie's "agent" at Glasgow when on a trip to view various aspects of the beef trade in Britain and continental Europe. The agent, he noted, was in the process of buying twenty-four head of the "best Ayreshires procurable" to import into Canada.[6]

Ogilvie's nephew-in-law, J.A. Gemmill, also invested in the Walrond company in 1898 and he joined the board at the same time.[7] Closely connected with the Ogilvies in business, and perhaps even wealthier, was Andrew Frederick Gault. Gault was known as the "cotton king of Canada," for the stranglehold he exercised over the industry as president of this country's three largest cotton textile firms – Dominion Cotton Mills Company Limited, Canadian Colonial Cotton Mills Company Limited, and Montreal Cotton Mills Company Limited.[8] W.J. Buchanan may have been brought into the company by James G. Ross. Along with Ross, he was a shareholder of the Guarantee Company of North America, so he may well have been connected to Ross through that business.[9] Joseph Hardisty, who also lived a considerable portion of his adult life in Montreal, worked his way to the upper executive offices of the Hudson Bay Company. He was the son of Richard Hardisty senior, a chief factor at the HBC for many years who paved the way for his sons Joseph and five others to attain careers there.[10] Joseph's brother Richard Charles was appointed to the Senate in 1888. Joseph's sister, Isabella, married Donald Alexander Smith who worked closely with members of the Hardisty family in the Hudson Bay Company before joining the directorship of numerous corporations including the Canadian Pacific Railway and the Bank of Montreal. As "one of Canada's richest millionaires," Smith was knighted and ultimately raised to the British peerage as Baron Strathcona and Mount Royal.[11] It is possible that Strathcona was de facto owner of the Walrond shares held by Joseph Hardisty. In 1905 McEachran claimed that he was "interested" in the company "to the extent of 2000 pounds."[12] The 1943 list of Walrond shareholders compiled when the company finally found a substantial buyer for its capital assets includes several of Strathcona's descendants and, ostensibly, none of Hardisty's.[13]

James Ross also of Montreal continued in his position as Secretary-Treasurer of the New Walrond though he was not on the board of directors. Along with the increase in Canadian participation in the company there was a significant British defection. Indeed, all the shareholders who decided to liquidate their stake in the ranch at this time were British. Besides the members of the Walrond family discussed above, they were George Stapylton Barnes, Aarchibald Herbert James (both of whom had bought in between 1888 and 1894,) James Ponley Dawes, William Herbert Evans, Julia Neville Grenville, Francis William Mitchell, William Maschwitz, Thomas Henry Goodwyn Newton, and Horace Newton. Yet the Walrond Ranche Company Limited was still far more British than Canadian. All the rest of the shareholders who along with Ramsay and Ross decided to reinvest were also from Great Britain. There were George Herbert Windsor-Clive, Lord Clinton, Henry Aubrey Cartwright, John Goring, Lady Jane Hotham, Walter Henry Holbech, Thomas Pakenam Law, Arthur Constance Mitchell, and Samuel Peshall. Moreover, several of their fellow Britons now joined the list of shareholders. As we have seen, Captain J.E. Acland, Sir John's grandson,[14] who resided with the family at Cullompton, Devonshire, was given a very small stake in the company. The rest of the new British shareholders seem almost certainly to have been attracted to the company by McEachran. Mrs. I. Dickie, A.H. Duncan, A.F. Huie, and D. McTaggart were from Campbeltown in Scotland, where McEachran had been born and raised. John Ferguson, D. McDonald, A. McWilliam, J. McWilliam, and R. Marshall were also Scottish. At the turn of the century they resided in Glasgow but their family names had all been plentiful in Campbeltown when McEachran was young.[15] At the time of his birth in 1841, along with the sixty-three McEachrans, sixteen Duncans, seventeen Huies, and sixty-five McTaggarts living in that town there had been five Marshalls, forty-three Fergusons, sixteen Duncans, seventy-two McDonalds, and twenty-four McWilliams. The one other new investor in 1898 was Sir George Thomas Brown, who lived in Harrow on the Hill in England (London). Even he may have been a McEachran recruit. In 1841 there had been sixty-four people with that last name in Campbeltown.[16] In total, of 5,041 shares in the New Walrond Ranche Company only 1,713 were held by Canadians, whereas 3,328 were held by Britons.[17]

On the surface the managers of the New Walrond Ranche Company maintained their earlier optimism as they commenced operations in the spring of 1898. "I am pleased to learn that you have been successful in your endeavour to reorganize the company," Warnock told McEachran in March. "I feel sure that the new company will find their venture a paying one."[18] Warnock now moved from his position as horse manager to take day-to-day charge of the entire ranch. One decision in which both Warnock and McEachran felt confident was giving up the Indian contracts in the spring of 1898. "I quite agree with you that beef gathering in the winter for Indian Contracts has been a detriment to the herd and probably did more damage in the past than was ever realised," Warnock wrote, clearly referring to the hundreds of undersized carcasses the ranch had sent to slaughter.[19] McEachran seems to have concluded by this time that he had to stop the frenetic cycle of marketing that he had adopted in the former period. He now had fewer shareholders than before, which would cost him just over $12,000 per annum in dividends rather than over $17,000, and he allowed his book inventory to fall considerably from the more than 12,000 head he had claimed earlier. "After deducting numbers sold and adding purchases and fall branding the books show a total of 7842," Warnock reported in November 1898.[20] That number seems to have been calculated on the basis of the rough estimate of 9,000 and therefore may also have been high.

McEachran's expectation was that he would sell fewer cattle, and principally only to the beef merchants after the roundup in the fall of each year. His hope was that then the animals would weigh up much better than before. This was a sensible approach. However, after 1898 settlement, and along with it fences, pushed ever more tightly around and onto the lands the Walrond had formerly leased. It was in this period that the great surge in western settlement long expected by both the Conservatives and the Liberals in Ottawa finally began to take place. In 1885 less than 9 per cent of the homestead entries that were eventually to be recorded on the prairies had been taken out and by 1900 just 20 per cent. By 1906, on the other hand, the figure would be circa 51 per cent and by 1914 nearly 89 per cent. As this process took shape settlers poured into the areas surrounding the Walrond's pastures, and the ranch's cattle were able to wander less freely than before to find greener pastures.[21]

What McEachran really needed to do was shut down operations completely for at least a year and then cut down his herd to no more than 4,000. This would have given his lands a chance to recover from years of overgrazing and then enabled the native grasses to maintain their health while keeping the cattle fit. From the standpoint of marketing one of the negatives with the loss of the Indian contracts was that it removed the outlet for the rough, substandard animals. Warnock soon had an answer for that. These cattle could now be sold to the Crowsnest Pass Railroad contractors to feed their army of largely immigrant construction workers who were considered to be, like the Indians, rather indifferent about quality. At this point John Lamar had quit the Walrond to work with the beef contractors specifically for that market and "all of the cowhands" who wanted to had got "work on the railroad, packing mail, freighting, herding beef and butchering."[22] The chief supplier was Patrick Burns, though A.J. McLean got a piece of the action. Warnock was able to sell the rough cattle to the latter in between the regular fall roundups and thus maintain a small percentage of the cash flows that had formerly come from the Indian sales. "McLean has a contract for 125 carcasses of dressed beef to go to the Kootenay and he is killing the cattle at Meads ranche" (which McLean had recently purchased), Warnock reported. "He is taking all the rough cattle and any cripples we find if they are fat. It is a fine opportunity for turning off cattle that we could not otherwise dispose of to advantage. We have turned off two steers suffering from incipient lump jaw, several affected with mange, and one of the suspected tubercular steers is now at Meads to be killed. McLean is to pay what the steer is worth if the meat turns out all right."[23]

The decision no longer to compete for the contracts to sell beef to the Indian agencies brought two disadvantages that were to prove more serious. From this point on the ranch would have to market most of its beef cattle at the same time as did the vast majority of the other ranchers in the North American West – i.e., after the fall roundup. Inevitably, year after year this helped to produce a glut of supply on both sides of the Atlantic Ocean, which caused the price of beef to plummet. This disadvantage was only partially offset by the international recovery of beef prices. It was in 1896 that the decline dating back to the late 1870s bottomed out and a period of gradual improvement began that was to continue until the Great Depression. The rise was far too slow to bring back the beef bonanza of the 1870s but it did give western Canadian producers a better break.[24] The other problem producers faced prevented them from profiting as they might have from the turnaround. It was the emergence of a syndicate that gained almost total control of the frontier beef marketing business and whose members knew exactly how to make money on the oscillating prices resulting from the annual glut.

By the late 1890s two frontier cattle merchant companies were gaining a stranglehold over the beef business from pasture to feedlot to packinghouse and finally to the retail trade. In the process they established a mutually beneficial system of co-operation that enabled them to enrich themselves at the expense of the ranchers. The two companies were those owned by Patrick Burns, operating principally out of Calgary, and James T. Gordon, Robert Ironsides, and William Henry Fares from Winnipeg. Together these men were able to manipulate the western cattle market to their own advantage. This made them very wealthy but it also eventually helped to force many of the early ranches, including the Walrond, out of business. While through to the present the remnants of their system have continued to be felt in the western cattle business, it is apparent that frontier conditions were particularly suited to its rise.[25] Foremost amongst these conditions were a scarcity of marketing facilities in Canada and a dearth of well-financed competitors for the two major merchant companies.

The story of the rise of a beef monopoly in the West starts with James Gordon and Robert Ironsides of Winnipeg. These two men got their start in the beef brokering business in the 1870s when they supplied meat to the troops during the North West Rebellion and to construction crews working on the Pembina Branch of the Canadian Pacific Railway. In the 1890s they formed a company known as Gordon and Ironsides and began shipping slaughter cattle to Great Britain. By 1896 the firm was shipping over 25,000 cattle a year across the Atlantic and had become "much the largest single shipper" out of Montreal.[26] In 1897 the two men took in a third partner, William Fares, and the name of the firm was changed to Gordon, Ironsides and Fares. To guarantee supply for their export business the firm branched into ranching. About 1896 the partners established the Two Bar Ranch in the Wintering Hills south of the Red Deer River. Here they ran between 5,000 and 10,000 head of cattle, mostly on free range owned by the crown or the Canadian Pacific Railway. In 1902 they bought the immense Bar U Ranch in the foothills of Alberta to the north of the Walrond in affiliation with George Lane. From then until the First World War they continued to expand their ranch holdings and they also entered the packing industry.[27] They built an abattoir in Winnipeg in the late 1890s, which by 1906 was killing about 1,000 hogs and 500 cattle per day. In quick succession they also built a slaughterhouse in Moose Jaw and established cold storage plants and distribution points in Kenora, Sault Ste. Marie, Fort William, Port Arthur, and Regina.

The rise of Patrick Burns was equally meteoric. Burns came west in 1878 to settle on land near Tanner's Crossing in Manitoba. There he began dealing in cattle, buying and selling from farmers in the area and trailing the animals to Winnipeg for sale. His business prospered for various reasons. The Canadian Pacific Railway link to eastern markets and a growing number of settlers raised the demand for beef. But Burns' big break came in 1886 when his friend William Mackenzie, in partnership with Donald Mann and others, formed the Mackenzie and Mann railway construction company and convinced him to take on the job of supplying meat to the construction camps. His first contract was for the Short-Line of the Canadian Pacific Railway in the state of Maine. It was followed by contracts for the Qu'Appelle, Long Lake and Saskatchewan Railway in 1888 and 1889 and later for the Calgary and Edmonton and the Calgary and Macleod branches of the Canadian Pacific Railway and finally the Crowsnest Pass Railway.[28]

In these years Burns also became a beef packer. He first set up his own "mobile slaughtering facility, which could move easily as the railhead was extended."[29] Then in 1890 he was able to build his first stationary slaughterhouse on the east side of the Elbow River in Calgary, and he went into the retail business selling beef to the city and surrounding area. He also developed contacts with merchants in British Columbia whom he supplied with both meat and wholesale livestock, and he set up his own retail outlets in that province. In 1903 Burns bought the string of meat shops and slaughterhouses owned by fellow meat marketer William Roper Hull of Calgary. At this stage, as L.V. Kelly noted, he became the "acknowledged beef king of the West."[30]

Like the Winnipeg entrepreneurs Burns also got into ranching in a big way in order to guarantee supply. In 1891 he bought a small parcel of land some twelve miles southeast of Olds (known as the "Olds ranch") with C.J. Duggan and started acquiring cattle both locally and from as far away as Manitoba to fatten on grass and hay. By grazing over countless acres of public domain all the way south to High River and by employing neighbouring farmers to both contract hay and custom feed for them in the wintertime, he and Duggan were able to run up to 30,000 head. The deal with William Roper Hull in 1903 included the latter's Bow Valley ranch at Fish Creek south of Calgary. Burns enlarged the ranch from 4,000 to about 12,500 acres by further land purchases, and he built a feedlot on the property for 5,000 head of cattle. In 1905 Burns incorporated under a Dominion charter using the title P. Burns and Company.[31] Thereafter he acquired numerous other ranching properties, presumably in part offsetting the contraction of public domain available as a result of settlement. Over the years several smaller ranchers from southern Alberta turned over their titles because they were unable to repay credit on loans he had extended to them. The bigger operations he obtained through purchase or lease.[32]

As early as the later 1890s, Burns and Gordon, Ironsides and Fares were working in co-operation to cut out competition in the beef trade. One of the secrets to their success was integration. These men made money on their own cattle when supply was low and demand, relatively speaking, high and on their packing and marketing facilities when supply was high and demand, in comparison, relatively low. In the frontier period the latter situation always occurred in the fall when all the ranchers were offering their mature steers and heifers and their dry cows for sale at the end of the summer grazing season. Burns and Gordon, Ironsides and Fares had the ability at that time to depress prices in order to give themselves very attractive profit margins. What having ranches with their own cattle did most for these men was give them the ability to maintain supplies at other times. They bought and kept steers that could be used to meet the demand when the regular fall glut was over. Some of these were animals that had originally been born out of season. They had seen their first light of day in the fall rather than in the spring calving season and thus were still growing too rapidly in the summer months of their fourth or so year to fatten up as well as their slightly older contemporaries. Others were cattle that came from overgrazed or drought-stricken pastures and had not put on as much weight as expected in the previous grazing season. Burns and Gordon, Ironsides and Fares would ship these animals to their own properties and feed them hay over the course of the winter in order to get them ready to kill the following spring or early summer when supplies in general were at their lowest. Thus, for instance, when Burns bought the fat cattle from the Walrond, Oxley, and Glengarry ranches in 1897 he separated out any that he considered not quite ready and sent them "to his feeding ranche sixty miles North of Calgary."[33]

The other secret to the success of the two beef companies was their ability to co-operate closely. That said, they were not the only buyers for the cattlemen to turn to. Before Burns bought him out in 1903, William Roper Hull must have been a strong contender in Calgary. From time to time throughout the frontier period A.J. Mclean, a rancher and partner in the beef brokering firm known as Mclean and Nanton, purchased a significant number of cattle.[34] On the whole producers seem to have liked dealing with Mclean. David Warnock felt he was "much more satisfactory to deliver to" than Burns.[35] However, Mclean did not have the integrated network of businesses or, indeed, the capital for the volume of cattle his competitors were able to handle. He also seems to have been a friend of Burns and may have colluded with him at times.[36] A Winnipeg dealer named Charlie Knox made numerous attempts to purchase cattle from the Alberta foothills. In the struggle against his stronger competitors, however, he met with a great deal of frustration. On 21 May 1902 he wrote to A.E. Cross, "regarding your beef cattle I think you and [William E.] Cochrane should give us a chance." But, "if you decide not to, we intend giving up attempting to buy in the High River District and you will find yourselves left to the mercy of Gordon and Ironsides and Burns."[37] Eight days later he told Cross that he was "prepared to increase

... [my] bid very considerably provided that we can get Cochrane's cattle also, but [I will not] make any further offer unless you say you are willing to sell to the highest bidder as it is not our object to keep up the price of beef in the country and allow you fellows to sell to the old lot."[38]

Other buyers who made some impact were Americans. The firm of Clay, Robinson and Company from Chicago contracted to market a good number of cattle for American ranchers in the Canadian West and for men like Spencer Brothers who operated on both sides of the border.[39] But American buyers generally had difficulty netting top prices for their Canadian customers, primarily because of an import duty of 27.5 per cent *ad valorem*.[40] In 1910 A.E. Cross informed Clay, Robinson and Company that for "many years past I have shipped ... export cattle to Liverpool and other English markets through Gordon, Ironsides and Fares" but "have never had any experience in shipping to your markets."[41]

There was also a dearth of local auction marts in the West. It was not until 1904 that one was established at Fort Macleod, and it was very small and dealt as much in farm equipment and probably household goods as livestock.[42] By that time ranchers also had the option of sending their slaughter cattle to the auction ring in Winnipeg, where buyers could bid on them for the local, domestic, and British trade.[43] Unfortunately, Gordon, Ironsides and Fares were by far the biggest buyers in Winnipeg, and they were more or less unchallengeable in setting prices for all good exportable cattle. It was probably for that reason that the owners of substantial herds preferred shipping directly to Britain. The Walrond did this in 1903, 1904, 1905, and probably 1906.[44] A.E. Cross at the A7 and William Roper Hull, who bought the Oxley Ranch, did so in 1900, 1903, and 1905.[45] This was very risky, however, firstly because of the transportation costs for the bulky freight.[46] It was also difficult to find space on the ocean steamers, not least because of the seemingly endless capital of Gordon, Ironsides and Fares. In 1905 a Montreal agent told Cross that "practically all the available space for July and August has already been engaged; the Gordon, Ironsides and Fares Co. stepped in and took the bulk of it at somewhat higher rates."[47] Once the ranchers got their cattle to Britain they had to take their chances that after paying all the transportation costs the market would hold up. Usually it did not, as the fall surplus normally also struck the British sales rings hardest when the cattle run from the West was at its height. When the *Pincher Creek Echo* reported the Walrond shipments in the fall of 1903 it also announced that prices in Liverpool had suddenly dipped to "the lowest mark ... in 25 years ... the high prices of last season have led to overproduction."[48] The ranch found itself in the same predicament virtually every year. After the fall run ended in 1904, H.A. Mullins of Winnipeg reported that "the trade for cattle is showing a firmness in all the principal markets in Great Britain. Now that the glut has cleared away in the British market, prices have advanced, particularly ... for good quality ranch cattle."[49] When the Walrond animals reached Britain the following year Mullins observed that "since our last report the markets have weakened in all points. Grass cattle are coming forward in big numbers and weather conditions in England are very unfavourable for the beef trade."[50]

It is seldom acknowledged that during the annual fall depression, prices for western Canadian range cattle in Britain tended to drop more precipitously than those from the American West. This was mainly because most of them were totally grass fed.[51] The range cattle that were exported to Europe from points further south normally went through a sales ring in Chicago, were purchased by farmers from the northern Corn Belt states, and fed for at least ninety days on surplus supplies of corn before being placed on steamers for the trip overseas.[52] This gave them a solid layer of hard fat to ensure that they would arrive in Britain looking properly finished and ready for the kill. Because there was no major livestock auction mart in Ontario, or any substantial surpluses of feed grains, Canadian cattle went straight to Europe from the western grasslands. Only a percentage were fat enough to be termed "well finished" when they left the West and, because of the stress of travelling such an enormous distance by train and ocean steamer, they invariably declined dramatically en route. Because their carcass weights were low compared to those from the United States, most of them were discounted significantly by British abattoirs.[53] Indeed, prior to the embargo in 1892, which stipulated that Canadian cattle had to be killed at the port of entry within ten days of disembarkation, many western cattle were bought by British farmers as "store cattle" (or what we would call feeders) to be finished properly over the winter on their surplus grains before being slaughtered.[54]

Time and again when the fall run was on, market reports for sales in London, Liverpool, Manchester, and Glasgow announced that: "from abroad the supplies of stock consisted of 700 cattle from Canada which were a moderate lot. Some of these were taken for keep [i.e. feeding], the rougher description meeting the worst trade of the season, entailing heavy losses for the exporters";[55] the Canadian cattle "were of a middling and ordinary quality receiving over the whole 56 s[hillings] to 62 s[hillings]" per hundred weight, while the American cattle received "60 s[hillings] to 63 s[hillings]" per hundred weight;[56] "foreign supplies for the week here comprised 1,083 Canadians, a fairly good lot, nearly half of which were bought for feeding purposes.... From the States there were 250 ..., which met a better demand."[57] In May 1904 the *Pincher Creek Echo* gleefully announced a brief respite in the "discrimination against Canadian cattle in favour of Americans which has existed during the past few years." The prices "this year at London, Liverpool and Glasgow for the best Canadians are almost equal to the top priced Americans."[58]

When they worked together, Burns and Gordon, Ironsides and Fares were able to prosper because they could utilize both the relatively small percentage of Canadian cattle that were fat enough for overseas markets and the ones that were not. They appear to have begun co-operating in earnest in 1897. Thus, for instance, in June of that year W.H. Fares and Burns negotiated the large purchase of draught horses from the Walrond ranch, and George Lane, who was soon to own the Bar U ranch in partnership with the Winnipeg firm, acted as Burns' agent to buy the Walrond slaughter cattle.[59] Once their relationship was cemented each company was positioned to get exactly what it most required in the cattle business. The Winnipeg entrepreneurs were concentrating on the local market in and around their home city and Moose Jaw and on the overseas trade. As exporters they were anxious to find prime steers and heifers that were well enough finished to satisfy the palates of consumers who were used to the best cuts. Burns was concentrating on the Calgary area and through the favouritism and backing of Mackenzie, he had by this time cut out all competitors except McLean to supply the railway construction crews and the mining and lumber towns of the British Columbia interior. Therefore he was happy for the most part to deal in the rougher, less well finished, and poorly bred animals.

In order to ensure that they were not ever competing with each other the two firms came to a very simple arrangement. Outside the Winnipeg and Moose Jaw areas Burns would purchase all the cattle, separate out the best ones for Gordon, Ironsides and Fares, and keep those of lesser quality. This naturally enough created suspicions of price fixing. In 1900 A.E. Cross, a close friend of Burns, expressed the opinion that "there are practically only two buyers here, and in fact it nearly all comes through one as he sells the exporters to the other after buying all the beef and uses the rough stuff himself, thus leaving the seller more or less at his mercy."[60] At that time Cross was prepared to forgive his friend because "he has shown far more mercy than any one could expect." Three years later, however, he sounded less accepting. "We are trying," he said, "to get a reasonable price, and not sell our cattle for far less than they are worth as was the case last year. What we want is to establish a fair market without any favors so that we know we can get at any time the right market value for all or any of our beef cattle and not go round with your hat in your hand at the mercy of one or two concerns."[61] In his annual report at the end of the same year McEachran bitterly announced "that prices were low due to 'rings' and 'combines'" and that "under the circumstances not much more than half the saleable cattle" on his operation had been marketed.[62] In fact this seems, in part at least, to have been another of McEachran's fabrications meant to obscure the ranch's deficiencies. That year spring and fall fires and early frosts had killed the grass in many districts and most of the beef herds were generally not in good shape. Consequently, "fifty per cent of the beef on some ranches" was held back.[63] However, the price of meat dropped as usual that fall, and a prominent fear of some sort of collusion among the buyers on both sides of the Atlantic was circulating. In September 1906 the *Pincher Creek Echo* informed its readers that a "notice" had been "brought to the House [of Commons] of vital importance to the settlers of this district in common with all farmers and ranchers in the North West Provinces: that is the beef combine that evidently exists among the beef buyers to keep down the price of beef cattle, paying the farmer as little as possible and taking all the profits of the business."[64] Some weeks later the paper urged local producers to get together and broker their own cattle. It is because producers do not have "confidence in one another," the writer argued, that they give "Burns and company ..." their "chance."[65] This kind of reasoning culminated in a government commission in 1907 to investigate the industry. Both Burns and Gordon were forced to testify, though suspicions against them could not be proved.[66]

To men like A.E. Cross there was no doubt that both parties were profiting from their arrangement. When Clay, Robinson and Company approached him in 1902 for advice on how to establish firmer roots in the Canadian West he told them that "the price paid for export cattle here to the stockman is $5.50" per hundred weight "less 5% off for shrinkage delivered at the railway." But, "a new man buying would have to pay more as P. Burns and Coy are the only people who can handle [both] the rough cattle" and the better types and thus he is able to "buy at better rates" than anyone else could.[67] Cross foresaw the coming of the modern system in which there are numerous local livestock auction marts in western Canada as well as at a large metropolitan distribution centre in Toronto, and he could see the benefits it would provide. "My idea for a cattle market," he stated, "is to establish one ... on the same basis as Chicago is towards the U.S. where a seller knows he can get the open market price for anything he ships no matter what grade of animal. The position in the [Canadian] west is not a very satisfactory one to the seller and will become more [problematic] each year as the number of cattle increases more than the requirements of the home market." Cross was trying to encourage the American firm to establish their own large sales rings in the East.[68] At present, he said, the best cattle nearly all go to Britain, which is too risky for the producer to ship to on his own account since "as a rule he only makes one sale a year and it would cripple him too much if he struck a poor market." Cross also commented that a smaller market should also be established "to supply the west and local trade and work in conjunction with the other market for the balance" of cattle. He clearly felt that lesser buyers like McLean and Knox would then be able to bid on all stock offered and would thus help to ensure a reasonable floor. This could bolster prices not just because of the competition. It would also provide for the establishment of more local slaughtering plants, which would be able to "utilize every part of the animal," including the heart, liver, and other organs which are "at present thrown away to some extent" when the meat from the "rough stuff is shipped out to" other localities such as the British Columbia interior.[69]

None of Cross's hopes were fulfilled before the First World War, and Burns, working in conjunction with Gordon, Ironsides and Fares, continued to have his way. The compact was not above "squeezing" suppliers when it suited them to do so. For instance, when some of the cattlemen tried to force prices up in 1900 by resisting early offers, the buyers were able to hold off "just long enough to lead some ... to think that there would be no market." As a consequence, a dearth of offerings turned into a rush to sell and "some cheap beef" was acquired. One producer sold his beef to Lane for Gordon, Ironsides and Fares "at 42.50 for 3 and 4 years olds, Lane to be allowed to cut back 10% of the threes.... Several small outfits ... sold at 42.00 and 43.00"[70] while others were holding out for as much as $50.00. L.V. Kelly believed that the arrangement between Burns and Gordon, Ironsides and Fares hurt large and small ranch operations alike in both the short and long terms. He felt that the two firms' immense purchasing power encouraged the ranchers to sell many cattle they should have been holding back. When Burns began supplying the construction crews for the Crow's Nest Pass Railway in 1896 he was rumoured to be buying some four hundred animals a month.[71] To get their cattle to full market weight on grass it was necessary for ranchers to keep them until they were at least four years old. However, to meet demand, Burns encouraged them to sell him younger steers as well. Kelly felt that this situation was general throughout the entire ranching country and that it had a negative impact later. "A shortage of fat steers was ... evidenced on the ranges, due to the good demand and fair prices ... when a large number of three-year-old steers were tempted off the range, consequently leaving a void in the ranks of the prime four-year-olds of the next year." Kelly also believed that Burns was responsible for sending too many cows to slaughter. The "demand for fat cows was the first step toward cutting into the breeding capabilities of the ranchers' herds, a condition of affairs that grew and in time hurt the industry considerably."[72]

Of course it might well be argued that the ranchers' own short-sightedness and greed rather than Burns' capital was the main problem. Certainly McEachran's need for cash for dividends to keep his shareholders happy had to have been one of his concerns in accepting Burns' bid in 1897. Kelly was sure, however, that monopolistic tendencies in the industry and the poor prices that resulted in the long term kept many ranchers desperate for cash at any one time and thus largely *incapable* of resisting the temptation to sell. "Combinations of buyers," held "the price low ... making it difficult for a rancher to go to the expense of putting up hay and feeding his stock." This also kept him "from being in position to purchase enough grazing land to allow ... [him] to expand."[73] And it put severe pressure on him to part with the cattle he most needed to maintain his livestock inventory for the future. "Certain ranches, declare that P. Burns and other buyers – but particularly Burns – harmed the ranching industry when a demand was made on the ranchers for fat cows, thus cutting down the breeding strength of the herds. Steers were always considered the only 'right' stock to market, but Burns opened a wide market for rougher meats, supplying construction camps and lumber outfits in eastern British Columbia, selling them cheap beef and calling on the ranchers of Alberta to supply it. Thirty dollars for a fat cow was as good as forty dollars for a fat steer, ready money was always welcome, and many ranchers cut cruelly into their herds to sell ... cows and steers alike."[74]

Over and above their stranglehold on the market, Burns and his associates were in a position to make sure they would come out ahead in each and every sale they negotiated with the ranchers because of their ability to judge dressed carcass weights.

To illustrate this point the Walrond sale in 1897 is instructive even though it took place prior to the period when the ranch had stopped supplying the Native bands. It is the only major sale for which there is a great deal of information and it does enable us to comprehend the position the ranch was in from 1898 on. By the contract, written out in June, McEachran agreed to deliver to Burns in the fall "all their four-years–old range steers estimated to be about eleven hundred head; as many of their three-years-old steers as the agent of the purchaser [George Lane] may select; and as many of their Ontario steers as the said agent may approve of. Also all their four-years old spayed heifers and such of their three-years-old spayed heifers as may be selected as above; and one thousand head of dry cows four years old and up, to be fat and fit for market provided that that number can be found on the range."[75] The price was to be $42 per head for the steers, $33 for the spayed heifers and $30 for the cows.

When he negotiated this deal Burns had every reason to expect that by the end of the grazing season a good proportion of the cattle would have a respectable carcass weight. There had been "great rains" by then and any cattle that could find grass near water that had not been badly overgrazed were "putting on flesh rapidly."[76] The Walrond had been abusing its grasslands particularly in riparian areas at this time, but as noted above a significant proportion of its animals were still able to wander far enough from home in the summer months to find good pastures when the weather behaved.[77] Burns himself was keeping thousands of animals roaming the distant expanse of the open range summer and winter, and he knew that even should the rains stop the natural prairie grasses would be sufficiently voluminous in places to keep them reasonably well fed for some time.[78] It is important to note, however, that he did not need the cattle to be very fat in order to profit on the contract. The going rate for beef carcasses that summer and fall was 6.15 cents per pound.[79] Since Burns was paying $42.00 for each steer he took and $33.00 for each heifer, he needed their carcasses to weigh only 682 pounds and 536 pounds respectively in order to be sure he in a sense was breaking even on the existing market ($42.00 ÷ $.0615 = 682 pounds; $33.00 ÷ $.0615 = 536 pounds).

Still Burns had to be careful with many of cattle described in the contract. Firstly there were the younger steers and heifers, the three-year-olds. While he was anxious to have as many of them as he could get, he knew that some would not have a sufficiently large frame by fall respectively to yield the critical 682 pounds and 536 pounds dressed. To protect himself, therefore, he insisted on the right to "select" the three-year-olds — in other words, to reject as many as he felt were not heavy enough to make him money. With this protection there can be little question that Burns got all the steers and heifers at well below their market value.[80] He must have easily attained at least 800 pounds net for all the Walrond steers. After a similarly good grazing season the previous year those that were delivered over a three-month period to the Indian bands had averaged 761 pounds.[81] A great deal of selectivity for those cattle had been impossible. Because they were delivered every month no general roundups could be held and the cowboys had to pick from the animals grazing relatively close to the reserves. Moreover, as the ranchers liked to get rid of any animals that were doing poorly in the Indian deliveries there must have been a number of carcasses in each delivery that were abnormally light and brought the average weight down. To gather the cattle for Burns in 1897, Lane rode with the roundup crews and was able to choose from the entire herd. Furthermore, he and then Burns liberally invoked their right to reject younger cattle. This created tensions between them and the Walrond management. Later Warnock told McEachran that "there was a good deal of difference of opinion between Mr. Burns and his agent, and myself re the ages of quite a number of the cattle especially the steers. The cattle ... have not been marked in any way as a guide to age and age had to be judged entirely from the appearance of the animals. A number of the steers and heifers rejected by Mr. Lane (Burns agent) were closely examined by Mr. Burns and myself and were accepted by him as being 4 years old. However, other steers and heifers classed in the hard-book as being 4 years old" were "small" and "Burns refused to accept" them.[82]

Burns was a veteran and he knew what he was doing. It seems likely, therefore, that he took virtually no steers that would have yielded less than about 800 pounds. It is evident, moreover, that a fraction of the Walrond cattle netted a lot more than that. Burns was able to cut out enough of them to fill four railway carloads for export to England.[83] At seventeen to eighteen a carload that would have amounted to a total of about seventy head.[84] Properly fattened steers, which these must have been, usually averaged about 1,580 pounds live and yielded at very least 58 per cent or some 916 pounds dressed.[85] If the best of the steers were about that size and the smallest were at least 800 pounds it is hard to image how Burns could have achieved an average weight of less than 820 pounds overall from the Walrond steers. At 6.15 cents per pound, 820 pounds of beef was worth $50.43. Since he was paying $42.00 for the steers by the head, the margin between what each animal cost him and their market value was at least $8.43. The same analogy can be done for the heifers. Younger female cattle were expected to yield about 720 pounds dressed when fat. Therefore one could conservatively assume that Burns would have been as likely to achieve, say, 680 pounds on the heifers as he was the 800-plus pounds on the steers. Six hundred and eighty pounds times $.0615 equals $41.82. Since he was paying only $33.00 per head for the heifers, Burns had a margin of no less than $8.82.

On paper the best deal for Burns may have been made on the dry cows. As fully grown and mature these animals have a good big frame and when not suckling calves really put on weight well. The meat is normally not as tender as that of the younger animals so cows were discounted by nine-tenths of a cent per pound dressed weight.[86] The Walrond cows tended to yield slightly less than the heifers on the Indian contracts. Because the ranch exploited that market to cull poor animals a large percentage of these were what the cattlemen referred to as "old and shelly." Burns' contract gave him the right, however, to take only those animals from four years of age and up that he considered "fat and fit." Therefore he could be very choosy. He could insist not only on the higher yielding cows but also the younger ones – i.e., those that were at or near four years of age – or only slightly older than the oldest heifers in the Walrond herd. If one continues to be conservative and estimates the average weight at 680 pounds and allows the regular discount, the cows were worth 680 times $.0525, or $35.70 apiece. At $30.00 a head Burns had a built in margin of about $5.70. The cows that were marketable as heifers, however, were worth 680 pounds times $.0615, or $41.82, giving him a margin of $11.82. As any experienced cattleman knows, good young cows are often graded heifer when processed through our modern packing plants. Considering that Burns and Lane were very selective and in the end took what David Warnock described as only a "small number" of cows and that Burns owned the packing plant through which they were processed, it is conceivable that the majority of their carcasses were classified as heifer meat before being shipped to the retailers or to the work crews in British Columbia.[87]

The final type of cattle mentioned in the contract that Burns had to be careful with were the steers the Walrond ranch had imported from the East as yearlings and two-year-olds to fatten on the grass over the summer months. These cattle were considered chancy by the beef merchants because so many were descendent from dairy stock of the Holstein, Guernsey, or Ayrshire breeds, which had a propensity to grow tall and lean and thus did not put on flesh at all well until fully mature. They were identified in the contract as "Ontario steers" and Burns agreed to take only those he or his agent "might approve of." Warnock deduced that he might not take any of these cattle and over the summer sent as many as possible to the Native bands.[88] He was not far off the mark. Ultimately "only about fifteen were considered good enough." We can be fairly sure that all fifteen netted over 800 pounds.[89]

Burns already had considerable control over the market at this stage and he seems to have been the only buyer who bid for the Walrond cattle.[90] The fact that he separated out the "exportable" ones for shipment to Britain suggests that he was already working closely with Gordon, Ironsides and Fares.[91] Moreover, money was no object. He had lots of capital, particularly with the backing of William Mackenzie, with whom he had a joint account at the Imperial Bank in Calgary.[92] He also had two places for the rougher cattle. The majority, those that were unlikely to put on much more weight, could go directly to his slaughter plant at Calgary, but any that he and Lane picked out that had a big frame but were not well finished could be fed until the fall glut was over. By then the cattle would weigh out better and the price per pound would rise.

The Walrond contract allowed Burns to take up to 1,100 four-year-old steers as well as any three-year-olds he felt suitable. Since the summer of 1897 had been a good growing season it would seem reasonable to suggest that he took at least 800 all told. The ranch normally had a lot fewer heifers than steers for sale, as most of the good young females born on the ranch were bred as they matured and used to replace older cows. Perhaps Burns took about 200. Though he had a right to take up to 1,000 dry cows Warnock considered the number he finally selected as small so he likely bought no more than about 100. Then of course he took a handful of Ontario steers. Altogether he probably ended up with about 1,100 Walrond cattle. His average margin on each animal must have been at least $8, so he came out ahead on the deal by about $8 times 1,100, or roughly $8,800. Considering that this was only one of a number of purchases Burns made in 1897 it is not difficult to see how he managed to amass a formidable fortune in the frontier cattle business.[93]

It is clear too that Burns prospered directly at the expense of the ranchers. To underscore what a bad deal the sale was for the Walrond one might compare it with what the ranch got from the Native bands when paid by the pound dressed weight. During the three-month period in 1896 when the steer carcasses weighed 761 pounds the ranch received only 5.8 cents per pound.[94] Still the return per head was $44.13. Thus in sales where some of the poorest animals were marketed and selectivity was severely limited, the average animal brought in nearly $2.00 more than that sold to Burns when only the cattle with the best carcass weights were purchased and when market price by the pound was higher.[95] There can be little doubt that Burns could have afforded to give much of his margin to the cattlemen. He had very little competition on the wholesale and retail side of the beef business as well, and therefore he was able to set prices for his processed meats. By this time he owned numerous meat shops stretching from Calgary to the British Columbia interior and he was the chief supplier for many other retailers and for the Crowsnest Pass Railway construction crews.[96] True, he had to carry the cost of slaughtering many of the cattle at his plant in Calgary. However, that cost was relatively low. In the 1890s Warnock kept close track of the costs at the ranch's own crude killing facilities for the Indian contracts for everything from bullets to kill the animals to salt for preserving the hides to living expenses for the butcher. When it killed over fifty cattle the cost to the ranch was about $2 per head and it was able to sell the hides of perhaps a quarter of the animals at $1 apiece.[97] Burns could surely have killed the cattle more efficiently than the ranchers. Therefore he would have been well protected had he allowed the cattlemen a full $6 of his $8 per head margin. For the sale examined here another $6 would have brought the

Walrond an extra $6,600 overall, or enough money to pay between a third and a half of its annual costs for labour and hay.[98]

McEachran does not appear to have dealt with Burns again until he sold out his entire cattle inventory after the 1906/07 winter. However, there is no doubt that the beef oligopoly hurt the Walrond ranch just as it did all the cattle operations on the prairies by keeping the price of range beef from rising as it might have in any given year. Historians have written a good deal about the impact of monopoly capitalism on the early grain farming community in the Canadian West. Railway, milling, and elevator syndicates assembled as the land was settled, and they helped to create a sense of disillusionment and disaffection when prices for wheat and other products were low. Perhaps more might have been written about collusion in the beef industry had it impacted farmers in general rather than just the cattlemen, and if between 1907 and the end of the First World War, beef was not replaced by "king wheat" as the major agricultural commodity in the West.[99] As the cattlemen continued to struggle over the decade following 1897 the beef brokers amassed incredible wealth. According to his own estimates Burns was worth $2,919,472.45 by 1915 and $9,211,222.41 by the time he sold out his meat-packing and other food-processing businesses in 1928.[100] Gordon, Ironsides and Fares were worth over $4 million by the First World War.[101] Historically, one of the main reasons the beef business has always fallen into few hands is the large amount of money it requires. Burns and Gordon, Ironsides and Fares were the only Canadian buyers who had access to what seemed limitless amounts of capital and therefore they were able to dominate the market. The purpose here is not to suggest that they acted maliciously. They did what any entrepreneur in a similar position would do – they got everything they could out of their business dealings. What seems irrefutable, however, is that the cattlemen would have been better off if there had been a lot more competition in the industry. Modern producers are making that same argument, and they have a good deal more choice when it comes to marketing their finished product than their frontier counterparts had.

9

DUNCAN McEACHRAN'S RANCH, 1898– 1903: FURTHER INTENSIFICATION, HIGHER PRICES AND HIGHER COSTS

With the Walronds now merely minor shareholders and himself the president and general manager, Duncan McEachran was in absolute control of the New Walrond Ranche Company Limited from 1898 on. One of his first undertakings was to make the operation as intensive in its methods as it was ever to be. During the summer months all the cattle were still turned loose on the open range but in the wintertime more than ever before were being fed in corrals on the ranch and on the holdings of small producers. During a "cold snap" in March 1901, Warnock told McEachran that with the cattle on custom lots and those on at home they were feeding 2,300 head. "The loss to date (among cattle being fed) counting small late calves ... has only been sixteen head. We have only lost one dogie [sic] since they were gathered. The dogies [sic] have done well and we have lost very few since last spring."[1] Some weeks later he told J.G. Ross that "approximately $2600.00 dollars will be paid out to feeding contractors by the 10th of April.... We turned out 300 head of yearlings yesterday. Those were wintered here and went out well grown and in fine condition. We have plenty of hay on hand and if we can turn loose most of the cattle being fed within the next two weeks, will have probably 200 tons of hay left over."[2]

To improve efficiency with the breeding stock Warnock also thoroughly embraced timed breeding. Prior to the 1898 summer grazing season the North-West Territories government passed an ordinance dictating that bulls be "pulled" off the range at particular points every year so that calving could be made to coincide with the coming of spring.[3] The system was far from perfect since the total removal of wandering "scrub" bulls was never achieved. However, over the course of a few years, noticeably fewer calves were born out of season. "We have finished our fall branding and the... number to be added to the spring brand is 313 – 174 steers and 139 heifers," Warnock reported in 1900. The overall count came to 1,429, which, at his estimation "of 1800 cows with the bulls last season" meant that some 79 per cent had given birth.[4] A year later he reported that the number of calves born in the spring only totalled 1,000 head because there were "a good many dry cows, as, owing to the bulls being taken up early last fall, fully three hundred cows ... did not get a chance of service."[5]

The other major adjustment the general manager attempted to make to the Walrond's practices beginning in 1898 centred on the attempt to revitalize his grasslands. The disappointing and consistently declining carcass weights, both McEachran and Warnock realized, could not continue. They also now recognized that they had to keep their herd numbers lower to allow the grass a better chance to flourish while selling fewer cattle each year in order to give them more time to put on weight. The latter objective they achieved by not renewing the Indian contracts. The former one they would attain by regulating the importation of eastern doggies. This meant purchasing large numbers each year only while the heavy culling process in quest of timed breeding was underway. Thereafter they would buy no more than necessary to maintain herd stability near Warnock's book figure of 7,842. This, they had no way of knowing, was still far more cattle than the ranch could handle on the two blocks of land it had originally leased and outside pastures to the east near Willow Creek and along the Oldman River.

During the first three or so years after incorporation McEachran and Warnock were able to maintain some of their optimism about the future. Initially, grazing conditions proved quite good, a reflection of ideal spring and summer weather. In 1898 rainfall was much better than average, and the cattle that were mobile enough to utilize the more distant pastures put on weight very well. In relative terms, a good percentage were in great shape in the fall. The numbers sold totalled only 816 head, but Warnock estimated that another 400 might have been marketed had storms not interrupted the gathering process.[6] Comparatively speaking, the animals that were sold yielded very well. When McEachran was to arrange a "good figure" for the fat steers some years later Warnock would regret that they did not have a bunch "like that of 1898."[7]

Prices also rose in this period, for two reasons. One was the gradual improvement in the international beef market.[8] The. other was that immigrant workers were still pouring in to man the construction crews for the Crowsnest Pass railway line and the coal fields and lumber yards that were being developed in its wake. By this time many ranchers had badly depleted their herds and in the short term there was considerable demand for what was left even during the fall run. In June 1899 McEachran contracted to supply A.J. McLean with all the exportable steers belonging to the company that were at least four years old and the exportable three-year-old steers at $46.00 per head cash. The exportable three- and four-year-old spayed heifers brought $37.50 per head. The lower quality animals in both categories that the Walrond wished to market brought $3.35 per hundred pounds live or approximately seven cents per pound dressed weight.[9] Thus the ranch got $4.00 more than Burns had provided in 1897 for its best steers, $4.50 more for its heifers and close to a cent a pound dressed above the going rate of previous years for the rest; and Warnock, rather than the buyer, assumed the right to decide which of the animals should be included in the deal.

A combination of factors over and above price made this a relatively profitable sale. First, Warnock's estimate at the end of 1898 that about four hundred head more could have been sold ostensibly was accurate.[10] Many of these cattle were among those that found good pastures again in the summer of 1899, and with a year more to mature and fill out they weighed up well. Further, the older doggies also prospered during the 1899 grazing season. These animals "turned out so much better than ... expected and largely contributed to the numbers sold."[11] This seems to have been the result of a combination of a reasonably good summer grazing season and the fact that in the late 1890s most of the doggies the ranch had bought came from Manitoba farmers who normally bred their dairy cows to Shorthorn, Hereford, and Angus bulls. This produced calves that "fleshed up" more efficiently than the calves from Ontario sired mostly by the lankier Holstein and Ayrshire varieties. By 1899, moreover, many of the doggies had been around for several years and had had a chance to mature fully and to fill out as much as could be expected of such breeds. Warnock had earlier declared these cattle a waste of time.[12] Now, however, he was convinced of their value. "If you can get good Manitoba steers at a reasonable figure for spring delivery I think it will be money well invested," he told McEachran. "I think range bred stockers are going to be higher priced in spring and am sure that the cattle purchased this year were cheap."[13] Nearly a year later he was still convinced. "Quite a number of Manitoba ... [doggies] have been brought into Macleod and High River districts this Fall," he noted, "John R. Craig" of the Oxley ranch, "purchased a bunch from Billy Stewart ... G[eorge] Emerson of High River bought over one thousand this year. He has been buying for some years and seems satisfied with results. I have gone over my memoranda of W.R dogies [sic] killed and shipped and find that fourteen hundred and twenty have been sold. It is a pity so many were killed on Indian Contracts.... There are a good many on the range yet even some of those brought in in /95."[14] In May 1900 McEachran bought 438 steers at $19.48 and 48 heifers at $16.00, primarily from George Lane.[15]

Of course, Patrick Burns and associates were still exercising considerable control over the local market and there can be little doubt that prices would have been better in a truly competitive system. Nonetheless, the improvement must have lifted the spirits of most producers. Prices were stronger again the following fall. McEachran got $48.00 from McLean for the Walrond steers in 1900 and $40.00 for spayed heifers.[16] Altogether 1,074 head were marketed for a total of close to $50,000.00.[17] The next spring McEachran was able to get "a good big bunch of dogies [sic]" again to put out on the ranges.[18] They must have cost about the same as previous ones. Warnock congratulated him on the purchase and told him that he was "convinced there is money in dogies [sic] bought as yearlings [i.e. over one year of age] at a figure under $20.00."[19]

It was August 1901 when much of the optimism both men had been feeling largely dissipated. The primary factor was a thorough count of the Walrond herds, which came up well short of expectations. On the 31 August Warnock sent a memo to head office showing the number and classification of cattle that were in the books, and number and classification actually counted.[20] The younger cattle, he noted, "counted up very well" but, unfortunately, there was also "a considerable shortage in the [overall] number counted principally in cows and aged steers." Some of the shortage he rationalized could be accounted for by the weather conditions at the time the count was taken, which he theorized had caused the cowboys to overlook quite few. "No doubt" a number were missed as the "outside roundups, especially on Willow Creek and East, were [not] very satisfactory owing to long delays at rivers and creeks." This "allowed cattle to drift back, and on the Little Bow [River] the roundup was held up for eight days and then all camp belongings had to be rafted across." The roundup crew "did not get through till the 8th of August and between extreme heat and almost unbearable torment from flies the work was hard on man and beast." A "considerable percentage" of the older steers must have eluded the riders. "We marked the cattle counted by squaring their plaits" (i.e. their tails) and marking them "with a smear of blue paint." Since then "we have seen a good many that were missed and have heard of a few as far East as Medicine Hat and Maple Creek."

Ultimately, however, Warnock had to admit that the deficiency was greater than he could explain away on that basis. Evidently, over the years, poor nutrition, harsh winter weather, two- and four-legged predators, and other natural and frontier forces or conditions had taken a lot more of the stock than he had realized. "We are short principally in cows ranging from six to ten years old, and I think this is largely due to the ravages of wolves in the early nineties.... In 93/94/95 and 6 wolves caused us heavy losses in horses, and I am afraid they did much more damage among cattle than we suspected. The winters of 95 and 96 too were severe, and the loss among breeding stock may have been heavier than we realized. At that time hay was fed to beef cattle for Indian contracts which perhaps could have been more profitably fed to weak cows."[21]

Warnock liked to blame setbacks on problems that had occurred before he became manager. There can be little doubt, however, that ecological and climatic factors had taken a significant toll during his watch as before. In the years of relative optimism both he and McEachran had failed to calculate the impact of severe weather such as that in the spring of 1898. "The past week has been the worst experienced during eight or nine winters," Warnock had reported. "Strong N[orth] East winds made the cold very piercing and cattle seemed to feel it very much. A number of the old cows heavy with calf ... had their feet frozen and are in bad shape to withstand prolonged cold. There is very little hay left and it is being carefully fed to carry as many weak cattle as possible over the next two or three weeks."[22] Two months later he told J.G. Ross that the calf brand would be extremely small everywhere and that the Oxley Company and some of the other ranchers had branded less than half the number of calves they had branded the previous year.[23] The overall brand that year was very small, and one suspects that a lot more of the cows and even younger yearlings than Warnock thought had by then been lost.[24]

What also contributed to the death loss during this period was the reduction of grazing space as a result of settlement. At this point the cattle were still able to utilize most of the free range on and relatively close to the land the ranch had originally held under lease. However, settlers and their livestock were beginning to crowd them. In 1901, Warnock told McEachran that numerous "entries have been made along the river."[25] As a result, "the fencing of a large acreage West of Beaver Creek," is bound to "interfere with cattle ranging between Tennessee Coulee and Beaver Creek." Even now "from three miles north of the Lower Ranche to its source Beaver Creek is ... fenced so that cattle cannot cross. In the event of the Reserve being fenced on the North side cattle would practically be shut in."[26] Five Mile Creek was also rapidly being settled and enclosed so that the open range there was getting distinctly smaller.[27]

Considering Warnock's comments about the steers that had been sighted as far away as Medicine Hat and Maple Creek, animals were obviously still finding their way through and around homesteader fences.[28] Some cattle will always evade containment when the food supply is short. However, overall the pastures were contracting. Many of the Walrond cattle thus suffered from low nutrition and were inordinately susceptible to the elements, particularly during the cold months.[29] The ranch may also have lost a lot more cattle than either manager supposed to predators. There appears to have been fewer wolves preying on the herds now, in part because of the new and better strychnine pellets and in part because of greater activity by Native hunters seeking "very encouraging" bounties from the territorial government and the stock association.[30] However, the fact that the bounties not only continued in these years but actually rose in monetary value suggests that the battle was far from won.[31] The depredations of human predators actually seem from the police reports as well as the ranchers' correspondence to have reached a peak during the New Walrond years as more professional rustlers and settlers arrived to take up residence in the area. It did not help that in an effort to reduce costs the Dominion government had more or less consistently trimmed the manpower of the North West Mounted Police.[32]

In the 1901 letter rationalizing the disappointing count Warnock gave McEachran a second jolt that he may or may not have been ready for. "The calf brand this spring was disappointing, only totaling 1000 head." Warnock had expected that even with timed breeding the cowboys would brand as many as they had the previous spring. He guessed that the small brand must be due to severe snowstorms that had occurred in April and May. To make the blow easier to accept, Warnock was reduced to falling back on the device he had employed on similar occasions in the past. Neighbouring ranchers he said, were in the same position and "many" had branded a third fewer calves than in 1900. Over the summer of 1901 environmental conditions did not improve. "Season very late," Warnock wrote in April, "grass is very poor ... we are most fortunate in having but a few head of two years old heifers in calf, as our neighbours that make a practice of breeding their yearlings are losing about 75%.... The Chinook and rapid thaw in February followed by cold weather so rotted the grass that cows have hardly been able to live on it and have rapidly lost condition." Mortality in some districts was heavy. Warnock felt that the Walrond losses were small, but he nearly always did. "Most stockmen ran short of hay and turned cattle loose early in March and have lost a good many since," he wrote. "So far our loss ... has not been 3% and during the last ten days a large number of calves have been dropped. Had the cows we are feeding at present been left to rustle the loss would have been" greater.

Prior to the August 1901 count, then, the challenges that confronted the ranch were relatively severe and neither Warnock nor McEachran had sufficiently considered the impact. After the count the challenges grew even more daunting. Prices for beef cattle held up fairly well. The Walrond got $48 again for its steers and $40 for its spayed heifers. However, very few cattle were ready for the slaughter market. In October, only 116 steers were fat enough to be accepted by the buyers[33] and in November when a second beef round up was undertaken, none of the cattle "had improved and some ... were not as fit" as they had been earlier. Mclean apparently took everything he could for slaughter,[34] but the cowboys were forced to turn loose over 100 animals the buyer refused because they were too lean.[35]

The next winter does not seem to have been horrendous, but many of the cattle entered it in rather poor shape and the death rate must have been relatively high.[36] The following spring appears to have been rather mild, but in May 1902 a very destructive rainstorm raised havoc with the herds. On the evening of Monday the nineteenth rain began to fall heavily, and in the early hours of the twentieth it pelted the countryside "in torrents." Then a driving wind from the north set in along with a "blinding storm" of sleet, which continued all the next day. Rain fell continuously over the course of that night and the next day. Callum Creek and the Oldman River "rose rapidly and ... were enormously swollen." Over four days Callum Creek "was a raging torrent carrying away hundreds of feet of its banks," some of the Walrond's bridges and buildings. One wall of the cook shack, some twenty-five feet from the creek, was completely washed out and the beef house had to be dismantled after the water had washed away the bank from under half of it. About eighty feet "of mud roofed shedding collapsed under the weight of mud and water and damaged the Democrat wagon, which was under it, rather badly." One of the Walrond cowboys who had crossed the Oldman River before the storm had to swim back. He reported "serious damage to the C.N. Railway and to Ranches along the Middle and South Forks of the Old Man's river." Most of the railway bridges from Macleod to

Calgary were "swept away." Numerous cattle and horses were "reported drowned on islands" along the river. It was believed that "the storm must have killed many young calves but nothing could be done for them as even the smallest creeks were impassable."[37]

The grazing year of 1902 turned out to be almost as bad as that of 1901. "The old and new settlers" near Beaver Creek "are quarrelling about land and fences and I should not be surprised to hear of a shooting scrape any day," Warnock wrote. This restricted the movement of the Walrond cattle further.[38] "We are busy weaning calves and gathering doggies," the onsite manager reported the next the fall. "Cattle are all up in the hills and take a lot of gathering. Many of the dogies [sic] are thin and will have to be fed from now on if this snow lies."[39] A week later he estimated that it was not just the doggies that were in poor shape. "We have had sharp frosts and the snow is now crusted, with, in some parts of the ranges, a good deal of ice. Weaning is being proceeded with but it is slow work as every ridge has to be ridden and cattle driven down out of the timber. Cattle are not [even] as fat as they were last fall and a good many cows will have to be fed later in winter."[40]

Though it has received very little attention from historians the winter of 1902/03 was among the worst on record.[41] In a December letter that also noted some of the other misfortunes that beset roaming livestock, Warnock reported that:[42]

The mercury has been ranging from 12 to 20 degrees below zero [Fahrenheit], and there has been a little more snow. We have been unfortunate in losing three of the 98 lot of Short-horn bulls. One died badly affected with Tuberculosis, and a second was killed by one of the range bulls ripping his abdomen open, and the third died while being fed.... The Galloways and range bulls are fat, but the old S[hort] H[orn] bulls are thin, and a number are blind in one eye from the effects of the <Cephthalmia>....[43] We have let out 1,342 calves and I got Baillie to take 125 dogies [sic] at 3.00 per head, instead of calves. A number of our calves are too small to let out.... We have gathered about 380 dogies [sic] of which number Baillie has 125; ... If the present severe weather and cold continues, and as more calves are gathered, it may be necessary to let out another hundred or more dogies [*sic*].... Hay is being fed as economically as possible and no hay has been fed at Damon creek yet. We have had more severe weather now than we had all last winter or the previous one, and if it should hold out for another month or two it will mean serious losses for many outfits.[44]

In 1903 the ranch produced about 1,580 calves. By this time, according to the book count, the cowherd had grown to about 3,000 head and McEachran had been leading his investors to expect better.[45] In his annual report, therefore, he again attempted to suggest that this situation was exceptional. "Owing probably to the severity of the winter, more particularly towards spring and especially owing to an unprecedented" May snow storm, "in which many newly born calves perished; the number ... branded fell short of expectations." The ranch sold 1,099 slaughter animals in the fall and McEachran felt the need to rationalize that as well since so many had been held over from previous years. "Rings" and "combines," he said in the same report, made it impossible to market about half the cattle that were ready.[46] The nutritional problem was compounded during the next summer as late spring and fall fires destroyed a good deal of pasture and early frosts killed much of the grass.[47]

The ranch also took losses in this period from two well-known diseases. In the correspondence, references to blackleg, an ailment that can be passed on from one animal to the other in their common feed and is nearly always fatal, had been discovered in the herd. "There is no snow, but cattle are not suffering for water as ... springs are open all over this range," Warnock noted, in early 1902. "I would like to see colder weather now as Blackleg has appeared among weaners [weaned calves]. We have lost two here, three at Elton's and four at the Mormons place in the last few days. ... Elton has been feeding timothy hay of excellent quality but is now feeding straw every second day. We have changed the feed here too, and there may not be any more cases, but if the disease continues to appear I think it will be necessary to vaccinate."[48] A new vaccine for blackleg had been developed commercially and Warnock had laid in five hundred doses.[49]

The total cost to the ranch from blackleg was not catastrophic, due to the vaccine and the fact that once all the cattle could be turned out on the open range none were any longer sharing hand-fed hay. The disease that was more destructive was the mange, for the spread of which the open range system was ideal. This disease is carried by a parasite that moves from one animal to another and lays its eggs in the hides. The Walrond cattle were unable to wander as freely as they had in earlier days, but since some invariably got well beyond the original leases at times, they obviously mixed with neighbouring animals. That was all it took for the disease to spread from one herd to another. Moreover, because of the sheer size of its pasture lands and the fact that they were very rough in many places and covered with trees it was impossible at any one time for the men to find all the infected animals. The mange parasites attack the hides, causing tremendous discomfort. This usually manifests in gigantic sores because the animals invariably scratch against trees, posts, buildings, or anything else they come across until their hair drops out and their hides are torn. While the death loss directly from the disease itself is not usually very high the ultimate loss can be substantial. As the animals continue to scratch the large sores on their hides are broken over and over again. The discomfort is heightened and ultimately the animals become so stressed that they stop eating, lose weight and become weak and subject to other diseases. Should the weather turn harsh for an extended period, they just cannot withstand it.

The mange spread north across the forty-ninth parallel, thoroughly infesting some Canadian herds in the 1890s. At that stage McEachran was still the Dominion Livestock Inspector and was involved in a campaign to eradicate the outbreak. Affected animals crossing the border into Canada were quarantined and treated. He also attempted to obtain subsidization for individual ranchers to help them cover the expense of building a dip and extra corrals and chutes for processing the cattle through it.[50] Some of the big ranches, including the Walrond, erected their own dipping vats and tried regularly to treat their infected animals. They continued to feel threatened, however, in the knowledge that the disease was rampant outside their own pastures. "I expect the mange question will cause some uneasiness among stockmen" Warnock told his manager in the spring of 1899, "evidently there is a great deal of it towards Lethbridge, especially amongst the Circle dogies [sic]. Last spring the Cochrane outfit spent some weeks treating their cattle down in that district. Quite a number of the thoroughbred bulls in the Willow Creek and Little Bow districts are affected, and I do not think that anything is being done to combat the disease." He felt quite sure that the problem was not yet severe among the Walrond livestock, but as a veterinarian himself, he understood how dangerous it could be and he promised that he would be outspoken at the next stockmen's meeting in insisting that something was going to have to be done to prevent further outbreaks.[51]

Over the winter the situation on the Walrond deteriorated. Many of the cows and bulls had to be dipped and some of the worst cases had to be treated three times. The men had to use a steel brush to rub it into the scabs to get it to penetrate the "thick crusts."[52] At this stage, however, Warnock was still in denial about the seriousness of the situation. "The quarantine regulations re mange are causing some inconvenience to shippers in this district," but "we have been very careful here about many cattle and have had no difficulty about shipping."[53] On a separate fall roundup to gather calves old enough to wean from their mothers, the cowboys treated every animal showing symptoms, and Warnock felt they had got the upper hand. He did admit, though, that there would be a lot to treat the following year.[54]

Warnock was right in the latter prediction. Thereafter, the disease swept through virtually all the herds in the southern foothills, and there is no question that the Walrond cattle were severely affected. In 1904 the outbreak became so ubiquitous that the government began erecting tanks along the international border so that all imported animals could be dipped. Even so, it took until after the First World War for the cattlemen to gain firm control over it. True to his nature McEachran insulated his shareholders from the truth. "This disease, which is more or less prevalent over the outside range, affected only a few of the Company's cattle," he told them in his December 1903 annual report, and it "was completely controlled by the immediate application of an effective remedy. A dipping vat or bath has been constructed, in which all animals showing signs of the disease, or vermin of any kind will be dipped as often as necessary."[55]

The one satisfaction David Warnock felt he could take in these years was that the system of nurturing the calves and doggies more carefully was actually working, since the main losses from all causes, he believed, were among the older animals.[56] The problem, however, seems to have been that even after doing a better job of bringing calves into the world through timed breeding and then keeping more of the "young stock" alive through feeding on the ranch and custom feeding, the operation was still experiencing heavy losses when the animals were left to their own resources. It would not seem unreasonable to argue that the managers were in fact wasting their precious money – that it would have been better to go to a fully intensive system or, indeed, perhaps even to stay with a fully extensive one, rather than trying to implement something of both.[57]

The shortage of cattle detected in 1901 strongly suggests that even Warnock's earlier book count of 7,842 head was on the high side. If it is difficult to know which environmental factors were *most* responsible for the failure of the ranch to maintain its cattle inventory over the years, it can at least be said that in a situation where single young men, alienated settlers, and hungry Indians lived among the stock, where Mother Nature could and did unleash devastation from time to time, and where natural pastures had lost much of their vigour, the Walrond's difficulties were inevitable. Under these circumstances an annual dividend should have been even more difficult to justify than before. However, McEachran's practice was to pay it in good years and bad. After informing his shareholders about the discouraging calf crop and marketing numbers in his 1903 annual report, he unflinchingly announced that a 5 per cent return of $12,249.59 would be paid as usual.[58]

SOMEBODY ELSE'S MONEY

10

DUNCAN McEACHRAN'S RANCH, 1903–1907: JOINING (AND ATTEMPTING TO LEAVE) THE LANDHOLDING CLASSES

The New Walrond Ranche Company became a large landholder for the first time in 1903. In his annual report McEachran announced that the directors had been "fortunate enough to secure by purchase about 34,000 acres of selected land: part from the Government and part from the Calgary and Edmonton Railway Company, at a cost of about $2.28 per acre." The purchase was achieved, the statement continued, immediately "before the withdrawal by the Government of all lands in that district from sale" and thus "before the influx of settlers led to a rise in value" of such property "from $3.00 to $5.00, and even $10.00 per acre."[1] Over the following year further smaller deals were made, which brought the total purchased to 37,966 acres.[2] With the quarter section the Walrond had owned from the beginning, it now had 38,126 acres all told.[3]

Notwithstanding McEachran's characteristic bravado it is apparent that his decision to invest in land had not been an easy one. It had occurred to him many years earlier that pasture security would become a problem once homesteaders began to crowd in on the open range where the Walrond cattle grazed.[4] Now, however, it took considerable pressure from David Warnock to get him to take each of the necessary steps to ensure the ranch would always have grasslands for its stock. This pressure began as early as 1898, when Warnock sent him information that a mutual acquaintance "intends to settle on Heath Creek this summer," which flows west out of the Porcupine Hills across the Callum Creek flood plain. This, Warnock pointed out, was vital property to the long-term viability of the ranch. "We cannot afford to let anyone settle on Heath Creek as it is our most valuable winter range on the West side of the Porcupines." There is an "abundance of feed there, open water all winter, and less snow ... than anywhere except on Beaver Creek."[5] Should anyone locate in the wrong place they could "practically control the whole creek" and cut off precious water supplies. Warnock advised McEachran to "arrange to lease" land along the creek "and have it exempted from settlement for a stated number of years," or if this could not be arranged to buy all the land in that area that settlers might find attractive.[6] McEachran did not take action despite further urgings from his onsite manager until, in September 1900, his attention was drawn to the fact that several prospective settlers had been exploring all the country from Cabin Creek, directly south of Heath Creek[7] to Black Mountain,[8] on the north end of the upper block. "At present two men from Utah are camped at the cabin. These men are most likely Mormons and we may have a ... colony [moving into this area if we delay establishing a proprietary right to the land]."[9] Warnock counselled McEachran either to talk to the Minister of the Interior, Clifford Sifton, about buying some of the Crown land they had previously leased or to attempt to acquire other holdings through Métis scrip.[10]

McEachran apparently responded this time by making application to the government for a number of sections, which then were surveyed.[11] But he did not immediately follow through by pursuing negotiations over price with the Department of the Interior.

As the wave of new settlers poured into the area after 1900, Warnock's anxiety that their pasture lands would be lost quite rightly grew even more pronounced, and he felt obliged once again to urge his boss to take action. "I am wondering whether you have had an interview yet with [the Minister of the Interior] ... re the land question," he wrote on 5 February 1901, "I expect it is not an easy matter to arrange a meeting with him; but I hope you will be able to make a deal." A week later he added that "several entries have been recently made on land around the fen, Cow Camp and Smithie's Ranche. Joe McFarland, Smithie and some of the other ranchers on Todd Creek," to the south of the upper block, "will soon be pretty well fenced in. I hope you will find Mr. Sifton willing to grant the land asked for on favourable terms."[12] In April Warnock sounded more anxious than ever. "Settlers are invading Macleod and Pincher Creek districts in hundreds and the people are land crazy. So far no settlers have come on this side of the [Oldman] river but from the south side to Pincher Creek land has all been taken up." Willow Creek is also "rapidly being settled."[13]

Even so, McEachran continued to move slowly. He finally made a tentative deal on some land from the government in November 1901,[14] and in December he came to "an understanding" with the Calgary and Edmonton Railway.[15] Application was made to purchase C & E lands over the course of the rest of 1902, and a contract was eventually signed with Sifton. However, the fact that actual purchases were not officially in place until sometime the following year suggests that McEachran's pace picked up only a little. His cautious approach may well have centred on concerns about the financial viability of the New Walrond Ranche. At $2.28 per acre the first 34,000 acres purchased cost the company $77,520.00, and once the smaller pieces were paid for, McEachran was forced to take some $86,562.48 out of the company's supply of cash.[16] This must have been difficult for him because it was cash he felt he badly needed to maintain the Walrond's livestock herds. To raise this capital he had to sell a lot of cattle and not replace them. If the average price the ranch was getting for fat steers and heifers off the grass was about $44.00, its herds would have had to undergo a numerical decline of some 2,000 head.[17] However, since this was considerably more cattle than the ranch usually marketed in a given year, it might well have meant selling off a large number of younger cattle with very light carcasses as he had done back in the 1890s. These could easily have reduced the average price by $5.00 to $10.00. In that case the Walrond numbers would have had to drop by as much to 2,500.[18] Of course, lowering the livestock numbers would have been a good step in order to give the Walrond's long overstocked grasslands a chance to replenish and to compete better with weeds in some areas. But McEachran must have felt the need to keep the value of his livestock at a level that was sufficient to enable him to pay off the shareholders, just as a farmer today would want his liquid assets to cover his operational loans at the bank. The Canadian dollar had strengthened since 1898 and, therefore, the £10 shares were worth about $48.60 when converted from sterling. Thus McEachran owed his investors $244,992.60. He could perhaps rationalize that all the cattle together were worth about $32.00 apiece – what they had cost way back in 1883. If he felt their numbers had increased since August 1901 to circa Warnock's earlier book count, he could convince himself that their total value was more than what was owed ($32.00 x 7,842 cattle = $250,944.00).[19] The book count he was showing his shareholders was considerably higher than that. The numbers he reported at the end of 1903 were 10,559, consisting of 5,390 cows and heifers, 1,745 steers under three years old, 1,788 steers three years old and up, 143 bulls, 1,491 weaned calves, and two stags.[20] Once all the land was paid for this number would have had to be adjusted down to between 8,000 and 8,500 head. However, McEachran knew full well that when tested in the past, book counts had almost always been too high. Indeed, as evinced below, the financial predicament the ranch was to be in when he had once and for all to take an honest look at it after the ferocious winter of 1906/07 strongly suggests that he had more like 5,000 head at this time.[21] In 1898, moreover, the average per head value had been less than $20. If he did the math after the turn of the century, McEachran should have realized that were he to liquidate all the old and young cows, the weaned calves, and the undersized steers and heifers as well as any that were fat, the average price per head might even now be well under $32.[22] It was impossible to escape the fact, therefore, that cutting the cattle inventory to buy the land could mean reducing liquid assets dangerously near or even below outstanding share value.[23]

No doubt what ultimately compelled McEachran to buy the 37,966 acres in 1903 and 1904 was that, subject to the warnings of his onsite manager, he came to fear that free range in general was disappearing so rapidly that it could eventually put him out of business altogether. Equally important was one very positive potential outcome from the investment that suddenly entered his mind. With all the settlement currently underway the price of landed property could dramatically appreciate in the near future. This could actually bring with it a substantial improvement in the net worth of the New Walrond Ranche Company that might more than offset its deficiencies in the cattle business. Soon after he bought the land McEachran began to dream of selling it not for $5 or $10 more per acre than he had paid for it but for a full $20 an acre. At that price the Walrond's 38,126 total deeded acres were worth a grand total of $762,520, about $517,000 more than was owed to the sharehold-ers.[24] If the ranch really were worth that much, he realized, a sale would enable him not only to pay back all his investors but to bring them (and himself) a very attractive profit. The fact that he started actively to try to sell the ranch merely two years after he bought the first 34,000 acres, and only a year after purchasing the last smaller parcels, underscores this thesis.[25]

It was in October 1905 that McEachran did a complete about-turn and began the process of marketing the Walrond property. On the twen-ty-first he wrote a letter to Arthur Walrond enclosing a second letter, which he said he hoped Walrond would "take seriously" and act upon. "Nothing, would please me more than to see the old W.R. have such a termination and that brought about by you and I."[26] In the first let-ter McEachran told Walrond exactly how to approach and represent his enclosed letter to parties in England who might be interested in buying the ranch. The enclosure is worth quoting at length because the mixture of fact and fiction in it speaks volumes about McEachran's nature. When reading it one wants to keep in mind all his past frustrations in attempt-ing to breed, raise, and finish livestock on the western ranges and that he had tried to defend the ranching industry in Ottawa by insisting that the foothills region was unsuited to farming.[27]

I notice in recent newspapers that "Great movements are on foot just now in the way of immigration and colonization schemes" in England. In view of the fact that our property is to my mind an ideal one for a model colony of good agri-culturalists, it might be worth while … to consult with the proper parties as to how best to put its phenomenal advantages before those interested in these movements – We own 37,500 acres and rent 2,500[28] – our purchased land is unequalled in this centre of fall wheat growing, constituting large valleys thoroughly watered – by seven streams in which there is excellent fishing – all of which may be said to rise from springs on our land and terminate in the Old Man river which runs about 10 miles along our south boundary, one of the best fishing rivers in this district. Most of these streams can be utilized for irrigation of the land....

We graze our herds the year round feeding only our calves and bulls with a few weaklings such as late calving cows – seldom over 3,000 in all and in most winters only for three months ... during bad weather. The climate can only be appreciated by residence here, and, most people like myself like it so much that scarcely any one is known to leave it. A healthier climate for livestock does not exist. Disease is unknown, not even the common ailments of animals. The excellence of our cattle is well known by our exportations. Horse breeding properly conducted is much more successful than in any other part of Canada. They graze out all winter, and are fat in spring. Our Clydes would be prize winners in any show in Britain – Light horses do equally well. The porcupine Hills our eastern boundary are covered by Douglas Pine, furnishing building logs, fencing posts and poles unlimited.... Coal of excellent quality exists abundantly.

The difficulty may be about the price of the land as compared with cheap railway lands in newly opened country, but the difference arising from the many advantages partly referred to above would be as gold to silver, and when land will produce 40 bushels to the acre of number 1 hard wheat, its value is easily estimated. Not many years will pass till it will be worth $30 – $50 per acre.

Farmers of the right class would much prefer to get such land and climate at $20 than lands in new regions at $3.00 per acre. I would not favour a less price – unless as part of a bargain for Land and Culture. Another advantage would be we can at once stock their farms on reasonable terms by highly bred cattle raised on the land – and we would undertake to stock them with high class agricultural horses of our own as far as they would go – and I would select and bring them from Ontario and Quebec.[29]

While he was attempting to market the Walrond property from 1905 on McEachran also, of course, had to continue to keep the ranch operating as before. The New Walrond Ranche papers in the Glenbow Archives in Calgary are incomplete for this period, in part because McEachran had retired from his post as Dominion Inspector of Livestock and was able to spend more time on the ranch, making it unnecessary for his onsite manager to communicate with him by letter.[30] It does appear, however, that even under normal circumstances the business climate proved more difficult than in the recent past. In part to escape the Burns/Gordon, Ironsides and Fares beef monopoly, the New Walrond consistently sold cattle in Britain in these years. Accessing that market was very risky because of the high costs of shipping and the glut that inevitably occurred during the fall run. It might be argued that the ranch's cattle should have been weighing up better than in the past. After the land purchases, herd numbers declined to the point where they were more proportional to the size of the Walrond's home pastures, including the land it owned along Callum Creek and the free range it had initially held under lease.[31] However, because these grasslands had been so badly abused for years it must have taken a long time for them to replenish. Therefore, it was still necessary to allow a considerable portion of the stock to access outside regions in the Willow Creek district and beyond. As settlement increased this became more and more problematic.

One thing that is perfectly clear is that the greatest environmental challenge the Walrond faced in this period was the celebrated winter of 1906/07, which coincided with the ranch's demise. It is tempting to assert that this event *single-handedly* brought the productive history of the ranch to a close. That would be painting the picture a little too simplistically, however. A deeper analysis suggests that it merely forced the ranch to terminate active operations sooner than would otherwise have been necessary. The destructive power of the blizzards and prolonged cold spells unleashed on roaming cattle herds starting in late 1906 was so great in part because the effects of these phenomena were bolstered by other natural forces. When the weather turned cold in fall many of the range cattle were already suffering from the mange. Moreover, an extremely dry late summer and almost unending hot winds had helped to stunt much of the grass across the entire country south of Calgary. Ironically, in late October and early November, when it was too late to affect the pastures, it began to rain. It continued to do so for about two weeks, and then on the night of November 15 the rain turned to snow and the temperature dropped to forty degrees below zero.[32] Some three feet of snow fell in only a few hours. Temperatures climbed above freezing for a short interval and when the blizzards returned and the thermometer dropped, a layer of hard crust formed under the fresh snow that made it even more difficult for the cattle to find sustenance. One blizzard followed another until late spring. By the middle of December all the available hay individual ranchers had put up was either gone or covered by gigantic snow drifts. The cattle began to die from starvation and cold. Soon many in the foothills headed east in a futile attempt to escape the northwest winds and to find food. Some ranchers tried to hold them back but in vain. Thousands of cattle piled up against the fences of the CPR and of the settlers, where they were found dead in the spring. Others pressed in on the fences in such large numbers and with such panic that they crushed them into the ground. They then painfully made their way out onto the flat and treeless prairie where there was little or no shelter. They ate everything in their path – supplies of hay stacked in farmyards, small sapling trees sticking through the snow, the hair off the backs of one another. Carcasses began to pile up all over the prairie against fences and in river valleys or low spots between hills where many had taken refuge before dying. For weeks starving cattle strayed hopelessly through urban centres, including Fort Macleod and Maple Creek.[33] In Medicine Hat, supplies of hay were brought in to feed the cattle, but still many died on the city streets "or became so emaciated that they had to be shot." At Fort Macleod, the town water carrier "dragged a frozen carcass to the dump each time he returned from his deliveries."[34]

The difference between the fortunes of the cattle that were left on the open range or in very large pastures and those in smaller sheltered enclosures is demonstrated in the A.E. Cross correspondence. On his A7 ranch at Nanton, Cross had fenced and cross-fenced his own holdings so that his cattle were restricted to areas near the home place with thick tree growth and ample supplies of stacked hay and green feed.[35] Cross's losses at Nanton were negligible. However, north of the Red Deer River near Bassano he had about three hundred head of yearlings running on the open range under the supervision of Charlie Douglass. On 20 January Douglass wrote to Cross informing him that the cost was bound to be heavy, as the cattle had drifted off their respective pastures into the river valley and were all mixed up. Those ranchers who had hay were unable to "get their cattle to it." Douglass had been rounding up the Cross stock to get as many as close to his ranch as possible. He had two horse-drawn wagons busy hauling hay to them and he thought they had enough feed to last to the end of January.[36] However, the cold weather and blowing snow continued, making the job more and more difficult. Cattle that stayed along the river were left to eat brush. By March Douglass had only about a hundred head of Cross's animals left in the field and these were "all I can possibly manage so its no use looking for the poorest any more."[37] He reported on 16 March that he was skinning the hides off the dead animals that were not too mangy and selling them for six cents a pound. This he realized was not very profitable. He could only offer the commiserating observation that at least it defrayed some of the cost of the chopped grain he was buying to feed with what little was left of his hay.[38] When the storms finally ended over two-thirds of the Cross cattle had perished.

Contemporaries realized that some ranches everywhere were harder hit than others. Early in the summer of 1907 the commanding North West Mounted Police officer at Macleod reported that the winter had been "an exceptionally long and cold one. It was said to be the coldest in twenty years. Cattle in consequence suffered a great deal, and large losses had to be recorded, especially by the owners of large herds who could not feed and look after their stock in the way small owners could." The latter, the officer believed, "suffered very insignificant losses."[39] Jerry

Paisley, who had worked on the Walrond from 1885 to 1890, had settled on his own outfit on Beaver Creek near where some of the big ranch's stock grazed. He later reported that "every evening a drove of ... [them] came to a bluff about half a mile from ... [my] house.[40] They would eat the branches and twigs off the brush that grew on the bluff and their legs were torn and bleeding from breaking their way through the crusted snow.... Each evening there would be three or four less until none survived."[41]

David Breen has posited the Walrond losses at 5,000 head, and rumours have circulated over the years that the ranch had as many as 20,000 cattle prior to the killing winter and lost at least half of them.[42] Neither of these estimates holds up to in-depth examination. To work out the extent of the damage it is instructive to jump ahead to 1923, when the ranch, by then merely a land holding company, was to be desperately short of cash and experiencing considerable difficulty servicing its debts. At that time McEachran's presidential successor, C.W. Buchanan, informed the shareholders that "to pay off our indebtedness for accrued salary and loans to Dr. McEachran and other charges and to give the shareholders their money back *without interest* from 1907 when the last dividend was paid, it would be necessary to sell [our land] for about eight dollars per acre net."[43] That figure will "doubtless appear as a very low price when compared with the amount which in the past it has been hoped to obtain for the property but the general conditions in the West are so unfavourable as to make large blocks of land such as ours almost unsaleable [sic] at present." These words were well chosen. At a shareholders' meeting resolutions passed "giving directors the right to liquidate at prices they see fit." Still, it was to take another twenty years to market a substantial piece of the property and then at only $6.50 an acre.[44]

The statement that $8.00 an acre was needed to get the shareholders' money back and pay all other debts provides an excellent opportunity to estimate the operation's net worth both in 1923 and in 1907, when McEachran terminated active operations. At this time the ranch owned exactly 37,806 acres.[45] Eight times 37,806 equals $304,448.00, which must have been the total of the ranch's liabilities, including what it owed

SOMEBODY ELSE'S MONEY

to the shareholders. The only asset it had left in 1923 was its land. The equipment was gone and the buildings were old, decayed, and worthless. The directors seem to have done everything they could to sell the property but to no avail. The aftermath of 1906/07 and the post–First World War depression had kept land prices soft. By the acre the property was probably worth very little more than McEachran had paid for it.[46] But if it was worth, say, the $5.00 an acre the Walrond accountants used in the company's annual balance sheets, this would give it an overall value of $189,030.00. In that case the net worth of the ranch was $189,030.00 less $304,448.00, or minus $115,418.00. At the very most in 1923 the New Walrond Ranche Company's net worth was $115,418.00 *less than nothing.*

The above amount, which really cannot be significantly disputed, one needs to keep in mind when attempting to come up with an appropriate valuation for the point when the outfit ceased production in 1907. McEachran realized as early as the spring of that year that the ranch was not financially viable, and he negotiated a contract with Patrick Burns to market all the cattle at the end of the summer grazing season. The contract gave the ranch $26.00 per head, with the few nursing calves that had survived the winter or been born in the spring thrown in free of charge.[47] The approximate amount of cash the ranch had on hand after the sale,[48] and thus how many cattle were actually sold, can be established fairly realistically by tabulating the Walrond's financial commitments. Once Burns paid him for the cattle McEachran used some of the money to pay the ranch's bills and earmarked the rest for miscellaneous expenditures he could foresee in the not-too-distant future. As usual the cowboys had all been paid regularly over the summer and, since the cattle had earlier been contracted to Burns, no haying costs had been incurred. Therefore, the only money owing at the end of the summer was to the shareholders. On that basis the shareholders had $244,992.60 invested in the company.[49] However, McEachran was able to reimburse them just $7.29 per share. The amount required for this was just $36,748.89.[50]

When he paid the shareholders McEachran must have had to hold back capital he needed for exigencies. Immediately following the dispersal of the herd he reduced the labour force to three men who were put to work looking for any cattle missed during the roundup. They also gathered and looked after the remaining horses until a decision could be made about what to do with them. McEachran would continue to try to sell the ranch so he did not expect to keep it for very long. Still, he believed that the prices he was quoting perspective buyers might well depend on the construction of a new railway to the area bringing more settlement and thus greater demand.[51] This, he had to know, could not happen overnight, so it would be sensible to assume that he kept enough capital in the bank to see the ranch through three years. In that case he would have had about $4,320.00 for wages.[52] From 1911 he took only a portion of his own salary.[53] However, in 1907 he may well have kept enough money to pay himself for three more years. At $8,000.00 per annum he needed another $24,000.00. To be safe it would have been logical for him to have on hand another, say, $4,000.00 for unforeseen expenses. It is possible, therefore, that at the time he sent $7.29 per share back to the investors McEachran had another $32,320.00 to cover the company's future financial obligations.[54]

Therefore, the total amount of money McEachran should have had on hand after the Burns sale was the $36,748.89 for the investors plus about $32,320.00 for future costs, or $69,068.89, which for simplicity could be rounded off to $70,000.00.[55] If every bit of this had come from the Burns cattle sale, the highest possible number of non-newborn cattle sold would have been 2,692 head.[56] This figure must be close. If McEachran had sold significantly more cattle than this he would have had more capital to return to the shareholders, some of whom were showing signs of impatience.[57] Instead, the $208,243.71 still owed them was to be kept on the books until the land was finally disposed of in the 1940s. After the 1907 cattle sale the three Walrond cowboys began to search for strays. In 1908 McEachran told Arthur Walrond he was "sorry to say that we have not found very many cattle, I could not have believed that we could make such a clean gathering."[58] The company balance sheet at the end of the year shows twenty-nine cows, fifteen calves, and one bull. At $26 for the cows and cows with calves and the bull, these animals were worth $780.[59] After that a few more strays wandered into the ranch headquarters. A year later McEachran reported to the company's accountant that he had sold just over a hundred cattle for $4,120.[60] At that point there were still two milk cows, one two-year-old heifer, and one yearling cow and calf on the ranch.[61] All told it would seem generous, then, to put the number of cattle found after the 1907 roundup at about two 200. This would make the grand total of non-newborns the company could have owned when the 1906/07 winter ended at roughly 2,892.

This supports the estimate that the ranch owned about 5,000 cattle before the 1906/07 winter. There can be little doubt that McEachran had previously been grossly overestimating his livestock inventory and that the vicious storms gave him the opportunity to put his books in order without admitting this. As the editor of the *Yellowstone Journal* had acknowledged about other managers in earlier days, he was suddenly able "bravely, and comprehensively" to write off "in one lump the accumulated mortality" of years.[62] The figure of 5,000 fits with Dominion Livestock Commissioner J.G. Rutherford's statement that the industry's loss on the range during the killing winter was about 50 per cent.[63] The Walrond was likely still feeding some cattle on its own lots and perhaps on custom lots.[64] These animals were relatively safe from the storms. Since the herd was smaller than prior to the land purchases; and since timed breeding had cut down on the percentage of calves born out of season; and as the 1906/07 winter came on very early without warning, making it impossible for the Walrond cowboys to round up many cattle for distribution to custom lots, the number corralled would have been much lower than in the past. If the operation had about 1,000 on feed during the winter, and 4,000 out on the range and half of the latter survived, it would have had about 3,000 all told when the storms ended (1,000 on feed + 2,000 that did not die on the range). Since, as was the norm, a small percentage of those on feed would also have died, reducing this to between 2,800 and 2,900 would be about right. At $26 per head these cattle were worth $75,000.00. The Walrond ranch still also owned 84 Clyde and Shire horses in 1907 and 67 saddle horses. Some of these were of the highest quality, but according to the records, 43 were very poor. Therefore the lot was probably worth on average about $70 apiece for a total of $8,050.00.[65] At that time the house and buildings on land the ranch owned might have brought a few extra dollars in a sale, and the haying, cultivating, sowing, and harvesting equipment was also worth something. Another $5,000.00 might therefore be added. At that time the Walrond owned 38,126 acres of land. After the disastrous winter ranching property was very difficult to sell because of the enormous losses in the industry as a whole. Therefore $2.50 an acre or $95,315.00 in total would seem realistic. In 1907 the ranch thus had assets of $183,365.00.[66] To arrive at a net worth the $244,992.60 owed to the shareholders would have to be subtracted. This would make the net worth $61,627.60 *less than nothing.*

In order to dispel any thought that the 1906/07 winter was the single cause of the Walrond's downfall rather than years of uneconomic operation, it can be shown from this that the company was valueless even before the storms. If at that time it had 5,000 cattle at $26.00 a head its total cattle inventory was worth $130,000.00, or some $54,808.00 more than it would be a few months later.[67] This means that in the fall of 1906 its total net worth was *below* the zero mark by about $6,819.60.[68] In the first few years after the killing winter the ranch stagnated financially. At first McEachran rented one section of land (640 acres) to W. and R. Lloyd,[69] and then, from 1909 to 1912, he leased out the bulk of the land to William Roper Hull of Calgary.[70] The Lloyds' rent was only $132.00 a year, but that to Hull brought in about $2,000.00.[71] Until 1911 this, along with the dispersal each year of some of the remaining livestock, was enough to cover all the costs including McEachran's hefty salary. However, from 1912 the last of the livestock were sold off and the ranch was subject to increasing taxation. School taxes, wild land taxes, and eventually corporation taxes grew to about $6,600.00 annually and total non-managerial costs to "at least $7,500.00."[72] At the same time rents, from 1914 on to Patrick Burns, consistently rose at a slower rate than expenses.[73] To prevent bankruptcy McEachran was forced to pare down his own annual salary and even to lend the operation some money.[74] He should not be lauded too loudly for generosity, however. As the next chapter underscores, of all the people involved in the Walrond venture he was the only one who amassed a substantial fortune.

11

CONCLUSION

From 1907 McEachran continued to pour most of his energies into the campaign he had started in 1905 to sell the Walrond ranch. Besides hoping to solve the financial predicament the company was in, he was feeling the effects of age,[1] and he was putting a good deal of money into his own farm in the countryside at Ormstown, Quebec.[2] "My expenditures" there, he claimed in a letter to Arthur Walrond, "are dependent on land sales. Like all others therefore I am desirous of seeing this land sold as soon as its value, or fair value, is offered."[3] Interestingly, his ultimate failure to find a buyer did not prevent him from building "a magnificent villa" at Ormstown on two hundred acres where he also operated a dairy and a stable of Clydesdale horses.[4]

In the letter to Walrond, McEachran mentioned two people who might take an interest in the ranch – Lord Strathcona, whom he identified as a shareholder with some £2,000 of stock[5] and Douglas I. Neame, who worked on the Stock Exchange, presumably in London. He also suggested that Walrond himself might "know the best men" in conjunction with his banking interests. In all his correspondence in this period McEachran continued to promote the idea that a new railway would soon be built to bring a multitude of settlers to the Callum Creek region who would in turn put intense upward pressure on land prices.[6] "You may be asked the distance from the railway," he advised Walrond, "at present Cowley station is about 19 miles" to the south. He proposed, however, that if the ranch were sold to a company or syndicate which came as a farmer colonization project, it would speed up the building of a new branch line based on increased demand for goods and services as well as a greatly enhanced grain and livestock trade. "We are," he said, "again seriously assured that the railway through our land will be built next spring. We are also promised a … Bridge across Old Man's River. This country is filling up rapidly with the homesteading class, but homesteads are all gone now and purchases must follow and will just as soon as the railway is built." The evidence McEachran offered was that in anticipation of this, land values were already trending much higher. "Some sales have been made between here and Pincher Creek, for speculative purposes at $25.00. Land is held all round us at $30.00."[7]

In another letter, which he sent directly to a prospective buyer, McEachran also employed the mode used by many other frontier speculators of inventing a town site – in this case not so aptly named Walrond – hoping that this would suggest incredible potential profits from sales of urban lots.[8] He even drew up a map that showed the town clearly marked at the upper ranch headquarters, and he eventually went so far as to apply to the Commissioner of Irrigation for water rights for the town.[9] He also once again outlined an array of natural resources in the surrounding countryside. Most of the land, he told the prospective buyer, is "wheat land" and "unlike ordinary prairie land it is most thoroughly watered, carries coal, probably coal oil – Fine clay, Brick clay, sandstone, Timber (Douglas Pine).… Whoever acquires it and can handle it properly is sure of a large profit."[10] Since that time very little of this land has ever been converted to wheat production, largely because of the short growing season in the foothills region and the fact that the terrain is uneven, the topsoil in places shallow and the subsoil very rocky. In the modern period the Walrond land is being utilized as a grazing co-operative for local ranchers. In subsequent letters McEachran consistently raised his estimates of the price the lands would bring. "They are easily worth $30 to $40 per acre judging from crops raised on adjoining farms;"[11] once "the railway is built" they will be worth "$40 to $50.00" per acre "within five years."[12] These prices were far above any sales that took place in these years. Some small pieces of fertile farmland that were some distance south and east of Callum Creek brought as much as $20 an acre. Indeed, McEachran did manage to market two quarter sections on Beaver Creek at that price. One, the southwest quarter of section 13, township 8, range

SOMEBODY ELSE'S MONEY

29, west of the 4th meridian, he had bought along with three other quarters to complete the section on which the lower ranch was located. The other was the northeast of section 19, township 9, range 29, upon which the Beaver Creek thoroughbred ranch was situated. These, he said in his annual report, "are isolated lands 25 miles south of the large block leased to P. Burns and Co." They are, he might also have mentioned, much better suited to farming.

There is no evidence a railway was ever seriously considered for the Callum Creek area and none has ever been built. The property, McEachran told people, "is on the market simply because most of the men who started the ranche with me in 1883, are dead and their executors desire to close their estates." I have "retired from my professional work to my farm near Montreal and wish to close this out so that I may take my ease – but neither they nor I will sacrifice too much to accomplish a sale."[13] At the same time that he was telling potentially interested parties of the great profits that were likely to ensue for anyone intelligent enough to buy the property, McEachran pled poverty when trying to extract concessions from the government, which he felt would make the operation look more attractive. For instance, when attempting to obtain public money for the bridge across the Oldman River to improve transportation facilities, he informed the minister of public works that his main concern was the "unprofitableness [sic] of the business."[14]

McEachran's failure to market most of the Walrond property left the company out of money, with a mounting debt, and dependent on a lease arrangement to pay its taxes and other expenses. In 1923 the shareholders came to the realization that their president and managing director had been grossly overstating the value of their property. The board "is of the opinion," Buchanan told them, "that in the past too optimistic a view was taken of the value of your land and ... a very considerably lower price may have to be accepted."[15] After years of frustration the directors finally managed to sell a few "small outlying sections" in 1940. This sale brought in a total of $5,484.64, which was immediately absorbed by outstanding bills. No figure is given in the company papers for the overall amount of land involved, but at $6.50 an acre, which seems to have been the going rate at that time, it would have been about 840 acres.[16] Three years later the directors made their first big sale – another 10,600 acres at that price.[17]

Ironically, much of the money from this sale went directly to McEachran's estate. The amount owed McEachran when he stepped down in 1923 collected interest for ten years and then, presumably by agreement because of the company's difficult financial state, the interest was waived for the future. By that time the debt had grown to $114,382.14.[18] In the 1940s Buchanan negotiated with the executors and got them to recalculate the amount on the basis of 3.5 per cent interest, thus lowering it by "about $34,000.00" to $80,382.14. The first big sale was not strictly for cash. The buyer paid $50,620.00 down and the company carried the remaining $20,500.00 at 5 per cent interest. McEachran's estate got all the cash and whatever principal the buyer paid off over the next few years. When all the remaining land was finally sold to John Miller of Las Vegas the estate got another $9,262.14.[19]

The amount of land left after the first big sale of 1943 would have been 26,366 acres.[20] At $6.50 per acre that land was worth $171,379.00. Once McEachran's estate was paid the $9,262.14, a member of the Ogilvie family got $2,626.34 to cover a long-standing debt for services rendered by A.E. Ogilvie after the company had run out of cash many years earlier. Thus the shareholders were left sharing about $159,490.52. The total number of shares in the company was still 5,041, so the value of each share at this point would have been $31.63.[21] Of course, McEachran also got some of that money. His 280 shares brought $8,856.00. With the $7.29 they had received back in 1908 the shareholders thus finally recouped a total of $38.92 per share, or about 78 per cent of their original investment.[22] After waiting thirty-six years from the time the company terminated ranching operations in 1907, the shareholders thus lost $10.71 per share. In the 1943 list of Walrond shareholders there are forty-nine names of both living and dead people (i.e., their estates) and the Royal Trust Company, which presumably held shares for people who had died without heirs.[23] Many of the shareholders had relatively little exposure, owning 20 to 50 shares. However, one feels some sympathy for men like William McWilliam, a Scot from McEachran's hometown of Campbeltown, who had bought into the New Walrond Ranche Company in 1898. McWilliam's estate owned 920 shares for which he originally paid over $45,000.00 – a considerable sum, indeed, in the early decades of the twentieth century. After sitting comatose for such a long time McWilliam's investment was finally worth $34,858.80 – a comparatively modest amount in the late 1940s. One suspects that McWilliam and others would have felt betrayed had they ever learned that it was by unloading a considerable number of shares on them that McEachran and the Walronds had managed to significantly diminish their own commitment so many years earlier.

There is something incongruous about McEachran's estate collecting so much in the 1940s, but it should not be forgotten that most of the money the managing director made from the Walrond ranch had come to him while still living. He collected $5,800.00 a year in shares and dividends between 1883 and 1887 and over $6,200.00 dollars a year in shares, wages, and dividends between 1888 and 1898.[24] He also got a windfall when he terminated the Walrond and instigated the New Walrond Ranche Company in 1898 by selling 535 shares at $50.00 each, or $26,750.00. At the same time he collected a commission of $7,750.00 for selling the Walrond Ranche Company Limited in effect to himself. Between then and 1911 McEachran also collected a salary of $8,000.00 a year.[25] When he dispersed the first $7.29 to the shareholders he collected another $2,041.20 on the 280 shares he owned at that time. Thus over the years as general manager of the various versions of the Walrond ranch, he received nearly $240,000.00 in wages, dividends, commission, and the dispersal. To convert that to today's values that figure would have to be multiplied by about eleven – great pay, particularly for work that was mostly part-time. We should remind ourselves, moreover, that McEachran did not ever risk a cent of his own money on any aspect of the venture. Even when he loaned the company some cash between 1916 and 1918 he was really only handing back a portion of the full salary he had continued to take between 1907 and 1911 when the ranch was effectively out of business; and between 1912 and 1922 he reimbursed himself by taking a percentage of his salary whenever there was a little extra cash left in the company's bank account at the end of a given year.[26]

As revelations go, however, the most important one in this book is that the Walrond ranch was uneconomic. The statement that the company was worth $115,418.00 less than nothing in 1923 is based on very simple figures supplied by the Walrond's own accountants. It cannot be more than a few dollars out and it makes the estimate of minus $61,627.60 in 1907 and minus $6,819.60 in 1906 look, if anything, on the generous side. It has been argued here that the annual dividend, though necessary to keep the shareholders steady, was an expense the ranch could ill afford. One wonders if the various versions of the Walrond would have flourished if this regular annual expenditure had been avoided. If so, some might reason that large-scale ranching on the western frontier was economic after all so long as the investors could be persuaded to keep their fingers out of the company purse. To be sure, if the $17,000.00+ and then $12,000.00+ payments had not been withdrawn each year from the company's funds, and if from the beginning McEachran had put this money back into the operation, it would have been in a better position financially. However, to argue that this would have made the Walrond viable would seem to be going too far. Today a bank would not consider a rancher or farmer a good risk unless his assets in the form of land, cash, livestock, feed, and other "liquid" produce such as wheat or canola, were worth at least 50 per cent more than his loans. Using that standard the Walrond should have had *net* assets in 1907 of at least $367,000.00. Or, it needed to be better off than it was by nearly $430,000.00. One doubts that the dividend made quite that much difference. Moreover, if McEachran had maintained more capital in the 1880s and 1890s he very well might have used it to augment his cattle herds, which would have made grasslands degradation even worse; and that would have magnified the problem of small carcass weights and raised his death loss even higher. In a way, however, weighing such questions is unnecessary. A good company with the Walrond's initial capital should have been able to pay interest at 5 per cent. Some of the shareholders who got out between 1896 and 1898 obviously thought so. These people were unimpressed though the company appeared capable of doing that every year. Historically, few if any companies have ventured into production with less than a 5 per cent projected return.

An economic business with a capitalization of a quarter of a million dollars at the turn of the last century should have been able to pay its managing director a fairly substantial annual salary too. One of the things that McEachran failed to understand, however, is that agriculture on the northern Great Plains tends for much of the time to be unlike other businesses in that it is *not* economic. Another lesson the Walrond experience helps to illustrate is that a key to survival for any farm or ranch in this area is close, personal management. Duncan McEachran was far from alone in failing to understand that. George Lane, who owned the Bar U outfit some thirty kilometres to the north, was one of many other cattlemen who missed the point. In the early stages of his career Lane appears to have taken a firm hand in running his outfit. He rode the range with the cowboys and gained a reputation as an expert in all the skills of his trade.[27] However, after he bought up a number of large holdings including the Bar U, Lane found himself providing less and less day-to-day control. In 1897 he moved to Calgary, began sporting a three-piece suit and largely turned over responsibility for daily operations to others.[28] There were lots of reasons why at his death in 1925 Lane was bankrupt and all his assets were seized by the banks. However, there seems little doubt that loose management practices were among them. Virtually every other similarly operated so-called great ranch about which we now know the financial circumstances fared as the Bar U did. The North Fork ranch near Pincher Creek ceased operations after only a few years because of heavy losses; the Stair ranch in southern Saskatchewan closed down in 1909 because of depleted resources; the Cochranes lost some $400,000 in their first two years of operation and then sold out when higher land prices enabled them to recoup some of their capital in the new century; the Ross ranch in southern Alberta and northern Montana essentially went bankrupt after the 1906/07 winter and then again after the 1919/20 winter; the Turkey Track and Bloom outfits pulled out of southern Saskatchewan after taking severe losses in 1906/07; and the Matador ceased active operations in the province in the early 1920s.[29]

The ranches that have endured on the northern plains have adopted three basic approaches. Firm control by the owner and his or her family is one. Another is some degree of grasslands conservation. The operations that outlived or replaced the great ranches entailed as few as three or four hundred or, in one or two cases, as many as some tens of thousands of acres, but none of them was nearly as big as the Walrond, the Oxley, the Bar U, or the Cochrane. Therefore, in time their owners were able to construct fences to separate summer from winter pastures in order to allow lengthy annual rejuvenation periods. Most of them also did enough cross fencing to rotate their cattle intra-seasonally from one area when the grass was eaten down to another. The other approach that surviving ranches have adopted is to make financial solvency the main objective rather than large profits. This has been the case with the biggest of the family owner-operated ranches as well as the smaller ones. Fergus constantly lectured his son about the need for frugality and attention to detail, and he and Pamelia accepted numerous sacrifices in their personal lifestyle.[30] The McIntyres in southern Alberta owned and operated some 55,000 acres from 1892 to the 1940s.[31] When they commenced operations on the Milk River Ridge, William H. McIntyre himself controlled the ranch. Then his oldest son, Billy, took charge. He raised a family on the place and at various times was able to keep the outfit from going under by adopting practices such as crop sharing arrangements with neighbouring farmers.[32] Clay and Avril Chattaway, Mac and Renie Blades, and John Cross and Shelley Wilson-Cross, still grazing large herds in the Porcupine Hills near Nanton Alberta, are widely recognized for their reliance on the best traditional and modern grazing techniques.[33] The Crosses are practising a fully organic approach, which involves not just a rest rotational system and a return to indigenous grasses but also the non-use of pesticides, herbicides, and fertilizers. They have even found a way to graze year round, which involves scraping away the snow from winter pastures with a bulldozer so that the cattle can get at the grasses below during winters when the snowfall is particularly heavy. This system has enabled them to reduce supplemental winter-feeding of hay pellets to an average of about thirty days.[34]

Many family ranchers have been able to content themselves with survival because it has allowed them to maintain a particular way of life. For the Walrond and other joint-stock companies like the Powder River ranch, however, mere survival was never enough. McEachran coloured the truth for his shareholders and sent them a dividend cheque even when cash was short because he knew he had to hold up hope that the business would eventually bring them great rewards. To do less, he rightly feared, might bring on a full-scale shareholders' revolt, dramatically lower the value of his own shares, put an end to his great remuneration, and possibly even ruin his squeaky clean reputation. In the final analysis, it is one of the greatest ironies of the Walrond story that a major reason why the managing director was unable to carry on in a more realistic manner, and possibly even to sustain the operation for a significantly longer period, was the same reliance on somebody else's money that enabled him to walk away from the venture with a sizable take.

NOTES

ABBREVIATIONS:

GA – Glenbow Library and Archives, Calgary

LAC – Library and Archives Canada, Ottawa

MHS - Montana Historical Society, Helena

MSU – Montana State University Library, Bozeman

NA – National Archives of England, London (formerly the Public Record Office).

PAA - Provincial Archives of Alberta, Edmonton

UM – University of Montana Library, Missoula

CHAPTER 1 –
INTRODUCTION

1   See K.H. Norrie, "The National Policy and the Rate of Prairie Settlement," in R.D. Francis and H. Palmer, eds., *The Prairie West Historical Readings*, 2nd ed., (Edmonton, Pica Pica Press, 1992), 239–63.

2   S. Evans, *The Bar U and Canadian Ranching History* (Calgary: University of Calgary Press: 2004). The Bar U lease encompassed 158,000 acres.

3   Ibid.

4   Quoted in R.H. Fletcher, *Free Grass to Fences: The Montana Cattle Range Story* (New York: University Publishers Incorporated, 1960), 91.

5   Elofson, *Frontier Cattle Ranching in the Land and Times of Charlie Russell* (Montreal and Kingston: McGill-Queen's University Press/Seattle: University of Washington Press, 2004), 132–47.

6   Geoff Cunfer, *On the Great Plains: Agriculture and the Environment* (College Station: Texas A & M University Press, 2005), 10–11.

7   Donald Worster, *Dust Bowl: The Southern Plains in the 1930s* (Oxford: Oxford University Press, 1979).

8   Cunfer, *On the Great Plains*, 51–54. Indeed, on the latter page Cunfer tells us that the "cattle population increased with human population and small-farm settlement."

9   See Elofson, *Cowboys, Gentlemen and Cattle Thieves; Ranching on the Western Frontier* (Montreal and Kingston: McGill-Queen's University Press, 2002); Elofson, *Frontier Cattle Ranching*.

10 GA, New Walrond Ranche papers, M8688.

11 GA, Cross papers, M 1543, M8780.

12   MHS, MC 29; MSU, Worthen, Fergus papers, MC 913; UM, Fergus papers, MC 10.

13   *The Canadian Prairie West and the Ranching Frontier, 1874–1924* (Toronto: University of Toronto Press, 1983), 164.

14   E. Brado, *Cattle Kingdom: Early Ranching in Alberta*, 2nd ed. (Surrey, BC: Heritage House, 2004), 133–34; A.B. McCullough, "Winnipeg Ranchers: Gordon, Ironsides and Fares," *Manitoba History* 41 (Spring/Summer 2001): 18–25; Evans, *The Bar U and Canadian Ranching History*.

15   Binnema, *Common and Contested Ground; a Human and Environmental History of the Northwestern Plains* (Norman: University of Oklahoma University Press, 2001). Binnema illustrates the relatively small impact early European traders and explorers had on most indigenous human groups as they continued to practice age-old traditions in conformation with the flora, fauna, and climate. See also G. Colpitts, *Game in the Garden; a Human History of Wildlife in Western Canada to 1940* (Vancouver: UBC Press, 2002).

16   C. Evans, *The War on Weeds in the Prairie West: an Environmental History* (Calgary: University of Calgary Press, 2002).

17   P. Voisey, *Vulcan; the Making of a Prairie Community* (Toronto: University of Toronto Press, 1988), 128–54.

18   Ibid., 139.

19   Ibid., 138–39. The Crystal Springs Ranch, "which apparently never earned a profit from farm operations," folded in 1921, and the major shareholder, Harry Marsden, "committed suicide." C.W. Carman "left an estate burdened with massive tax arrears on extensive holdings of farmland and town lots." These collapses were small, however, "beside the spectacular 1922 bankruptcy of Charles S. Noble's gargantuan forty-eight-section empire." That event "stunned the farm press, for it had not only hailed Noble as perhaps the world's largest wheat farmer but as one of its most capable and knowledgeable."

20   *Edinburgh Courant*, 13 January 1880.

21   Prentice Ingraham wrote most of the dime novels about Buffalo Bill; see, for instance, *Buffalo Bill, from Boyhood to Manhood, Deeds of the Daring Scenes of Thrilling Peril and Romantic Incidents in the Early Life of W.F. Cody, the Monarch of the Borderland* (New York: [Beadle and Adams], [c. 1882]).

22   J.S.C. Abbott, *Christopher Carson familiarly known as Kit Carson* (New York: Dodd, Mead and Company, 1874); S.S. Hall, *Stampede Steve; or, the Doom of the Double Face* (New York: Beadle and Adams, 1884); G. St. Rathbourne, *Sunset Ranch* (1902); O. Wister, *The Virginian: A Horseman of the Plains* (New York: Macmillan, 1902); R. Connor, *Sky Pilot; a tale of the foothills* (Chicago, New York, Toronto: R.H. Revell, 1899).

23   J.S. Brisbin, *The Beef Bonanza or How to get Rich on the Plains; being a description of cattle-growing, sheep-farming, horse-raising, and dairying in the West* (Philadelphia: J.B. Lippincott, 1881); H. Latham, *Trans-Missouri Stock Raising; the Pasture Lands of North America; Winter Grazing* (Omaha; Daily Herald Steam Printing House, 1871); J. S. McCoy, *Historic Sketches of the Cattle Trade of the West and Southwest* (Kansas City: Ramsey, Millett & Hudson, 1874); W. Baron von Richthofen, *Cattle Raising on the Plains of North America* (New York: D. Appleton, 1881).

24   J.S. Brisbin, *The Beef Bonanza*, 47–48.

25   W. Baron von Richthofen, *Cattle-Raising on the Plains*, 57–58.

26 Voisey, *Vulcan*, 310. Voisey cites the following works: Morton Rothstein, "The Big Farm: Abundance and Scale in American Agriculture," *Agricultural History* 49, no. 4 (October 1975): 585; Paul Wallace Gates, "Large-Scale Farming in Illinois, 1850 to 1870," *Agricultural History* 6, no. 1 (January 1932): 14–25; Harold E. Briggs, "Early Bonanza Farming in the Red River Valley of the North," *Agricultural History* 6, no. 1 (January 1932): 26–37; Stanley Norman Murray, *The Valley Comes of Age: A History of Agriculture in the Valley of the Red River of the North, 1812–1920* (Fargo: North Dakota Institute for Regional Studies 1967), 131–38; Hiram M. Drache, *The Day of the Bonanza, A History of Bonanza Farming in the Red River Valley of the North* (Fargo: Institute for Regional Studies 1964); idem, "Bonanza Farming in the Red River Valley," *Historical and Scientific Society of Manitoba Transactions* 3, no. 24 (1967–68): 53–64; E.C. Morgan, "The Bell Farm," *Saskatchewan History*, 19, no. 2 (Spring 1966): 41–60; Don G. McGowan, *Grassland Settlers; the Swift Current Region during the Early Years of the Ranching Frontier* (Regina: Canadian Plains Research Center 1976), 57–59; Grant McEwan, *Illustrated History of Western Canadian Agriculture* (Regina: Western Producer Prairie Books, 1980), 57–79.

27 See Elofson, *Frontier Cattle Ranching*, 132–74.

28 Cunfer, *On the Great Plains*, 37–68.

29 Elofson, *Frontier Cattle Ranching*, 9, 136, 140.

30 See below, chapter 5.

31 *The Beef Bonanza*, 79. See also Moreton Frewen's comments in Elofson, *Frontier Cattle Ranching*, 151–53.

32 J. Macoun, *Manitoba and the Great North-West; the Great Wheat Fields and Stock Raising Districts of Canada; Facts and Information for Settlers with a Map of the Country* (Guelph: World Publishing Company, 1882). See also G.M. Dawson, *Montreal Gazette*, 17 November 1881.

33 Thomas Spense (clerk of the legislative assembly of Manitoba), *Useful and Practical Hints for the Settler on Canadian Prairie Lands and for the Guidance of intending British Immigrants to Manitoba and the North-West of Canada*, 2nd ed. (St. Boniface, Manitoba, Jan. 1882), 22–26. See also J. Dussault, *Farming in the North West of Canada, Actual Results* (Ottawa: Office of the Minister of Agriculture and Statistics of the Dominion of Canada, 1884).

34 McEachran, *A Journey Over the Plains from Fort Benton to Bow River and Back* [1881], 23.

35 In Wyoming Moreton Frewen was terribly disappointed in the results of grazing crowded plains (Elofson, *Frontier Cattle Ranching*, 151–53).

36 F. Wilkeson, "Cattle Raising on the Plains," *Harper's New Monthly Magazine*, April 1886, 790.

37 West, "Families in the West," reprinted from the *Organization of American Historians Magazine of History* 9 (Fall 1994), online: www.oah.org/pubs/magazine/west/west.html.

38 See Elofson, "Other People's Money, Patrick Burns and the Beef Plutocracy," *Prairie Forum* 32:2 (Summer 2007): 235–36.

39 In 1931, 40.4 per cent of all farms were in this category, in 1941 36.9 per cent were in this category, and in 1951 25.5 per cent were in this category (Census of Canada, 1971, Agriculture, Alberta, table 4.1, p.35).

40 Ibid.

41 "Total farm area, land tenure and land in crops, by province (1986–2006 Census of Agriculture," www40.statcan.ca/101/cst01/agrc25j.htm); Census of Canada, 2001, Agriculture, Alberta, "Average acres in hectares per farm reporting."

42 Ibid., Agriculture, Alberta, "Total number of Farms."

43 Ibid., Agriculture, Alberta, "All operators in the province."

44 Ibid., 1971, Agriculture, Alberta, Table 1, "Large farms and census farms by province."

45 Ibid., 1971, Agriculture, Alberta, p. 8.

46 Ibid., 1971, Agriculture, Alberta, Table 30. The vast majority of farms – 58,857 of 62,707 – were between 90 and 1599 acres.

47 See below, chapter 4.

48 See GA, New Walrond Ranche papers, count books, M8688–37, and below, chapter 4.

49 Ibid. Figures are also given from time to time in the company letters and annual reports. Thus, for instance, on 21 October 1905 McEachran wrote to A.M. Walrond informing him that the ranch had branded nearly 2,300 head (New Walrond Ranche papers, M8688–8); see also ibid., M8688–2: "Sixth Annual Report of the New Walrond Ranche Company Limited," for the year ended 31 December 1903.

50 See below, chapter 7.

51 This is about what cattlemen expect to get today; it is also what I normally achieved when running my own cow/calf operation in the 1980s.

52 Neth, Preserving the Family Farm: Women, Community, and the Foundations of Agribusiness in the Midwest, 1900–1940 (Baltimore: Johns Hopkins University Press, 1995), 17–70.

53 Teachers in 1911 were paid between $641 and $973 per annum and farm labourers got on average $421 per annum ("Canada Farm Labor Higher than Here," New York Times, 2 April 1911).

54 In 2005, total net income for farmers in Alberta was $622,508,000 ("Net Farm Income, Alberta and Canada … 1998–2005," www.1.agric.gov.ab.ca/$department/deptdocs.nsf/all/sdd5477). In that year there were about 50,000 farms in Alberta ("Total farm area, land tenure and land in crops by province 1986 to 2006, Census of Agriculture, Alberta," www.40.statcan.ca/lo1/cst01/agrc25). $622,508,000 divided by 50,000 is just over $12,450, which would be the average farm income. In Montana in the same year, 28,000 farmers netted $818,246, for an average of just over $29,000, and in 2006, 28,100 farmers in the state brought in $256,840, for an average of $9,140 (Montana State Fact Sheet, USDA Economic Research Service, Farm Financial Indicator, online: www.ers.usda.gov/statefacts/XLSfiles/MT-fact-sheet.xls).

55 "An Exceedingly Dicey Business; Frontier Horse Ranching on the Northern Great Plains," Agricultural History 79, no. 4 (Fall 2005): 462–77; "Figures Don't Lie: Reinventing the Walrond Ranche, 1897–98," Prairie Forum 32, no. 1 (Spring 2007): 67–86; "Other Peoples' Money; Patrick Burns and the Beef Plutocracy, 1890–1914," Prairie Forum 32, no. 2 (Summer 2007): 235–50.

CHAPTER 2 – THE WALROND CATTLE RANCH: PERSONNEL AND CHALLENGES

1 The original leases were: Walrond Ranch – 100,000 acres; Sir John Walrond – 100,000 acres; Duncan McEachran – 16,640 acres; Duncan McEachran – 29,000 acres; Duncan McEachran – 30,000 acres (Canada. *Sessional Papers*, 21, no. 4 [1888]), 201. These later passed to the company.

2 See below, chapter 5.

3 See Chapter 10, note 16.

4 GA, New Walrond Ranche papers, M8688–2: "Twentieth Annual Report of the New Walrond Ranche," for the year ended 31 December 1917. This report describes this as one of two quarter sections 25 miles south of the large block the ranch then owned on Callum Creek and leased to Patrick Burns.

5 Ibid., M8688–2: inventory for 31 December 1893.

6 See below, chapter 6.

7 It appears it was abandoned when McEachran decided to get out of the purebred horse business in 1896.

8 New Walrond Ranche papers, M8688–4: Warnock to C.E.D. Wood, 16 October 1895. "Enclosed herewith I send you diagram descriptive of the buildings on the Loring Ranche situated on the East side of Beaver Creek, East of the Porcupine Hills. The Ranche described as the 'Thoroughbred Ranche' in policy No: 14182 is no longer the property of the Walrond Ranche Co. Therefore please have it deleted and the Loring Ranche [instated]." It appears that the Loring site was sold in 1902 (M8688–6: Warnock to Campbell, 15 March 1902. "McEachran informs me that he has put the Loring Ranche in your hands to sell and that G.F. Johnston is negotiating for it. W. S. Brady of Five Mile was here to see me on Monday and he also would like to purchase").

9 Ibid., M8688–4. Buildings and corrals for all the sites are shown on the early district survey maps.

10 See below, chapter 6.

11 New Walrond Ranche papers, M8688–43; M8688–oversize 1–3.

12 Ibid., M8688–11: see the ranch inventory for 1892.

13 See NA, Walrond ranch company papers, BT 31/3169: "Special Resolutions of The Walrond Cattle Ranche, Limited, 16 June 1887; BT 31/3925, "Special Resolution. The Walrond Ranche, Limited, 24 December 1896; New Walrond Ranche papers, M8688–1: "The New Walrond Ranche Company, Limited." The New Walrond ranch was officially in existence as a company until it finally sold its lands in the 1940s. However, it stopped active operations when it sold its cattle to Patrick Burns in 1907. It began leasing its lands shortly thereafter (see below, chapter 11).

14 MHS, Power papers, MC55–448–2, McEachran to T.C. Power, 18 December 1882.

15 For the ranching fraternity's influence with the dominion government, see D.H. Breen, *The Canadian Prairie West and the Ranching Frontier, 1874–1924* (Toronto: University of Toronto Press, 1983), 90–93.

16 Elofson, *Frontier Cattle Ranching in the Land and Times of Charlie Russell* (Montreal and Kingston: McGill-Queen's University Press, Seattle: University of Washington Press, 2004), 8, 138–39.

17 This was the arrangement he made with Sir John Walrond and associates when

he became their general manager (below, p. 39).

18 P.J. Cain and A.G. Hopkins, *British Imperialism: Innovation and Expansion, 1688–1914*, vol. 1 (Harlow: Longman Group UK Limited, 1993), 22–25.

19 These properties are referred to in "codicils" Sir John Walrond Walrond made to his will in the 1880s; see Devon Record Office, Anstey and Thompson Collection, M1926B–W/F–2/15. The Pembina River property was advertised for sale soon after Sir John's death in 1889; see M1926B–W/E–29/1.

20 For descriptions of this and the other major ranches, see E. Brado, *Cattle Kingdom; Early Ranching in Alberta*, 2nd ed. (Surrey, BC: Heritage House, 2004); D.H. Breen, *The Canadian Prairie West and the Ranching Frontier 1874–1924* (Toronto: University of Toronto Press, 1983), 23–69; S. Evans, *The Bar U and Canadian Ranching History* (Calgary: University of Calgary Press, 2004).

21 According to the census reports all the original Walrond investors except the Canadian merchant Lionel Boyle, who was temporarily renting quarters in London, had four or more servants living with them.

22 Hon. Charlotte Margaret Lothian Coats married Hon. William Lionel Charles Walrond, son of Sir William Hood Walrond, on 18 June 1904.

23 *The Walrond Papers Compiled by Charlotte Walrond* (London: Arthur L. Humphreys, 1913), 34–35.

24 Clinton's second wife was Sir John Walrond Walrond's daughter, Margaret.

25 Goring was anything but a poor vicar. In the 1891 census he is shown living with four sons, two daughters, and no fewer than nineteen servants.

26 Lieutenant-Colonel Lionel Richard Cavendish Boyle was born in Cape of Good Hope, 24 November 1851. In the English census of 1871 he is listed as Acting Sub-Lieutenant in the Royal Navy stationed at Portsmouth. He is identified in the English census of 1881 staying with friends at Stanley V, Western Road, Hornsey (a London suburb). His parents were Charles, JER/LTF/171).

27 Boyle had five brothers and one sister.

28 Anstey and Thompson Collection, M1926B–W/F–2/15: "Draft, Sixth Codicil to the Will of Sir John W. Walrond."

29 NA, Walrond ranch company papers, BT 31/3169.

30 Ibid.

31 Ibid. The contract was signed on 18 May and registered on 28 May.

32 Ibid., "Memorandum of an Agreement."

33 In 1884 Arthur Walrond gave his address as that of his father's London residence, 45 Brook Street (NA, Walrond ranch company papers, BT 31/3169, "List of Persons Holding Shares in the Walrond Cattle Ranche Company Limited," 9 January 1884). However, in a list of shareholders composed in 1887 he would give his address as Pembina Crossing, Manitoba and he would describe his occupation as "farmer" ("List of Persons Holding Shares in the Walrond Cattle Ranche Company Limited," 30 June 1887). In Britain Arthur Walrond was in the banking business.

34 C. Walrond, *The Walrond Papers*, 76.

35 Like the other clergymen in the company Newton was anything but a *poor* vicar. The 1891 census shows him living with six daughters, one son, and nine servants.

36   The 1901 census report lists three servants living with Peshall, his wife, and two sons.

37   Listed in the 1891 census living with his wife, two daughters, and eight servants.

38   Listed in the 1881 census living with his wife, two sons and a daughter, and five servants.

39   For whatever reason, Arthur Constance Mitchell does not appear in the census reports.

40   NA, Walrond ranch company papers, BT 31/3169: "Agreement between D.M. McEachran Esqu and The Walrond Cattle Ranche Limited, 1 November 1883."

41   Teachers in 1911 were paid between $641 and $973 per annum and farm labourers got on average $421 per annum ("Canada Farm Labor Higher than Here," *New York Times*, 2 April 1911).

42   NA, Powder River ranch papers, BT 31/3033: "Memorandum of Agreement," 3 August 1882 between Moreton Frewen and C.W.M. Kemp of Walbrook, London "as Trustee for a company intended to be incorporated under the Companies Act, 1862 to 1880 by the name of The Powder River Cattle Company, Limited ..." Frewen to get "52,000 pounds" for his operation in Wyoming through "8000 Ordinary shares" and "12,000 pounds in cash." Vendor not to sell "more than 4000 shares" for five years – "4000 shares to be retained by the Company." "No salary or other annual remuneration shall be payable to the Vendor, unless and until a dividend of 10 pounds per centum on the whole subscribed capital of the Company shall have been declared by the Directors, payable out of the net profits of any year, and in such case the Vendor shall be entitled to receive one-third of the surplus net profits for that year remaining after payment of such dividend of 10 pounds per centum. The directors shall be the sole judges of what shall in each year constitute the net profits of the Company for the purposes of this Article."

43   Later the Ontario Veterinary College.

44   *Dictionary of Canadian Biography Online*: www.biographi.ca/EN/ShowBio.asp?BioId=42417&query=Duncan%20AND%20McEachran.

45   Canada, *Sessional Papers*, 21, no. 4 (1888): 201: Annual Report of Cattle Quarantines.

46   Power papers, MC55–448–2: McEachran to Power, 27 February 1883; ibid., Power to McEachran, 9 March 1883; ibid., 10 March 1883.

47   See above, note 46.

48   Power papers, MC55–448–2: 7 July 1883, "Copy of Receipt to D. McEachran, Cattle Business."

49   Ibid., Power to John H. Power and J.H. McKnight, 4 July 1883.

50   Ibid., McEachran to Power, 2 July 1883.

51   Ibid., McEachran to Power, [July 1883].

52   See below, p. 82.

53   L.V. Kelly, *The Range Men*, 75th Anniversary ed. (High River, AB: Willow Creek Publishing, 1988), 2–3.

54   Power papers, MC55–448–2: McEachran to Power, 28 February 1883.

55   Ibid., McEachran to Power, 30 April 1883.

56   Ibid., 10 May 1883; 23 May 1883.

57   GA, New Walrond Ranche papers, M8688–3: William Bell to McEachran 28 April 1887; "Joe got back from Montana last Friday he bought 28 head of saddle horses. He paid fifty seven dollars

and a half ($57.50) per head for them.... They are a good lot of horses similar to those bought three years ago but better as they are ... on the average larger. He hired the ... Mexican who you may remember broke for Payet at Benton four years ago. He does a first class break and I think by the round up will have most of them pretty well in hand."

58 Elofson, *Cowboys, Gentlemen and Cattle Thieves; Ranching on the Western Frontier* (Montreal and Kingston: McGill-Queen's University Press, 2002), 9–15.

59 Power papers, MC55–448–2, McEachran to Power, 21 September 1883. For McEachran's "anxiety ... to get the cattle on early consignment" so that the cattle drives would not run into inclement weather, see idem, McEachran to T.C. Power and Brother, [June/July 1883].

60 Ibid., McEachran to Power, 21 September 1883: "I am happy to say we got the herd in, in good order and Sir John Walrond and myself are well pleased with it."

61 Ibid., McEachran to Power, 4 September 1884.

62 This seems likely, as McEachran had bought from those companies when managing the Cochrane ranch (Ibid., McEachran to Power, 18 December 1882). Edward Brado mentions that "additional stock was bought near Bismarck, Dakota Territory and from various outfits near Fort Benton and points south of the Missouri River" (*Cattle Kingdom*, 133).

63 Power papers, MC55–448–2, McEachran to Power, 18 December 1882; see also McEachran to Power, 28 February 1883; McEachran to Power, 30 April 1883.

64 Ibid.

65 "Ranch Deal a Triumph," *Lethbridge Herald*, 9 November 1962.

66 Power papers, MC55–448–2, McEachran to Power, 12 October 1883; Kelly, *The Range Men*, 78.

67 Elofson, *Frontier Cattle Ranching*, 48–52.

68 "Ranch Deal a Triumph," *Lethbridge Herald*, 9 November 1962.

69 Kelly, *The Range Men*, 116.

70 New Walrond Ranche papers, M8688–3, Bell to J. G. Ross, 9 July 1888.

71 MHS, Memoirs of Lady Katherine Lindsay, SC 1692.

72 New Walrond Ranche papers, M8688–5, Warnock to McEachran, 23 January 1899.

73 "A Scene of 'Real Western Life,'" *Nanton News*, 21 July 1904; "Drew a Six Shooter," *Rocky Mountain Echo*, 8 March 1904.

74 "The Six-Shooter Again is Called in to Settle a Dispute," *Macleod Gazette*, 21 July 1885.

75 Kelly, *The Range Men*, 109. See also New Walrond Ranche papers, M8688–4, Warnock to McEachran, 23 December 1895 and 4 May 1896.

76 New Walrond Ranche papers, M8688–5, Warnock to McEachran, 23 July 1900.

77 Ibid., Warnock to McEachran, 29 January 1901.

78 See Elofson, *Frontier Cattle Ranching*, 81–95.

79 McEachran, *Impressions of Pioneers of Alberta as a Ranching Country* (commenced in 1881 but completed and published sometime after 1915), 12–13.

80 As did the Mounties; see, for instance, Canada, *Sessional Papers*, 31, no. 11 (1897): n. 15, 9, Report of the North-

west Mounted Police, Annual Report of the Commissioner, 10 December 1896.

81 New Walrond Ranche papers, M8688–5, Warnock to McEachran, 5 February 1901.

82 Ibid., Warnock to J.G. Ross, 4 March 1898. For Fallis, see ibid., M8688–3, W. Bell to J.G. Ross, 6 November 1887.

83 "Arrested for Cattle Stealing," *Nanton News*, 14 April 1904. This event is also recorded in Kelly, *The Range Men*, 183.

84 Kelly, *The Range Men*, 183.

85 Elofson, *Frontier Cattle Ranching*, 90–92.

86 New Walrond Ranche papers, M8688–3, W. Bell to J. G. Ross, 18 September 1887. List of men and time worked for the year 1886; total 140 months 22 days. Including Bell – 11 men worked 7 to 12 months but only 6 for 9 to 12 months.

87 Ibid., Mathison memo, 31 August 1889: "Baker and Coy. took delivery of two hundred and one three year old steers this week. They looked a very satisfactory even lot when bunching up"; M8688–4, Warnock to McEachran, 16 October 95; Warnock to J.G. Ross, 11 November 1895; Warnock memo, 24 October 1896.

88 Monthly tallies kept by Bell and then David Warnock are in ibid., M8688–3.

89 Ibid., W. Bell to McEachran, 9 April 1887; M8688–3, Bell to J. G. Ross, 6 November 1887: "The intention is to have two men there for the winter who will do their own cooking and take care of the hides as Black Bros. do not care to take the hides any longer. At the Piegan (sic), Fallis boarded himself and his Indian assistant in a cabin purchased from I.G. Baker & Co. along with their improvements there and when he quit on the 24th. Oct. everything was removed from him and the killing is now done from the ranch."

90 New Walrond Ranche papers, M8688–11, inventory for 1892.

91 Ibid., M8688–28.

92 Ibid., M8688–3, Bell to McEachran, 9 April 1887.

93 McEachran, *A Journey over the Plains from Fort Benton to Bow River and Back* [1881], 17.

94 New Walrond Ranche papers, M8688–3: Warnock to McEachran, 8 August 1894.

95 Ibid., M8688–5, McEachran to Watson, 21 June 1898.

96 Ibid., M8688–3, J.F. Scott to McEachran, 11 December 1890; Warnock memo, 11 March 1894, "List of Employees on Horse Ranche," 2 July 1893. J. <Shrock> and wife and Adam Ferguson and wife are listed at $60.00.

97 Ibid., Warnock to McEachran, 11 March 1894.

98 Ibid., M8688–5: Warnock to McEachran, 27 November 1902. Warnock told McEachran that he was "glad to know that you have got a young man whom you think will suit you. I shall be very pleased to turn over everything at 3rd Dec as I will likely run over to Glasgow and see my parents before settling down to business in spring." Subsequent letters demonstrate that he actually stayed on for a week or two after 3 December.

99 Warnock was living on the ranch when the census was taken in 1891 (PAA, 1891 Census of Canada, Alberta, Pekisko District, T- 6425, T- 6427).

100 The wedding was recorded under "Local and General," *Calgary Daily Herald*, 8 October 1897.

101 1901 Census of Canada, Alberta District, Sub-District A1, T–6551.

102 New Walrond Ranche papers, M8688–5, Warnock to McEachran, 31 August 1901.

103 1906 Census of Canada, District 18, Sub-district 21, T–18361.

104 Elofson, *Frontier Cattle Ranching*, 119–31.

105 UM, Fergus papers, MC 10–17, Fergus to Pamelia Fergus, [1879]. In this letter Fergus is seen admonishing his wife over her atrocious spelling. "You spell stade for stayed, kepped for kept, haled for hauled, herd for heard, levle for level, bye for buy, eny for any, calvs for calves."

106 Ibid. "The things I instructed you to do after I left home in the East you ignored. You did not copy the bills as I directed, nor stop at Chicago, nor ask Thomas to fix the wagon, nor put your flour in double sacks." If my own wife "pays no attention to my directions, how can I expect" other people of standing in the community "to do it."

107 Ibid., MC 11–65: Fergus to "friend Mills," 7 May 1883.

108 *Fergus County Argus*, 18 December 1908.

109 UM, Fergus papers, MC 11–65: Fergus to Mrs. Harding, [1887].

110 MHS, Stuart papers, MC35: sketch by Mrs. Allis Stuart.

111 I.F. Randall, *A Lady's Ranch Life in Montana*, ed. R.L. Saunders (Norman: University of Oklahoma Press, 2004), 117–18.

112 University of Texas, Austin, Harry Ransom Humanities Research Center, J.F. Dobie Collection, C.M. Russell Miscellaneous material, 18–3, interview with Mr. Charles L. Sheridan. For other powerful frontier women, see Elofson, *Frontier Cattle Ranching*, 119–31.

113 Numbers of men employed over the years can be found in New Walrond Ranche papers, M8688–25 and M8688–26.

114 MHS, Power papers, MC 55–448–2: McEachran to Power, 9 April 1883. Ostensibly, after Bell's years the onsite manager handled the clerk's duties as well as his own.

115 See New Walrond Ranche papers, count books, M8688–37.

116 Ibid., M8688–5: Warnock to McEachran, 31 August 1901. Mclean was concerned about the loss of body weight as a consequence of stress.

117 See below, p. 195.

118 New Walrond Ranche papers, M8688–37, "Rough count of Herd," June 1888; idem, M8688–7.

119 Ibid., M8688–3, W. Bell to McEachran, 28 April 1887.

120 Ibid., McEachran to Boyle, Campbell, Burton & Coy, 10 July 1887: "We have cut out every old cow with a barren udder or frozen teats, and have put them on good pasture up North fork, and will wean their calves as soon as they can live. And let them fatten for … [Indian] contracts before winter sets in and will feed the calves during part of winter if need be."

121 Ibid., Bell to McEachran, 25 September 1887.

122 Ibid., 10 July 1888: "I, W.D. Bailey do hereby contract and agree with the Walrond Ranche Company for the sum of one thousand dollars to build a stable and furnish all the material, and to have the same complete to the satisfaction of the Local Manager not later than October 10th next."

123 Ibid., M8688–7: McEachran to G.C. Fielding, 28 June 1909.

124 See above, p. 43.

CHAPTER 3 – THE WALROND CATTLE RANCH: UPPER MANAGEMENT

1 D.H. Breen, *The Canadian Prairie West and the Ranching Frontier, 1874–1924* (Toronto: University of Toronto Press, 1983), 20, 55; L.V. Kelly, *The Range Men*, 75th anniversary ed. (High River, AB: Willow Creek Publishing, 1988), 87.

2 See D.H. Breen, "The Canadian Prairie West and the Harmonious Settlement Interpretation," *Agricultural History* 47 (1973): 68–73.

3 Kelly, *The Range Men*, 106, 118; E. Brado, *Cattle Kingdom; Early Ranching in Alberta*, 2nd ed. (Surrey: Heritage House Publishing, 2004), 190; LAC, RG 15 B12–1–4–184–M3799, McEachran to Fred White, 27 January 1891: "A fire recently occurred by which about 300 tons of hay was destroyed at our cattle Ranche [near] Beaver Creek, which fire I have every reason to believe was incendiary in its origins." McEachran blamed the Dunbars, Dave Cochrane, or a man named Jerrod Paisely to whom he also refused access to Walrond lands.

4 "A Hard Case," *Macleod Gazette*, 27 August 1891.

5 Ibid.

6 Kelly, *The Range Men*, 106.

7 Canada, *Official Reports of the Debates of the House of Commons*, seventh parliament, first session, 6155.

8 "An Enemy to Southern Alberta," *Macleod Gazette*, 29 August 1891.

9 *Debates of the House of Commons*, seventh parliament, first session, 6156.

10 Ibid. The eviction notice might have appeared to Dunbar as a mistake had he not been warned several months before by the land office in Lethbridge, the same office that had granted his patent.

11 GA, Dewdney papers, M320: J. Lamar to McEachran, 4 August 1891.

12 F.G. Bundy, "In the Foothills of the Rockies," *Pincher Creek Echo*, 3 August 1961.

13 Canada. *Debates of the House of Commons*, seventh parliament, first session (1891), 6148–6166.

14 Ibid., 6160; "An Enemy to Southern Alberta," *Macleod Gazette*, 29 August 1891.

15 Ibid., 6166.

16 See below, p. 109.

17 Kelly, *The Range Men*, 109, 118.

18 *Debates of the House of Commons*, 29, 6156.

19 "The Walrond Ranche Again," *Macleod Gazette*, 27 August 1891.

20 Below, p. 162.

21 New Walrond Ranche papers, M8688–3: McEachran to D.I. Campbell, Stock Association, Fort Macleod, 22 July 1888. See also "Dr. McEachran Speaks," *Macleod Gazette*, 11 July 1888.

22 See below, p. 202.

23 Kelly, *The Range Men*, 109.

24 Brado, *Cattle Kingdom*, 190.

25 Kelly, *The Range Men*, 73; see also W.M. Elofson, *Cowboys, Gentlemen and Cattle Thieves* (Montreal and Kingston: McGill-Queen's University Press, 2000), 132–33.

26 "Wanted to Get Even," *Nanton News*, 1 September 1904.

27 Kelly, *The Range Men*, 151.

28 Ibid., 183–84.

29 Ibid., 157.

30 New Walrond Ranche papers, M8688–5, Wanrock to McEachran, 5 February 1901.

31 GA, Stair Ranch Letter Book, D.H. Andrews to Glengarry Ranch Co., 10 September 1892.

32 New Walrond Ranche papers, M8688–4, Warnock to P. Burns and Coy, 12 November 1900.

33 See below, chapter 8.

34 New Walrond Ranche papers, M8688–8 McEachran to A.J. McLean, 7 December 1889.

35 "Town and Country," *Rocky Mountain Echo*, 15 August 1900.

36 Below, chapter 8.

37 Canada, *Sessional Papers*, 41, no. 11 (1906, 1907), n. 28, 62: Report of the Northwest Mounted Police, Annual Report for K Division, 1 October 1906.

38 J.W. Bennett, *Northern Plainsmen; Adaptive Strategy and Agrarian Life*, 1st paperback ed. (Chicago & New York: Aldine & Atherton, 1971), 185.

39 New Walrond Ranche papers, M8688–5, Warnock to McEachran, 13 April 1898. He told McEachran that "I am not in a position to purchase an appreciable amount. There had been numerous chances to loan money at a good rate of interest during the past autumn and winter and whenever I could get good security I arranged the loans for a year at from 6 to 8%."

40 Ibid., M8688–4, Warnock to McEachran, 20 April 1897; see below, p. 194.

41 New Walrond Ranche papers, M8688–5, Warnock to McEachran, 31 August 1901; this is taken from the rewritten letter in which Warnock made a more concerted effort to soften the blow and sidestep any possible criticism of himself.

42 For instance, on occasions when an owner goes into his corrals to examine cattle that his hired man has just checked he often finds one or two with colds or shipping fever that really do need attention. I found this a number of times on my own feedlot operation in Alberta.

43 The ranch grew from 320 acres with 100 horses, 1,900 sheep and 950 cattle in 1883 to 8,600 acres deeded and 2,500 acres rented land, 1,000 horses, 9,000 sheep and 2,500 cattle in 1900 (R.M. Horne, "James Fergus: Frontier Businessman, Miner, Rancher, Free Thinker," University of Montana Ph.D. thesis, 1971, online: www.dangel.net/AMERICA/Fergus/JamesFergusThesisTableOfContents.html).

44 UM, Fergus papers, MC11–64: Fergus to F.E. Bright, 5 December 1895.

45 Ibid., MC11–60: J. Fergus to W. Fergus, 10 August 1885.

46 In the 1890s, a few years before his death, Fergus was, himself, very dissatisfied with the economic performance of the ranch and he spelled it out in black and white (R.M. Horne, "James Fergus").

47 Fergus' careful financial management is seen in a letter he wrote to his son in 1892 in which he counselled him to "buy nothing we can get along without, I have been looking over our books since you went away and our Expenses are Even More than I Expected. Our Total Expenses during the year and half a Month to come yet is $10050.73. Our credits leaving out the Steers and heavy horses $740.05 leaving a balance of 9716.70. $897.62 is for goods at Lewistown, 4172.21 for expenses there, $3775.00 for wages, $165 for mess Expenses /92, Steer drive/91 $89.38 for Pool Expenses $330.48, Stock bought

$206.00 You have drawn out $637.25 More than you put in one way or another . Not adding in your doctors bill, or crediting you with Steers Sold & the rest in includes My little Expenses for papers, books clothing interest and odds and ends, the only way we can get out of dept is to Spend less" (Fergus papers, MC11–60, Fergus to Andrew Fergus, 17 December 1892).

48 In 1899 Fergus was 86 years old.

49 Fergus papers, MC11–65, memo by James Fergus, March 1899.

50 GA, A.E. Cross papers, M8780–109, Cross to Cochrane, 9 June 1898.

51 Kelly, *The Range Men*, 72–74. Kelly believed that in bringing in the two big shipments of cattle in 1881 and 1882 Walker was forced to take some steps that eventuated in major death losses by McEachran's orders from Montreal. This argument seems well founded and there can be no doubt that McEachran was responsible for putting both purchases on the trail to the Cochrane ranch late in the fall and that this more than anything else caused them to be caught in the inclement weather that destroyed so many.

52 Ibid., 72–74; H.F. Lawrence, "Early Days in the Chinook Belt," *Alberta Historical Review*, 13, no. 1 (Winter 1965): 13–14.

53 Kelly, *The Range Men*, 74.

54 I.e., domesticated animals then recently imported from the East that were unaccustomed to fending for themselves on the open range.

55 See note 51 above. Years later the Cochranes themselves would admit that in their first two winters they lost a total of $400,000: see J.J. Young, "A Visit to the Cochrane Ranch," *Alberta Historical Review* 22, no. 3 (Summer 1974): 28.

56 See below, chapter 11.

57 D. McEachran, *Impressions of Pioneers of Alberta as a Ranching Country* (commenced in 1881 but completed and published sometime after 1915).

58 Ibid., 4.

59 Ibid.

60 Ibid., 6.

61 Ibid., 11.

62 Ibid.

63 D.H. Breen, *The Canadian Prairie West and the Ranching Frontier, 1874–1924* (Toronto: University of Toronto Press, 1983), 35.

64 McEachran, *Impressions of Pioneers of Alberta as a Ranching Country*, 6, 11.

CHAPTER 4 – THE FIRST GREAT KILLING WINTER

1 S. Evans, *The Bar U and Canadian Ranching History* (Calgary: University of Calgary Press, 2004), xiii, 2, 18.

2 Figures provided by Statistics Canada (www.statcan.gc.ca/pub/11-516-x/sectionm/M228_238-eng.csv).

3 GA, New Walrond Ranche papers, M8688–37. In 1886 there were 1,794 and in 1887 there were 1,464 that were branded in the summer and fall.

4 Ibid., M8688–3, McEachran to Boyle, Campbell, Burton and Co., 10 July 1887. In the same letter he also implied that they should continue the practice: "We have cut out every old cow with a barren udder or frozen teats, and have put them on good pasture..., and will wean their calves as soon as they can live. And let them fatten for ... contracts before winter set in and will feed the calves during part of winter if need be."

5   Ibid., Bell to McEachran, 9 October 1887.

6   Ibid., M8688–6, Warnock to McEachran, 15 March 1902. "A few calves are beginning to appear on the range but these are brought in as found and are being sheltered. The cows must have been served by bulls running loose in Willow Creek district last spring. Quite a number of Circle bulls were found running at large on last Spring Roundup."

7   Ibid., M8688–3, McEachran to Boyle, Campbell Burton and Co., 10 July 1887.

8   Ibid., W. Bell to McEachran, 9 October 1887.

9   See, for instance, ibid., M8688–4, Warnock to McEachran, 29 April 1898: "In compliance with the new ordinance all bulls are being gathered and herded this spring. The ranchers between the N. fork and Pincher Creek are going to hold their bulls in Elkhorn Park and I think it would be a good plan for us to go in with them and put our range bulls there too.... So far we have gathered about 30 head" (M8688–4: Warnock to J.G. Ross, 20 June 1898). Warnock to McEachran, 28 October 1899; Warnock to McEachran, 23 July 1900.

10 Ibid., M8688–6, Warnock to McEachran, 15 March 1902; see also M8688–4, Warnock to McEachran, 31 August 1901.

11 To the east of Beaver Creek.

12 Ibid., M8688–3, W. Bell to McEachran, 9 April 1887.

13 Ibid., W. Bell to McEachran, 28 April 1887.

14 Ibid., McEachran to Boyle, Campbell, Burton and Co., 28 June 1887.

15 Ibid., 10 July 1887.

16 Ibid., M8688–37, New Walrond Ranche count books.

17 Ibid., M8688–3, W. Bell to J. G. Ross, 18 September 1887.

18 Ibid., M8688–37.

19 Ibid., McEachran to Boyle, Campbell, Burton and Co., 10 July 1887.

20 Ibid., M8688–6, McEachran to [A.R.] Springett, 10 November 1902.

21 "The Roundup of 1887," *Alberta Historical Review* 13, no. 2 (Spring 1965): 23.

22 Evans, *The Bar U and Canadian Ranching History*, 30–31.

23 Kelly, *The Range Men*, 100.

24 New Walrond Ranche papers, M8688–3, W. Bell to McEachran, 28 April 1887.

25 "Winter Feeding of Cattle," *Pincher Creek Echo*, 29 November 1904; carcass weights of fat, mature steers will average about 60 per cent of live weight.

26 New Walrond Ranche papers, M8688–3, W. Bell to McEachran, 9 October 1887.

27 Ibid., Bell to McEachran, 22 October 1887.

28 Ibid., McEachran to L. Vankoughment, Deputy Superintendent General of Indian Affairs, 7 July 1888. "Stags" are steers that have been poorly castrated and therefore have a great deal of muscle in their meat that makes it comparatively tough.

29 Packing plants like Cargill or Tyson Foods in Canada today would discount this kind of meat by a lot more.

30 New Walrond Ranche papers, M8688–3, McEachran to Messrs Boyle, Campbell, Burton and Co., 28 June 1887.

31 Ibid.

32 See Elofson, *Frontier Cattle Ranching in the Land and Times of Charlie Russell* (Montreal and Kingston: McGill-Queen's University Press; Seattle: University of Washington Press, 2004), 151–53.

33 American Heritage Society Archives, Laramie, Frewen papers, MC9529–2–11, M. Frewen to T.C. Sturgis, 9 June 1883; Frewen to J.M. Carey, 9 August 1883; Frewen to Sturgis, August 1883; Frewen to Clare Frewen, 16 July 1883; Frewen to Clare Frewen, 28 August 1884; Frewen to Vernon, 20 August [1885]; Frewen to Lord Rosslyn, [October 1885].

34 Ibid., MC9529–2–19, Frewen to Board of Directors, [9] June 1883.

35 Ibid., Frewen to Clare Frewen, 1 October 1883.

36 Ibid., Frewen to Kali, 24 October 1883.

37 Ibid., MC9529–3–5, Frewen to Clare Frewen, 28 August 1884.

38 Ibid., MC9529–3–6, Frewen to Clare Frewen, 12 September 1884.

39 Ibid., Frewen to W.H. Hulbert, 10 May 1883; Frewen to A. Pell, 23 June 1883; Frewen to E.F. Kemp, 8 August 1883. See also L. Woods, *British Gentlemen in the Wild West: the Era of the Intensely English Cowboy* (New York and London: The Free Press, 1989), 84.

40 See above, p. 76 and below, Chapter 10.

41 "Local Notes," *Macleod Gazette*, 7 June 1895.

42 See McEachran's prospectus of February 1898, below, p. 156.

43 Evans, *The Bar U and Canadian Ranching History*, 197–201.

44 See below, Chapter 7.

45 J.R. Craig, *Ranching with Lords and Commons, or Twenty Years on the Range* (Toronto: William Briggs, 1903), 64.

46 See MHS, Power papers, MC55–448–2, "Copy of Rect. To D. McEachran, Cattle Business," 7 July 1883.

47 Ibid., McEachran to Power, 4 September 1884.

48 Elofson, *Frontier Cattle Ranching*, 81–85.

49 Indeed, this must have been the case for McEachran and others in 1887.

50 R.H. Fletcher, *Free Grass to Fences; the Montana Cattle Range Story* (New York: University Publishing Corporation, 1960), 91.

CHAPTER 5 – THE SECOND WALROND RANCH, 1888–1898: A NEW STRATEGY

1 NA, Walrond ranch company papers, BT 31/3169, "Summary of Capital and Shares of the Walrond Cattle Ranche Company, Limited," 30 June 1887.

2 Ibid.

3 5 x £2,500.

4 5 x £1,550.

5 Lady Sarah Hotham had two shares, and George H.W. Windsor Clive had one share.

6 Teachers in 1911 were paid between $641 and $973 per annum and farm labourers got on average $421 per annum ("Canada Farm Labor Higher than Here," *New York Times*, 2 April 1911).

7 He was married to Sir John's eldest daughter, Katherine.

8 In the 1881 census Mason is shown living with his wife and three servants.

9   In the 1881 census Cartwright is shown living with one son, two daughters, and thirteen servants.

10 In 1881 he lived with his wife, two sons, and twenty-five servants/labourers.

11 In 1881 he lived with his brother, sister, and seven servants.

12 With the loss of Boyle's £1,550 ($7,750.00).

13 See NA, Walrond ranch company papers, BT 31/3925, "Memorandum of Agreement," 6 December 1887; ibid., "Memorandum of Agreement," 10 December 1887.

14 See below, p. 160.

15 Exeter, Devon Record Office, Anstey and Thompson Collection, M1926B–W/F–2/15, codicil dated 12 December 1883.

16 Evidence suggests that Sir John worried a good deal about Arthur's future. In 1888 he also bought him a partnership in the Exeter banking firm, Sanders and Company (ibid., M1926B–W/E–8/15: see May 1888 correspondence between Sir John and his lawyer and the 1888 draft of an agreement between Sir John and Arthur on one hand and Sanders and Company on the other).

17 Anstey and Thompson papers, M1926B–W/F–1/5, draft dated 14 February 1887 and labelled the seventh codicil.

18 Ibid., M1926B–W/F–2/15, 1888, draft of the "Sixth Codicil to the Will of Sir John W. Walrond."

19 Maschwitz appears in the 1901 census living with his wife and four servants at 22 Augustus Road, Edgbaston, which address is also cited in the Walrond papers

20 Aurelius Bruce Mitchell lived next door to Francis William Mitchell with his wife, two daughters, three sons, and just three servants. He also listed his occupation as "pen maker."

21 See www.Deloitte.com.

22 NA, Walrond ranch company papers, BT 31/3925, "D.M. McEachran Esq and The Walrond Ranche Limited, Agreement," 18 July 1888.

23 Ibid., "Summary of Capital and Shares of the Walrond Ranche Limited," November 1893. The shares are valued at £10 apiece or $50 Canadian.

24 Ibid., "Summary of Capital and Shares of the Walrond Ranche Limited," 22 December 1896.

25 Ibid., "Summary of Capital and Shares of the Walrond Ranche Limited made up to the 29th day of November 1893."

26 $17,212.50.

27 The frost-free period is longer due to the fact that the altitude is lower than at the other ranches.

28 GA, New Walrond Ranche papers, M8688–3, W. Bell to McEachran 25 September 1887.

29 Ibid.

30 Ibid., Bell memorandum, 20 July 1887: "rain and snow made it a very bad week for haying"; Bell to McEachran, 25 September 1887: "We got the hay finished in the early part of week before last and on Friday the round up started."

31 Ibid., Bell to J. G. Ross, 6 November 1887. Bell informed Ross that he had bought hay on contract and that "both amounts are more than the contract actually calls for but it is not an easy matter to judge the amount exactly and as the hay is of good quality and well stacked should the winter prove severe it can be used to good advantage as the grass owing to late rains and early frosts will not be first class."

32   Ibid., 20 July 1887, Hay contract with William Farmer.

33   Ibid., to J.G. Ross. The Belly River is south of the Oldman River.

34   Ibid., M8688–5, Warnock to McEachran, 31 August 1901.

35   Ibid., M8688–3, McEachran to Boyle, Campbell, Burton and Co., 10 July 1887.

36   Ibid.

37   The following is an amusing incident that occurred when one of the cowboys played a trick on Murray: "he had one of the riders plait a horse-hair rope to put around his bed as he had heard that snakes will not cross such a barrier. This was too much for the Waldron [sic] boys and they didn't rest until they had got a rattlesnake skin and stuffed it. They placed it well over the circle of horse-hair and Billy Ferguson imitated the rattles of an energetic rattlesnake. It worked, for Murray leaped out of bed and out on to the prairie in two seconds flat" ("Ranch Deal a Triumph," *Lethbridge Herald*, 9 November 1962).

38   Lamar apparently came up to Alberta in 1888 (Kelly, *The Range Men*, 109).

39   "A Famous S. Alberta Ranch; The Walrond or 'W.R.'," *Lethbridge Herald*, 2 February 1963. When Scott quit Warnock fulfilled the duties of both the horse manager and the general onsite manager until the ranch got out of the horse business in 1897, when he officially took over as general manager.

40   See above, p. 53.

41   $5,600.00 + $2,400.00 + $2,400.00 + $1,800.00.

42   GA, New Walrond Ranche papers, M8688–3, Warnock to McEachran, 13 November 1893; "Particulars re fodder etc. Horse Ranche, 417 tons of hay put up by contract at 3.75 per ton.... Of this quantity about 280 tons will be hauled by contractor @ 2.50 per ton. Of this quantity about 137 tons will be hauled by ranche teams. Five Mile Ranche, 48½ tons of hay put up and delivered by contract @ 4.50 per ton. 20 tons of hay put up by Ranche employees, 5 tons of that hay grown on the farm. Hay contract for 250 tons to be stacked in the hay corrals at the Horse Ranche for 4.75/ton ranche lands." M8688–4, Warnock to McEachran, 18 August 1897: "Contractors are taking a great deal of hay now and are paying good prices. Wilson is putting up one hundred tons for us at Mill's place at 6.00 per ton"; M8688–4, Warnock to McEachran, 11 November 1895: "When the contractors all get through hauling we will have about 1150 tons of hay."; Warnock Memo, 7 December 1895: "A few hundred of the eastern steers have been let out to farmers to be fed by contract for the winter."

43   550 tons x $5.00.

44   Ibid., M8688–6, Warnock to McEachran, 7 December 1901, "Feeders of beef cattle for Indian contracts get 3.00 per head per month."

45   Ibid., M8688–5, Warnock to J.G. Ross, 28 March 1901.

46   In the same letter Warnock reported that "we have plenty of hay on hand and if we can turn loose most of the cattle being fed, within the next two weeks, [we] will have probably 200 tons of hay left over." This tells us that to that point the winter had not been tough enough to force the ranch to feed up a disproportionate amount of its feed reserve. From that time on, however, the weather seems to have deteriorated and more of the reserve had to be used (ibid.).

47 This is assuming that the cow would have had to be fed during the worst 100 days of weather and the steer the worst 150 days to keep it at least maintaining, but hopefully, gaining weight. The cows would have needed about 20 pounds of dry hay a day and the steers, depending on age and size, would average about 20 pounds.

48 This included the yearling heifers from previous calf crops that were bred to replace older or poorer cows as they were sold off to the Native bands.

49 1.5 x 8,500.

50 13,600 x $5.00.

51 It can be assumed that had the Walrond put up all its own hay without contract the costs would have been very close to the same. The management would have had to hire many more men, purchase a great array of haying, hauling, and stacking equipment, and provide housing and a food supply for the men.

52 With horse-drawn equipment one man could put up about 60 tons of hay.

53 There were two waves of settlement: the first started in the 1890s and brought farmer/ranchers to the area, many of whom took 160-acre homesteads supplemented by free range or small grazing leases. It was not until the second wave, beginning in the early years of the twentieth century, brought homesteaders, most of whom initially settled on 160-acre parcels, which they later doubled through pre-emption, that modern density levels were reached (Elofson, *Cowboys, Gentlemen and Cattle Thieves*, xviii, 149). At the turn of the century all of southern Alberta and Assiniboia had only 100,000 people, while the State of Montana, which covered almost as large an area, had 243,000: *Fourth Census of Canada* (1901), vol. i, 9; A. Merrill and

J. Jacobson, *Montana Almanac* (Helena: Falcon, 1997), 46.

54 Elofson, *Cowboys, Gentlemen and Cattle Thieves; Ranching on the Western Frontier* (Montreal and Kingston: McGill-Queen's University Press, 2000), 81–82.

55 Throughout the early to mid-1890s the horse manager David Warnock reported on the devastation wolves were wreaking on both cattle and horses; on 12 November 1894, he told McEachran that "we have finished rounding-up counting and marking the horses and I am sorry to inform you that we have only gathered forty nine yearlings out of one hundred and one turned out in May last. Myself and Rennie have thoroughly ridden all the surrounding country within a radius of 20 miles from the ranche and are satisfied that we have found all that are alive.... The number of wolves in this part of the range at present is I think unprecedented, and they are following the foals and yearlings right into the pastures" (M8688–3).

56 See J.G. Nelson, "Some Reflections on Man's Impact on the Landscape of the Canadian Prairies and Nearby Areas," in P.J. Smith, ed., *The Prairie Provinces* (Toronto: University of Toronto Press, 1972), 43.

57 The severe losses the Walrond took from them in both cattle and horses inclines one to empathize with modern day livestock owners who have vociferously resisted government efforts to re-introduce and revive the species in Idaho, Montana, and Wyoming. The ranchers' stand against wolf recovery programs has been well covered by the media in ranching areas: see, for instance, "Ranchers Want Feds to Start Killing Wolves," *Bozeman Daily Chronicle*, 16 April 2004; "Livestock Losses Leave

Ranchers Worn Down by Wolves," *Billings Gazette*, 16 May 2004; "Impact of Wolves Grows," *Casper Star Tribune*, 18 January 2005. The advocates of recovery are many: see B.H. Lopez, *Of Wolves and Men* (London: J.M. Dent, 1978); T. McNamee, *The Return of the Wolf to Yellowstone* (New York: Henry Holt, 1997); R. Bass, *The Ninemile Wolves: an Essay* (Livingstone: Clark City Press, 1992); K. Jones, *Wolf Mountains: a History of Wolves along the Great Divide* (Calgary: University of Calgary Press, 2002); M.A. Nie, *Beyond Wolves: the Politics of Wolf Recovery and Management* (Minneapolis: University of Minnesota Press, 2003).

58   GA, New Walrond Ranche papers, M8688–3, Warnock to McEachran, 31 July 1894.

59   Ibid., M8688–4: Warnock to J.G. Ross, 13 December 1897.

60   See below, chapter 6.

61   D.H. Breen, *The Canadian Prairie West and the Ranching Frontier, 1874–1924* (Toronto: University of Toronto Press, 1983), 58.

62   T. Binnema, "The Case for Cross-National and Comparative History: the Northwestern Plains as Bioregion," in S. Evans, ed., *The Borderlands of the American and Canadian Wests: Essays on Regional History of the Forty-Ninth Parallel* (Lincoln and London: University of Nebraska Press, 2006), 29.

63   Both creeks flow out of the east side of the Porcupine Hills and join the Oldman River.

64   Bob Creek to the west of Callum Creek flows into the Oldman River, and Damon, Sharples, and Meadow Creeks flow into Callum, which ends in the Oldman River to the south. Heath and Cabin Creeks feed into the Oldman

River from the Porcupine Hills to the east of Callum Creek.

65   See, for instance, "Holistic Cow! Why ranchers are going green," www.albertaviews.ab.ca/issues/2003/julaug03/julaug03cow.pdf.

66   See L. Fitch, B. Adams, P. Ag, K. Oshaughnessy, *Caring for the Green Zone; Riparian Areas and Grazing Management*, 3rd ed., 22, online: www.cowsandfish.org/riparian/caring.html; see also Geoff Cunfer, *On the Great Plains: Agriculture and the Environment* (College Station: Texas A & M University Press, 2005), 67.

67   See C. White, *Revolution on the Range*, 10.

68   *Caring for the Green Zone*, 33.

69   Ibid., 32; T. Bennima, "The Case for Cross-National and Comparative History," 28.

70   McEachran, *A Journey Over the Plains from Fort Benton to Bow River and Back*, [1881], 23.

71   The photograph is from the Glenbow Archives in Calgary and the two copies are from L. Fitch, B. Adams, P. Ag, K. Oshaughnessy, *Caring for the Green Zone*, 23. Note that at present the Walrond land along Callum Creek is now a grazing co-operative erroneously named Waldron.

72   See Alberta, Forestry, Lands and Wildlife, Public Lands Division, *Range, Its Nature and Use* (Edmonton, 1986), 11.

73   L. Fitch, B. Adams, P. Ag, K. Oshaughnessy, *Caring for the Green Zone*, 38.

74   In *Range, Its Nature and Use*, 11, the average stocking rate in this area is shown as 1.72 acres (0.7 hectares) for each "animal unit month." This would be 20.64 acres per animal unit year (12 x 1.72). Under the extensive practices of

the early ranchers, however, this would have been about 63 acres per animal. I rounded this off to 70 acres to allow for the fact that on portions of the range that are too far from a drinking water source, or on hill/mountain peaks where the coniferous and/or willow growth is extremely thick, grazing is impossible.

75 $275,640 \div 70 = 3,938$.

76 New Walrond Ranche papers, M8688–3, McEachran to Messrs Boyle, Campbell, Burton and Co., 28 June 1887.

77 The 2,000 removed from pastures for 100 days would be like removing about 600 for the year since 100 days is between a quarter and a third of a year. I am arbitrarily assuming that something like another 1,000 could have been handled on land the cattle had access to outside the lease even though, as has been seen, the positive impact of this was offset by outside cattle that commonly roamed *onto* the Walrond lease.

78 See below, chapter 6.

79 T.G. Jordan, *North American Cattle-Ranching Frontiers; Origins, Diffusion, and Differentiation* (Albuquerque: University of New Mexico Press, 1993), 239; R.H. Fletcher, *Free Grass to Fences; the Montana Cattle Range Story* (New York: University Publishing Corporation, 1960), 86–87; L.V. Kelly, *The Range Men*, 191; Elofson, *Frontier Cattle Ranching*, 135–41. C. White, *Revolution on the Range*, 131–43.

80 Geoff Cunfer, *On the Great Plains; Agriculture and Environment* (College Station: Texas A & M, 2005), 66–67.

81 Thus, for instance, when Patrick Burns purchased the Walrond cattle from the 1897 fall roundup he was able to find very few cows or "eastern" cattle that were fat enough to kill (below, p. 186). In 1904, wandering cattle from the New Walrond, Circle, and IV ranches were found mingling together in Tennessee Creek coulee to the west of the lower Walrond ("Local and General," *Pincher Creek Echo*, 13 June 1905).

82 Some of the more aggressive among these animals could end up as far away as Medicine Hat or even Maple Creek (below, p. 195).

83 They appear monthly in New Walrond Ranche papers, M8688–3.

84 Seeds of leafy spurge and sow thistle are often transported in animal digestive systems and those of Canada thistle are carried in the fur. All three compete at least reasonably well with native grasses in the West, particularly on land that is overgrazed.

85 Above, chapter 1. For the spread of eastern weeds on western farms, see C. Evans, *The War on Weeds: An Environmental History* (Calgary: University of Calgary Press, 2002).

86 New Walrond Ranche papers, M8688–4, Warnock to McEachran, 9 November 1896.

87 Ibid., Warnock to McEachran, 20 April 1897.

88 Each year the pattern was about the same at each reserve.

89 Prior to the 1897 sale to Burns the ranch sold about a thousand each year to the Peigan and Blood bands. In 1898 the company stopped supplying the Indians and sold principally to Burns or other cattle buyers or else shipped directly to Britain in the fall of each year.

90 At an average of about $42, the 80 could have brought in another $3,000 to $3,500 annually. The heifer calves were normally allowed to mature to be incorporated into the breeding herd. This would eventually have given the ranch the ability to cull and sell another 80 or

so of its older cows every year. Fat cows normally brought in about $30 apiece – thus annual cash flows would have increased by another $2,400. That would of course have added to ranch income, firstly because in four to five years the steer calves would have been full-grown and available to sell on the slaughter market. A percentage of them would succumb to severe winters, drought, disease, or predation. However, about 80 could be expected to survive. In the late 1880s and early 1890s steers were worth between $40 and $45 apiece (see below, chapter 7).

91 R.H. Fletcher, *Free Grass to Fences: the Montana Cattle Range Story* (New York: University Publishers, 1960), 115.

CHAPTER 6 – ELEGANT HORSES IN A RUGGED SETTING

1 See, for instance, R.H. Fletcher, *Free Grass to Fences: the Montana Cattle Range Story* (New York: University Publishers, 1960); D.H. Breen, *The Canadian Prairie West and the Ranching Frontier, 1874–1924* (Toronto: University of Toronto Press, 1983); T.G. Jordan, *North American Cattle-Ranching Frontiers; Origins, Diffusion, and Differentiation* (Albuquerque: University of New Mexico Press, 1993).

2 For a brief evaluation of the sheep industry, see W.M. Elofson, *Frontier Cattle Ranching in the Land and Times of Charlie Russell* (Montreal and Kingston: McGill-Queen's University Press; Seattle: University of Washington Press, 2004), 160, 179–80. For a brief assessment of the horse ranching industry in the late nineteenth and early twentieth centuries, see W.M. Elofson, *Cowboys, Gentlemen and Cattle Thieves: Ranching*

on the Western Frontier (Montreal and Kingston: McGill-Queen's University Press, 2000), 27–28; for the horse business on the Bar U ranch, see S. Evans, *The Bar U and Canadian Ranching History* (Calgary: University of Calgary Press, 2004), 149–75.

3 In early 1898 McEachran decided to liquidate the Walrond Ranche Company and put its assets into the New Walrond Ranche Company Limited (below, Chapter 7). To further the latter objective he composed a prospectus that he hoped would attract investors (GA, New Walrond Ranche papers, M8688–1, "The New Walrond Ranche Company, Limited," 26 February 1898). In that document he announced that the horse business had not paid financially and he promised that the new company would have nothing further to do with it. He indicated that its downfall had principally been "competition from electric motors." Evidence from the ranch correspondence strongly suggests that this was only one of the problems.

4 New Walrond Ranche papers, M8688–3, Warnock memo, [November 1893]; [2 July] 1894.

5 Ibid., Warnock to McEachran, 19 September 1894.

6 Ibid., 12 November 1894.

7 Ibid., 31 October 1894.

8 Ibid., Warnock to McEachran, 12 November 1894.

9 Ibid. It is clear that the Walrond did not face this menace alone. L.V. Kelly reported that many others paid a heavy price. In 1890, he recalled, "one old wolf, who hunted alone, and who had been responsible for damage amounting to thousands of dollars, was finally roped and killed by a man who had followed him a month to secure the fifty

dollar reward that was offered" (L.V. Kelly, *The Range Men*, 75th anniversary ed. (High River: Willow Creek Publishing, 1988), 130). For the owner of a small herd the destruction could prove critical. In 1894, a settler in the Pincher Creek district had "no less than nineteen head of young stock," out of a herd totalling some 40 or 50 taken in one grazing season (New Walrond Ranche papers, M8688–4, Warnock's "Remarks re Wolves," June/July 1894).

10   New Walrond Ranche papers, M8688–4, Warnock to McEachran 18 April 1896.

11   Ibid., Warnock to J.G. Ross, 16 May 1894.

12   Ibid., J.F. Scott to McEachran, 3 August 1892.

13   Ibid., J.W. Mathison memo, 7 November 1888.

14   Ibid., M8688–3, Warnock to McEachran, 23 January 1894.

15   Ibid., M8688–4, Warnock to McEachran, 25 March 1895

16   Ibid.

17   Ibid., M8688–3, Warnock to Major Bell, 6 April 1894.

18   Ibid., Warnock to J.G. Ross, 16 May 1894.

19   Ibid., Warnock to McEachran, 13 November 1893.

20   Ibid., 2 February 1894.

21   Ibid., 14 November 1894.

22   Ibid., M8688–4: Warnock to S. Reid, 25 May 1895.

23   Ibid., Warnock to McEachran, 22 April 1895.

24   Ibid., 2 April 1895

25   Ibid., Warnock to J.G. Ross, 11 November 1895.

26   Ibid.

27   Ibid., Warnock to McEachran, 11 November 1895.

28   Ibid., Warnock to McEachran, 15 April 1895.

29   Ibid., M8688–3: David Warnock to McEachran, 13 November 1893: "We have all WR. Horses on the North side of the river and I have instructed Murray to [use] the greatest vigilance in preventing Coy. Horses from going south and strange horses from coming north of the river."

30   Ibid., Mathison memo, 27 April 1889.

31   Ibid., M8688–4, Warnock to McEachran, 15 April 1895.

32   Ibid., "List of Employees on Horse ranche," 2 July 1895.

33   Ibid., M8688–3, 28 February 1894.

34   Ibid., Warnock to McEachran, 12 March 94.

35   Ibid., M8688–4, Warnock to J.G. Ross, 26 May 1896 "I went up to [Edmonton] to take possession of the horses sold to Jas. Dimmer in March /95; also to Antonio J. Allen re the Allen and Essery notes. Essery died very suddenly in February and left his affairs in a very muddled state. Allen is a hard man to make pay, and I only succeeded in collecting $205 on the 350 note due 15th Feb. Times are extremely hard in that district owing to the almost total failure of crops last summer... I found it an impossibility to dispose of the Dimmer outfit of horses for cash, so decided to trade them off for young cattle."

36   Ibid., M8688–6, Warnock to Beck and Essery, 18 November 1902: "I beg to acknowledge receipt of yours of 8th inst. Enclosing draft value 320.00 to cover balance on G. Allan claim. Personally I am very pleased to have this a/c closed

as I am leaving the Walrond Ranche Coy: service in Spring."

37 Ibid., M8688–4, Warnock to McEachran, 15 April 1895.

38 Ibid., Warnock memo, 2 May 1896; Warnock memo, 25 July [1896]; Warnock memo, 1 August 1896. In all three cases the vast majority of the 52 head are listed as "aged." For the rest see Warnock memo, August 1896; Warnock memo, 17 October 1896; Warnock memo, 28 November 1896.

39 Ibid., "Memo. of sale and agreement between the Walrond Ranche (Ld) and Messrs W.H. Fares and P. Burns re the draught horses the property of the Ranch Company," 26 June 1897.

40 Ibid., Warnock reported to McEachran on 18 April 1896 that he had bought 15 saddle horses "well broken and sound at $40."

41 See Elofson, *Frontier Cattle Ranching*, 47, 58–59.

42 GA, A.E. Cross papers, M8780–112, Cross to A.R. Springett, 10 November 1902.

43 Ibid., Cross to George G. McNeil, 2 January 1901: "we purchase a limited quantity of hay but can get it so easily from the farmers here we find it suits our purpose best."

44 Ibid.; see also Elofson, *Cowboys, Gentlemen and Cattle Thieves*, 31.

45 A.E. Cross papers, M8780–112, Cross to McNeil, 2 January 1901.

46 Ibid., M8780–470, Cross to L. McKinnon, 23 January 1908.

47 Kelly, *The Range Men*, 130.

48 A.E. Cross papers, M8780–112, Cross to Mr. Hodson, November 1900.

49 Ibid., Cross to A.R. Springett, 10 November 1902.

50 C. White, *Revolution on the Range: The Rise of a New Ranch in the American West* (Washington: Island Press, 2008), 54–58.

51 New Walrond Ranche papers, M8688–2, "Report of the New Walrond Ranche Company," for the year ended 31 December 1903.

52 The number McEachran had on hand when closing down the ranch after the 1906/07 winter was 70 mature animals and a few foals; see ibid., inventory for year ending 31 December 1907.

53 Elofson, *Cowboys, Gentlemen and Cattle Thieves*, 27–28. For an excellent indepth discussion of the horse business in the late nineteenth and early twentieth centuries, see M. Derry, *Horses in Society: a Story of Animal Breeding and Marketing, 1800–1920* (Toronto: University of Toronto Press, 2006).

CHAPTER 7 – FIGURES DON'T LIE: THE BIRTH OF THE THIRD WALROND RANCH

1 GA, New Walrond Ranche papers, M8688–1, "The New Walrond Ranche Company, Limited," 26 February 1898.

2 Ibid. Sir William Hood Walrond agreed to act as one of the provisional directors of the new company and its president. Some time later he stepped down and McEachran became the president and general manager (below, p. 173).

3 D.H. Breen, *The Canadian Prairie West and the Ranching Frontier, 1874–1924* (Toronto: University of Toronto Press, 1983), 76.

4 "Local Notes," *Macleod Gazette*, 7 June 1895.

5 New Walrond Ranche papers, M8688–1, "The New Walrond Ranche Company, Limited," 26 February 1898.

6 As we will see (below, p. 155), before he decided to reorganize the company he received fairly reliable evidence that the cattle herd was substantially smaller than his own estimate based on a book account.

7 New Walrond Ranche papers, M8688–1, "The New Walrond Ranche Company, Limited," 26 February 1898.

8 See below, chapter 11. In the *Pincher Creek Echo* of 21 June 1907, it was reported that the Walrond herd had been sold for nearly $250,000.00. The *Echo* got its facts wrong. The actual contract is in the New Walrond Ranche papers (M8688–29). By it P. Burns and Company agreed to take all the Walrond cattle at $26.00 a head with suckling calves thrown in. Burns provided a down payment of only $2,500.00. The cattle were to be delivered between 1 September and 31 October 1907 and, of course, the final payment was to depend on the number of cattle actually delivered. $7.29 x 5041 shares amounts to only $36,748.89. The total value of all the cattle sold could not have been much more than this, and therefore, the number of cattle sold could not have been more than about 2,500; see below, chapter 11.

9 New Walrond Ranche papers, M8688–7, McEachran to H.W. Hooper, 6 July 1912. In 1903 he got about 34,000 acres of land for 2.28 per acre from the C. & E. Railway and "from the government," (M8688–2, "Report of the New Walrond Ranche Company, for the year ended 31st December, 1903"). It is in fact doubtful given the disastrous condition of the ranching industry in general after the 1906/07 winter whether this land would have brought the original price had it been put on the market in 1908.

10 See L.V. Kelly, *The Range Men*, 75th anniversary ed. (High River, AB: Willow Creek Publishing, 1988), 190–93. The Walrond was reputed to have lost over half of its 20,000 head of cattle at that time (*Lethbridge Herald*, 2 February 1946).

11 Edward Brado implies that this was indeed the case with the Walrond itself: *Cattle Kingdom: Early Ranching in Alberta*, 2nd ed. (Surrey, BC: Heritage Books Publishing, 2004), 135.

12 New Walrond Ranche papers, M8688–1, "The New Walrond Ranche Company," 26 February 1898. In the same document he also claimed that he was going to invest $30,000 in the New Walrond Ranche.

13 The northeast quarter of section 19, range 29, township 9, west of the 4th meridian. The quarter was surveyed in 1889 and then turned over to the ranch in 1891.

14 In 1896 the leaseholders were told that they were allowed to purchase a tenth of their leased land at that price: D.H. Breen, *The Canadian Prairie West and the Ranching Frontier, 1874 to 1924* (Toronto: University of Toronto Press, 1983), 76.

15 New Walrond Ranche papers, M8688–3, J.F. Scott to McEachran, 17 September 1892; M8688–7, McEachran to G.C. Fielding, 22 February 1909.

16 In his prospectus, M8688–1, "The New Walrond Ranche Company, Limited," 26 February 1898, McEachran said that no count had been taken since 1891. By the count books, however, it appears that it actually had been done one year later than that.

17 Ibid.

18 The request was from a W. Hoile: New Walrond Ranche papers, M8688–4, Warnock to J.G. Ross, 13 December 1897.

19 Ibid., Warnock to McEachran, 2 December 1897.

20 Ibid., Warnock to J.G. Ross, 13 December 1897.

21 Ibid., Warnock to McEachran, 2 December 1897. Warnock used the phrase "on the range." It is clear, however, that he was referring to virtually all the cattle, as very few had been brought in off the range by late November: see Warnock memo of 20 November 1897; Warnock to McEachran, 22 November 1897; Warnock Memo of 27 November 1897. Also, 9,000 is the number McEachran used as his conservative estimate in his prospectus for the New Walrond Ranche: M8688–1, "The New Walrond Ranche Company," 26 February 1898.

22 Ibid., M8688–4, Warnock to McEachran, 18 December 1896; Warnock to McEachran, 18 March 1897.

23 A comparison with 1894/95, which approximated what had at one time been the norm, helps to illustrate this. In January 1895 the steers at the Blood reserve had averaged 718 pounds, and through to May dropped by less than 50 pounds. In the same period the female stock managed to net no less than about 535 pounds.

24 New Walrond Ranche papers, M8688–1, "The New Walrond Ranche Company," 26 February 1898.

25 In fact, after the prospectus was written in February the ranch sold a total of just over 1,000 head all the rest of the year – 816 to A.J. Mclean and about 200 to the Blood and Peigan Indians. Warnock said there were another 400

that he felt could have gone to market in the fall had the weather held out a little longer to enable the cowboys to round them up: ibid., M8688–5, Warnock to McEachran, 26 November 1898. So the total that either were or could have been marketed was just over 1,400 – not 2,000 as McEachran claimed. Moreover, many of those marketed in 1898, as in the 1897 sale, must have been three-year-olds. Therefore, McEachran's estimation seems a bit outrageous. If 760 of the animals that were sold to Mclean in the fall were steers and if 300 of the 400 that could have been sold were steers the total would have been 1,060. The 1898 grazing season was ideal and apparently those cattle fattened up very well. At the turn of the century Warnock would single them out as the best the ranch had produced in years (below, p. 193). The other steers marketed went to the Blood and Peigan Indians in March and April 1898. We know that virtually none of them was ready for market. So if we go by what McEachran referred to as "saleable" stock we could allow him all 1,060 but probably no more. If we also use saleability to count up the heifers and cows that were ready for market we really just get the 56 sold along with the steers to McLean in the fall of 1898.

26 New Walrond Ranche papers,, M8688–4, contract between the Walrond Ranche and P. Burns and Co., 26 June 1897.

27 Ibid., Warnock to J.G. Ross, 18 September 1897.

28 Ibid., M8688–3, Bell to McEachran, 20 August 1888.

29 MHS, Fergus papers, MC 28–2–5, 22 August 1887.

30 Calculated by taking the average of the four deliveries between January and April.

31 One could argue that 4 cents is too much for the female animals, as normally they brought a lower price than steers. The discount, however, was based on the fact that female carcasses are smaller than male carcasses. I have allowed 4 cents under the assumption that all of the carcasses were discounted the same amount for size. In other words I am, if anything, erring on the high side in setting the value of the female cattle.

32 Many of the calves born late in the previous grazing season, of which there were usually several hundred, were worth very little because they were too young to survive on their own and anyone buying them would have needed to figure wintering costs into the price. Yearling steers were commonly bought a few years later, when the price of beef was significantly higher than in 1897/98, for $19.00 per head and yearling heifers for $16.00. Thus if we allow $15.00 for all the calves and one- and two-year-old steers and heifers, any error would likely be on the high rather than the low side. The pregnant cows would have varied immensely depending on age and quality; but a few years earlier McEachran had tried unsuccessfully to sell them at $27.50 with calves at foot. Therefore, if we allow $20.00 for them in the wintertime before they had given birth, we would probably not be very far out. If half the 7,000 Walrond cattle that were farthest from the beef market were cows and half calves and one- and two-year-olds, the total value would thus have been $15.00 x 3500 = $52,500.00 + $20.00 x 3500 = $70,000.00, or $122,500.00.

33 New Walrond Ranche papers, M8688–4, McEachran to [A.R.] Springett, 8 July 1897. I am guessing at the value of the bulls, but in 1911 the ranch would sell some at $40.00 a head (M8688–1,

McEachran to J.G. Ross, 17 October 1911), and in May 1899 Warnock and McEachran discussed purchasing breeding bulls for 75.00 each (M8688–5, Warnock to McEachran, 1 May 1899). During March the bulls would have brought less than in May because of the need to look after them until the grass was ready. Moreover, there would have been some old bulls in the Walrond herd that would have brought the average down.

34 The ranch needed about that many horses for the roundups, for which up to 10 per rider was the norm. For the value of horses see above, p. 149 and ibid., M8688–3, W. Bell to McEachran, 28 April 1887

35 $41,920 + $122,500 + $2,500 + $5,000.

36 Ibid., M8688–1, "The New Walrond Ranche Company," 26 February 1898

37 There are two shareholder lists for the New Walrond ranch. The other one was published in 1913 by Charlotte Walrond (*The Walrond Papers compiled by Charlotte Walrond* (London: Arthur L. Humphreys, 1913), 34–35).

38 One wants to recall his attempts to sell his personal stake in the Cochrane outfit to T.C. Power back in 1883 as that company was experiencing severe losses (above, pp. 76-77).

39 There were 7,170 shares outstanding for which the shareholders had paid $50 apiece. McEachran had started the liquidation process in 1896 and he may well have allowed some of the shareholders who most wanted out to redeem their shares. Even if at that point he had paid none of them, however, the $187,000 would have allowed redemption for all the shareholders to the tune of $26 per share, or just over half the original value. McEachran would thus have got

$26 x 815 = $21,190. Given his powers of rationalization, however, he almost certainly figured the cattle to be worth considerably more than the amount I have allotted.

40 New Walrond Ranche papers, M8688–1, "Shareholders Meeting of the Walrond Ranche Limited on 23 February 1898." It was moved by Lieutenant Colonel Holbech and seconded by Major Mason that the sale to the New Walrond Ranche should proceed. One of the conditions was articulated as follows: "the Old Company to pay out of the purchase money to Dr. McEachran the sum of 775 pounds being one half of his Commission on a sale at 48,000 pounds calculated upon the basis of his Agreement with the Company dated 6th November 1894, the remaining half of the Commission to be paid to Dr. McEachran by the New Company."

41 New Walrond Ranche papers, M8688–2, "Fourteenth Annual Report of the New Walrond Ranche Company Limited." For the year ended 31 December 1911, "Ranche Expenses, Management, etc." is shown as costing $8,752.31. Expenses had been reduced drastically at this time to $50.00 a month in the wintertime. Thus about $8,000.00 must have been McEachran's salary. This seems verified by his habit of looking after himself as well as possible in every transaction. On that ground it is very unlikely that he would have taken less per year out of the company now than in the past when, as we have seen, he had been taking over $6,156.00 in salary, stocks, and dividends. The other evidence that McEachran did not take shares is provided in company papers in the Government of the Province of Alberta, Office of the Registrar of Joint Stock Companies, which show the

company with 5,041 shares outstanding from beginning to end.

42 The name of the banking firm was Sanders and Company.

43 Exeter, Devon Record Office, Anstey and Thompson papers, M1926B–W/F–3/12: H. Houlditch to William Walrond, 16 February 1894. There are also several other letters about Sir William's financial problems and the eventual solution in this file.

44 C. Walrond, *The Walrond Papers*, 34–35.

45 From over $91,000.00 to $23,650.00.

46 New Walrond Ranche papers, M8688–1, "The New Walrond Ranche Company, Limited," 26 February 1898.

47 Government of the Province of Alberta, Office of the Registrar of Joint Stock Companies for the year ended 1913, Report of the Director of the New Walrond Ranche Company and Statements of Account, "Paid up shares 5041." "Total amount of shares that have never been allotted or subscribed for 4959." McEachran valued the shares in the new company at £10, or $50.00 (New Walrond Ranche papers, M8688–1, "The New Walrond Ranche Company, Limited," 26 February 1898). In 1914 the shares were valued at $48.60, possibly reflecting changing currency values: ibid..

48 Anyone reading the general manager's letters discovers many other exaggerations. One of the most glaring in the 1898 prospectus is that the company could be expected to produce 5,000 calves annually.

Nothing even approximating that number had at any time been achieved in the past; indeed, the highest post-1887 calf count ever mentioned in the Walrond papers is "nearly" 2,300, and that was not until 1905: New Walrond Ranche papers, M8688–8: McEachran to Arthur Walrond, 21 October 1905.

49   Ibid.

50   Ibid.

51   Ibid., M8688–4, Warnock to McEachran, 2 December 1897.

52   Ibid., M8688–3, Warnock to McEachran, 25 Sept. 1894.

53   Ibid., Warnock memo, 9 November 1895; M8688–4, Warnock to McEachran, 2 December 1897.

54   Both Creeks flow south and west out of the west side of the Porcupine Hills and join the Oldman River miles below where Callum Creek joins the same river.

55   New Walrond Ranche papers, M8688–4, Warnock to McEachran, 13 December 1897.

56   Ibid., M8688–6, Warnock to McEachran, 4 September 1902.

57   Ibid.

58   Ibid., M8688–1, "The New Walrond Ranche Company, Limited," 26 February 1898.

59   Ibid.

60   Ibid., M8688–4, Warnock to McEachran, 22 November 1897.

61   Ibid., Warnock to McEachran, 22 November 1897.

62   Ibid., M8688–1, "The New Walrond Ranche Company, Limited," 26 February 1898; M8688–5: Warnock to McEachran 16 April 98; "dogie [sic] steers are in demand for the Yukon trade, they are gentle and can be made to pack if necessary."

63   In July 1897, the steamer Portland arrived at Schwabacher's dock on the Seattle waterfront and discharged a number of successful Klondike gold miners, weighed down with bags, sacks, and boxes of gold. The newspapers and telegraphs spread word of this shipment, and the similar one to San Francisco, all over the nation and the world. For the gold rush see P. Berton, *Klondike: the Last Great Gold Rush, 1896–99*, revised ed. (Toronto: McClelland and Stewart, 1974).

64   New Walrond Ranche papers, M8688–5, Warnock to McEachran, 24 March 1898.

CHAPTER 8 – CONFRONTING THE FRONTIER BUSINESS ENVIRONMENT

1   GA, New Walrond Ranche papers, M8688–8: McEachran to Walrond, 21 October 1905: "President and Managing director D. McEachran, Secretary-Treasurer, James S. Ross, Vice President W.H. Ramsay, all of Montreal."

2   See University of Manitoba, Archives and Special Collections, Ogilvie Flour Mills fonds, 1847–1983, MSS 120 PC 122, MC3; *Dictionary of Canadian Biography*, xiii, 1901–1910.

3   J.A. Gemmill, *The Ogilvies of Montreal* (Ottawa, 1904).

4   In 1887, William Bell wrote to James G. Ross to inform him that he had "received notice last week from the Ogilvie Milling Coy. Winnipeg, that two sets of bob sleighs had been shipped to Lethbridge for us and I arranged with [I.G.] Baker's people to have them forwarded to Macleod without delay." New Walrond Ranche papers, M8688–3, 6 November.

5 Ibid., M8688–5, Warnock to S. Reid, 25 May 1895; see also above, p. 146-47. .

6 D. McEachran, *Report of a Visit to Great Britain and the Continent of Europe in the Winter of 1897–98* (Government Printing Bureau, 1898), 7.

7 Gemmill was married to the daughter of Ogilvie's brother Alexander Walker Ogilvie: see J.A. Gemmill, *The Ogilvies of Montreal.*

8 See *Dictionary of Canadian Biography*, xiii, 1901–1910. Ogilvie sat on the Board of the Exchange, Bank of Canada, and the Montreal Loan and Mortgage Company, which were Gault enterprises.

9 Guarantee Company of North America List of Shareholders, online: www.rootsweb.com/~ote/canada/shareholders_gna.htm.

10 J.G. MacGregor, *Senator Hardisty's Prairies, 1849–1889* (Saskatoon: Western Prairie Books, 1978); S. Smith, "Richard Charles Hardisty," *Dictionary of Canadian Biography*, xi (Toronto: University of Toronto Press, 1982), 383–84.

11 MacGregor, *Senator Hardisty's Prairies*, 3–5. At his death Smith was worth 28,867,635 (*Dictionary of Canadian Biography*, xiv, 1911–1920, 939–51).

12 New Walrond Ranhe papers, M8688–8, McEachran to Walrond, 21 October 1905.

13 See below, p. 226.

14 Sir John Walrond Walrond's daughter Gertrude was married to Sir Thomas Dyke Acland: C. Walrond, *The Walrond Papers* (London: Arthur L. Humphreys, 1913), 34–35, 76.

15 British Library, New Walrond Ranche Company, Letters Patent, By-laws, Shareholders, Montreal.

16 This information is taken from the 1841 census reports, which are found at www.ancestry.co.uk.

17 New Walrond Ranche papers, M8688–9, C.W. Buchanan to the New Walrond Ranche Company shareholders, 15 February 1923.

18 Ibid., M8688–5, Warnock to McEachran, 24 March 1898

19 Ibid., Warnock to McEachran, 13 February 1899.

20 Ibid., Warnock to McEachran, 26 November 1898

21 K.H. Norrie, "The National Policy and the Rate of Prairie Settlement," in R.D. Francis and H. Palmer, eds., *The Prairie West, Historical Readings*, 2nd ed. (Edmonton: Pica Pica Press, 1992), 245.

22 Ibid., Warnock to McEachran, 24 January 1898: "John Lamar quit last month and the only man I could get to take his place was J. Ferguson"; Warnock to J.G. Ross, 7 November 1901: "We are holding thirty six head of beef cattle (big jaws, cripples etc.) for Mead to kill for his shop in Crows Nest Pass. McLean is to settle for these cattle."

23 Ibid., Warnock to McEachran, 11 December 1899.

24 Between 1898 and 1907 the average price paid to Canadian producers per pound live rose from $3.80 to $4.24.

25 One of the problems cattle producers in western Canada complain about today is the lack of competition among the purchasers of finished beef. In Alberta they point out there are only three companies to call when it is time to market their slaughter animals. The three are Tyson Foods, which owns the huge Lakeside packing plant at Brooks, Cargill Incorporated, which operates out of High River, and XL Foods of Calgary, owned by Nilsson Brothers. These companies

together process more than 90 per cent of Alberta's beef. Moreover, their participation in the industry goes far beyond their packing plants. They finance cattle owned by individual cattlemen, thus gaining full rights to process them when finished; they "lock in" prices in "forward contracts" with owners to slaughter their cattle when ready; and they purchase and feed large numbers of cattle themselves on private feedlots. Nilsson Brothers also runs the busiest livestock auction mart in western Canada at Clyde Corners north of Edmonton as well as smaller marts at Grande Prairie and Vermilion. The potential for these three companies to make money from the twists and turns in the market place is enormous. When supply is short and prices high they profit through the "lock-in" system and by processing their own animals, and when prices are low and supply high they are generally able to pass on any losses to other producers. Thus, for instance, during the BSE crisis when the American market was cut off and there was suddenly a glut of finished cattle in Alberta and Saskatchewan, they were able to nearly triple their net returns by simply paying the other feeders far less for their animals than they had been getting previously. While their system obviously places major obstacles in the way of a profitable cattle industry at the primary production level, I would argue that it is less destructive than its counterpart in the frontier stage. At least now the giant corporations are forced by anti-collusion laws to compete for supply and western cattlemen have a number of alternatives for selling their finished product. They can, for instance, ship their animals to sales rings here in the West or in Toronto where buyers are forced openly to bid against each other. Moreover, tariff agreements, including NAFTA, have made the United States much more accessible to Canadian producers than it was a over a hundred years ago: Elofson, "Other Peoples' Money; Patrick Burns and the Beef Plutocracy, 1890–1914," *Prairie Forum* 32:2 (Summer 2007): 235–50.

26 A.B. McCullough, "Winnipeg Ranchers: Gordon, Ironsides and Fares," *Manitoba History* 41 (Spring/Summer 2001): 18–25.

27 From 1903 Gordon, Ironsides and Fares were also part of a consortium that grazed 3,000 to 5,000 head of cattle on a 219,000-acre lease on the Blood Indian Reserve; in 1909 and 1910 the partners bought the 76 Ranch, the Turkey Track, and the T-Bar Down in southwestern Saskatchewan, where they kept another 12,000 head; and, between 1902 and 1912, the partners owned and operated a 200,000-acre ranch in Chihuahua, Mexico.

28 See Elofson, "Other People's Money."

29 S.M. Evans, *The Bar U and Canadian Ranching History* (Calgary: University of Calgary Press, 2004), 206.

30 L.V. Kelly, *The Range Men*, 75th anniversary ed. (High River, AB: Willow Creek Publishing, 1988), 189; in later years Burns established packing plants at Edmonton, Vancouver, Regina, Prince Albert, Winnipeg, and Seattle. He bought out or started over a hundred retail meat shops in the provinces of Alberta and British Columbia and he set up export agencies in London, Liverpool, and Yokohama, Japan.

31 In 1909 it became P. Burns and Company Ltd.

32 He bought the 7,000 deeded acres of the C K Ranch on the north side of the Bow River about 8 miles west of Calgary in 1905. In 1906 he bought the 3,300-acre Ricardo Ranch near Shepard on the

north side of the Bow River 15 miles east of the city. In 1910 he purchased the 2,768 deeded acres of the John Quirk outfit near High River and the Kelly Palmer Ranch south of the Little Bow River, and he took over the 150,000-acre lease of the Colonel A.T. Mackie spread in the Milk River District. Then he added the Imperial Ranch on the north side of the Red Deer River to his collection and the nearby Circle Ranch.

33 New Walrond Ranche papers, M8688-4, David Warnock memo, 6 November 1897.

34 Thus, for instance, on 23 June 1899 McLean agreed to buy "all the exportable steers belonging to the [Walrond] Company four years old and up, and such three year old steers as the manager consents to turn in at forty six dollars per head cash, also all their three and four year old spayed heifers at thirty seven dollars and fifty cents per head cash … and to pay three dollars and thirty five cents per 100 lbs for all other steers or heifers which the manager may select to ship of the above ages": ibid., M8688-5. See also Warnock to McEachran, 31 August 1901.

35 Ibid., Warnock to McEachran 23 June 1900.

36 He, like Burns, was one of the "Big Four" cattlemen who helped finance the first Calgary Stampede in 1912.

37 GA, A.E. Cross papers, M1543-443, C. Knox to Cross, 21 May 1902.

38 Ibid., Knox to Cross, 29 May 1902.

39 For the actual figures on shipments of live cattle to the United States and Britain see D.H. Breen, *The Canadian Prairie West and the Ranching Frontier, 1874–1924* (Toronto: University of Toronto Press, 1983), 66, 204.

40 A.E. Cross papers, M1543–470, Clay, Robinson and Company to Cross, 29 July 1907; *Macleod Gazette*, 7 May 1897. For Spencer Brothers see W.M. Elofson, *Frontier Cattle Ranching in the Land and Times of Charlie Russell* (Montreal and Kingston: McGill-Queen's University Press; Seattle: University of Washington Press, 2004), 93–94.

41 A.E. Cross papers, M1543–480, Cross to Clay, Robinson and Company, 5 August 1910.

42 "Macleod Stock Yards Company," *Pincher Creek Echo*, 21 June 1904.

43 "Weekly Livestock Market Report: H.A. Mullins & Co.," *Pincher Creek Echo*, 6 September 1904.

44 "Town and Country," *Pincher Creek Echo*, 15 August 1900; "Local and General," 19 July 1904; "Local and General," 3 August 1905.

45 A.E. Cross papers, M1543–451, Cross and Hull to unknown, 19 September 1900; M1543–450, W.C. Bowles to Cross, 27 August, 28 August, 2 September, 4 September, 17 September 1903; M1543–458, unknown to Cross, 1 August 1905.

46 The cost of shipping by steamer ran from 35 to 50 shillings per head: A.E. Cross papers, M1543–458, W.W. Craig to Cross, 12 June, 3 July, 6 July, 28 August 1905.

47 Ibid., 6 July 1905.

48 "Additional Local," *Pincher Creek Echo*, 6 October 1903; see also 1 September 1903; A.E. Cross papers, M1543–458, W.W. Craig to Cross, 1 August 1905.

49 "Weekly Livestock Report: H.A. Mullins & Co.," *Pincher Creek Echo*, 22 November 1904.

50 "Livestock Report: H.A. Mullins & Co.," *Pincher Creek Echo*, 22 August 1905.

51 See Dr. J.G. Rutherford, Veterinary Director-General and Live Stock Commissioner of the Dominion Government, "The Cattle Trade of Western Canada" (1909), quoted in L.V. Kelly, *The Range Men*, 197–212. In 1906 the number of cattle shipped east from Winnipeg that were fed on dry feed (hay, or hay and grain) – 9,435, the number fed only on grass – 81,609. The difference for 1907 was significantly greater than that in 1906, largely because of the rush by ranchers to sell out of the business after the losses of the previous winter, and for 1908 the difference was about the same.

52 Minnesota, Wisconsin, Illinois, and Ohio.

53 In 1906 the *Pincher Creek Echo* reported that cables from Liverpool on Canadian cattle were weaker and 1/2 cent lower at 9 1/2 to 10 1/2 cents, and on [poorly finished] rancher cattle 1/3 to 2/3 lower at 8 1/3 to 8 2/3.

54 Breen, *The Canadian Prairie*, 94.

55 "Yesterday's Markets," *Edinburgh Courant*, 12 September 1885.

56 Ibid., 18 September 1885.

57 Ibid., 30 October 1885.

58 "Weekly Live Stock Meeting Report: H. Mullins & Co.," *Pincher Creek Echo*, 24 May 1904.

59 The contract for the horse sale was made with Fares and Burns as partners: New Walrond Ranche papers, M8688–4, "Memo of Sale agreement between the Walrond Ranche (Ltd) and Messrs W.H. Fares and P. Burns re the draught horses the property of the Ranche Company 26th June 1897". Lane was working as Burns' agent in completing the cattle

sale: Warnock to J.G. Ross, 13 December 1897.

60 A.E. Cross papers, M8780–112, Cross to Mr. Hodson, November 1900.

61 Ibid., Cross to Lanigan, 13 August 1903.

62 New Walrond Ranche papers, M8688–2, "Sixth Annual Report of the New Walrond Ranche Company Limited."

63 Kelly, *The Range Men*, 178–79.

64 "Beef Combine," *Pincher Creek Echo*, 28 September 1906.

65 "Better Price for Cattle in the East," *Pincher Creek Echo*, 2 November 1906.

66 A.B. McCullough, "Winnipeg Ranchers: Gordon, Ironsides and Fares." A.E. Cross was also summoned to give evidence before the commission: see A.E. Cross papers, M1543–470, H. [Kraig] to Cross, 7 June 1907.

67 A.E. Cross papers, M8780–112, Cross to Mr. Hodson, November 1900.

68 He designated Fort William but presumably would have been just as pleased with the Toronto sales rings that modern beef producers are able to utilize.

69 A.E. Cross papers, M8780–112, Cross to Mr. Hodson, November 1900.

70 New Walrond Ranche papers, M8688–5, Warnock to McEachran, 23 July 1900.

71 Kelly, *The Range Men*, 151.

72 Ibid.

73 Ibid., 21.

74 Ibid.

75 New Walrond Ranche papers, M8688–4, "Memo: of sale and agreement between the Walrond Ranche Ltd and P. Burns and Coy, done in duplicate this the 26th day of June, 1897."

76 A Warnock memo of 12 June 1897 states that "the grass is luxuriant, stock of all classes are putting on flesh rapidly": ibid., M8688–3. See also Warnock memos of 5 June and 19 June 1897.

77 See above, p. 135.

78 In fact the grass continued that summer to be plentiful; Warnock reported to McEachran on 18 August 1897 that the "cattle are fat and are still putting on flesh": New Walrond Ranche papers, M8688–4.

79 Ibid., Warnock told J.G. Ross on 18 September 1897 that he had "supplied 1307 lbs to St. Paul's mission at same price as reserves – viz. 6.15 per 100 lbs."

80 "British Trade with Canada," *Macleod Gazette*, 20 June 1888.

81 New Walrond Ranche papers, M8688–29, "Beef Contract."

82 Ibid., M8688–4, Warnock to J.G. Ross, 13 December 1897.

83 Ibid., Warnock to McEachran, 18 August 1897. After a similarly good grazing season in 1903 the Walrond was able to put together three shipments of fat cattle for the British market. In one of the shipments 348 head of steers and cows were sent: see *Pincher Creek Echo*, 10 June 1903.

84 Kelly, *The Range Men*, 193.

85 See, for instance, A.E. Cross papers, M1543–450, W.E. Cochrane to Cross, 15 October 1903.

86 New Walrond Ranche papers, M8688–29, "Beef Contracts."

87 Ibid., M8688–4, Warnock to J.G. Ross, 13 December 1897.

88 Ibid., Warnock to McEachran, 20 September 1897.

89 Ibid., Warnock to J.G. Ross, 13 December 1897.

90 There is no mention of other bids in the Walrond papers.

91 Ibid., M8688–3, Warnock to McEachran, 18 August 1897.

92 Balance sheets for the account are in GA, Burns papers, M7771–24.

93 The Walrond kept accounts of the men's wages: see, for instance, New Walrond Ranche papers, M8688–28.

94 See above, p. 184.

95 New Walrond Ranche papers, M8688–29, "Beef Contracts." The Walrond delivered to the Peigan and Blood reserves. Unfortunately the ranch could not deliver all its fall slaughter cattle to the Native bands. In the average month the two reserves combined consumed fewer than 100 head.

96 This is confirmed by the fact that in some of the other deals he made with other cattlemen that summer he paid as much as $45 by the head for steers and $37.50 for cows: Kelly, *The Range Men*, 158.

97 Monthly costs for butchering are given in the New Walrond Ranche papers, M8688–3 and M8688–4. There is also a statement (M8688–4, September 1897), of hides sold between July 1896 and September 1897.

98 From time to time David Warnock recorded labour costs on the ranch. The average number of men over the course of twelve months was about 15 and the average wage was about 480 per annum: New Walrond Ranche papers, M8688–3 and M8688–4. The hay contracts cost the ranch about $2,000 a year: see Elofson, *Frontier Cattle Ranching*, 167.

99 See T.D. Regehr, "Western Canada and the Burden of National Transportation Policies," in R.D. Francis and H. Palmer, eds., *The Prairie West Historical Readings*, 2nd ed. (Edmonton: Pica Pica

Press, 1992), 264–84; C.W. Anderson, *Grain: The Entrepreneurs* (Winnipeg: Watson and Dwyer Publishing Ltd., 1991); D. Baron, *Canada's Great Grain Robbery* (Regina: Don Baron Communications, 1998); L.A. Wood, *A History of Farmers' Movements in Canada; The Origins and Development of Agrarian Protest, 1872–1924* (Toronto: University of Toronto Press, 1975); L. Dick, *Farmers "Making Good": The Development of Abernathy District, Saskatchewan, 1880–1920,* 2nd ed. (Calgary: University of Calgary Press, 2008), 171–221; D.S Spafford, "The Elevator Issue, the Organized Farmers and the Government, 19089–1911," *Saskatchewan History* 15, no. 3 (Autumn 1962): 81–92.

100 These figures are found in statements in Burns papers, M7771–43.

101 A.B. McCullough, "Winnipeg Ranchers: Gordon, Ironsides and Fares."

CHAPTER 9 – DUNCAN MCEACHRAN'S RANCH, 1898–1903: FURTHER INTENSIFICATION, HIGHER PRICES AND HIGHER COSTS

1 GA, New Walrond Ranche papers, M8688–5: 5 March 1901.

2 Ibid., Warnock to J.G. Ross, 28 March 1901.

3 Ibid., Warnock to McEachran, 29 April 1898. "In compliance with the new ordinance all bulls are being gathered and herded this spring. The ranchers between the N [orth] fork and Pincher Creek are going to hold their bulls in Elkhorn Park and I think it would be a good plan for us to go in with them and put our range bulls there too."

4 Ibid., M8688–5, Warnock to McEachran 17 October 1900.

5 Ibid., Warnock to McEachran, 31 August 1901. The following year they were to have branded 1,656 head by 18 August (M8688–6, Warnock to J.G. Ross, 18 August 1902). While that was not quite what Warnock expected, it was a return of well over 50 per cent – better than the average rate normally achieved under the open range system. In a letter of 28 March 1902 (ibid.) Warnock told his boss that "this year we will have over three thousand cows with the bulls and with favourable seasons I think we will get all the increase we can take care of." With decent weather "I shall be very disappointed if we do not brand from 1800 to 2000 calves." No herd count was undertaken that spring and summer so Warnock's figures were imprecise. They do, however, reflect ranch policy.

6 Ibid., M8688–5, Warnock to McEachran, 26 November 1898.

7 Ibid., M8688–6, Warnock to McEachran, 29 April 1902.

8 See above, p. 81.

9 The contract is dated 23 June 1899 (ibid.).

10 These cattle would have been at least 4 years old.

11 New Walrond Ranche papers, M8688–5, Warnock to McEachran, 1 January 1900.

12 Ibid., Warnock to McEachran, 14 March 1899.

13 Ibid., Warnock to McEachran, 1 January 1900.

14 Ibid., Warnock to McEachran, 14 November 1900.

15 Ibid., Warnock memo: "re Stockers purchased May 9th to 12th 1900."

16 Ibid., Warnock memo, "re cattle shipped 13ᵗʰ and 14ᵗʰ Aug:/[19]00."

17 Assuming 800 steers and 274 heifers – about the usual proportion the ranch sold.

18 New Walrond Ranche papers, M8688–5, Warnock to McEachran, 29 January 1901.

19 Ibid., Warnock to McEachran, 29 January 1901.

20 Ibid., Warnock to McEachran, 31 August 1901.

21 Interestingly Warnock rewrote the above letter to insert this passage. Clearly he was attempting to put the best appearance on the disappointing count as he could.

22 New Walrond Ranche papers, M8688–5, Warnock memo, 26 March 1898.

23 Ibid., Warnock to J.G, Ross, 12 June 1898.

24 Ibid., Warnock to McEachran, 21 November 1898: "To date we have gathered Five hundred and thirty seven calves of this seasons brand which leaves forty six still to account for. Of these we have weaned 442; the balance of 95 head being too small to wean are being held with their dams in the pasture to be fed later in the winter."

25 Pincher Creek was often referred to as the "South Fork" of the Oldman River. It joins the Oldman River several kilometres west of where Beaver Creek joins the river.

26 New Walrond Ranche papers, M8688–5, Warnock to McEachran, 18 November 1901.

27 Ibid., M8688–6, Warnock to McEachran, 4 September 1902: "We are nearly finished with the fences across the river and will then move the fence up in the field. We are cutting some green oats as

the wind is breaking it down and there is no chance of it ripening. I expect to hear from you today about the land. I trust you have secured a portion of [range] 11."

28 See above, p. 195.

29 Above, p. 136.

30 New Walrond Ranche papers, M8688–5, Warnock to J.G. Ross, 4 March 1898: "In ... Montana last year 16,384 wolves and coyotes were killed and the bounty paid amounted to nearly 60,000."

31 Ibid.: the amounts of the bounties were "10.00 for bitch wolves, 5 for dogs and 2 for cubs under three months."

32 In that year there had been 1,000 men stationed in the West. In 1901 there were 450: see Elofson, *Cowboys, Gentlemen and Cattle Thieves* (Montreal and Kingston: McGill Queen's University Press, 2000), 102.

33 New Walrond Ranche papers, M8688–5, Warnock memo "re beef shipment of Oct. 28ᵗʰ [19]01."

34 Ibid.

35 Ibid., Warnock to McEachran, 18 November 1901.

36 The fact that the company then still had quite a large number on feed must have helped temper the impact but since at least two-thirds of the stock was still being left to their own resources the losses must still have been severe.

37 New Walrond Ranche papers, M8688–6, Warnock to J.G. Ross, 24 May 1902.

38 Ibid., Warnock to McEachran, 7 December 1901. "I am very pleased to know that you have sold the beef at a good figure," Warnock wrote on 29 April 1902, while warning his boss that there were not going to be a lot of good fat animals to pick from.

39 Ibid., Warnock to McEachran, 12 November 1902.

40 Ibid., Warnock to McEachran, 19 November 1902.

41 Ibid., Warnock to McEachran, 12 November 1902. "We are busy weaning calves and gathering dogies etc," Warnock wrote. "Cattle are all up in the hills and take a lot of gathering. Many of the [dogies] are thin and will have to be fed from now on if this snow lies."

42 Ibid., Warnock to McEachran, 19 November 1902; Warnock to McEachran, 4 December 1902.

43 Perhaps he meant Xerophthalmia, known as "dry eye," which sometimes does lead to permanent blindness.

44 New Walrond Ranche papers, M8688–6, Warnock to McEachran, 11 December 1902.

45 See above p. 161, note 48.

46 Ibid., M8688–2, "Report of The New Walrond Ranche Company, for the year ended 31st December, 1903."

47 L.V. Kelly, The Range Men, 75th anniversary ed. (High River, AB: Willow Creek Publishing), 178–79.

48 New Walrond Ranche papers, M8688–6, Warnock to J.G. Ross, 6 January 1902; see also Warnock to McEachran, 28 March 1902: "In the early part of last week Blackleg reappeared among the yearling so we vaccinated all those being fed at Eltons and the Mormons and all likely subjects here, using 500 doses altogether of 'single' vaccine."

49 Ibid., Warnock to McEachran, 28 March 1902; see also Warnock to McEachran, 20 January 1902: "Kennington has lost five of his doggies and weaners from backleg so the season would seem to be favourable to it. Some of the Ranchers on Willow Creek used Blackleg vaccine i.e. a cord saturated with the vaccine – very successfully last year. Its use is much less complicated than the syringe method."

50 New Walrond Ranche papers, M8688–5, McEachran to Minister of Agriculture, 24 May 1899: "I regret to have to report that Mange is very prevalent in cattle in southern Alberta...," he wrote, "it will be necessary to establish quarantine over a considerable area."

51 Ibid., Warnock to McEachran, 17 April 1899. Warnock did as he promised. "I was at the stock meeting on the 19th," he later reported. "The mange question was discussed and the members resolved to take active measures to eradicate the disease. It is reported to be very prevalent on the Little Bow" (Warnock to McEachran, 25 April 1899).

52 Ibid., Warnock to McEachran, 11 December 1899.

53 Ibid., Warnock to McEachran, 7 October 1899.

54 Ibid.

55 Ibid., M8688–2, "Sixth Annual Report of the New Walrond Ranche Company," for the year ended 31 December 1903. McEachran is supposed to have stated that had he known the mange was to become such a grave threat "the New Walrond Ranche Co. would never have been formed" ("The Mange," Macleod Gazette, 14 July 1899).

56 New Walrond Ranche papers, M8688–5, Warnock to McEachran 31 August 1901.

57 Ibid., Warnock to McEachran, 16 April 1901.

58 Ibid., M8688–2 : "Sixth Annual Report of the New Walrond Ranche Company," for the year ended 31 December 1903.

CHAPTER 10 – DUNCAN MCEACHRAN'S RANCH, 1903–1907: JOINING (AND ATTEMPTING TO LEAVE) THE LANDHOLDING CLASSES

1   GA, New Walrond Ranche papers, M8688–2: "Sixth Annual Report of the New Walrond Ranche Company," for the year ended 31 December 1903.

2   Ibid., M8688–8, J.G. Ross to McEachran, 25 April 1904: "I was in Ottawa on Friday and Saturday and saw Mr. Ryley of the Department of the interior and Mr. Belcourt in reference to the water rights which have been under consideration." [I pressured the minister to sell them and asked] "if there was any chance of the company being able to purchase the lands outright at an upset price of $3.00 per acre without being put up to auction."

3   For all the land purchased on Callum Creek and five quarter sections on Beaver Creek, see note 16 below.

4   GA Dewdney papers, M3799–1–16, RG 15 B22, vol. 19, file 177068, McEachran to E. Dewdney, 8 December 1890. Requesting purchase of 13,559 acres of land; New Walrond Ranche papers, M8688–5, Warnock to McEachran, 17 October 1900: "A commissioner has been appointed to visit this district and look into the water right question. I expect him here any day and will accompany him over the range. I shall do my best to have all the best springs and creek frontages as surveyed by Wilkins reserved."

5   Heath Creek flows southwest out of the west side of the Porcupine Hills and joins the Oldman River several miles below where Callum Creek joins the same river.

6   New Walrond Ranche papers, M8688–5, Warnock to McEachran, 1 April 1898.

7   Cabin Creek flows into the Oldman River from the northeast a few kilometres to the south and east of where Callum Creek enters the river.

8   Black Mountain about twenty kilometres north of the ranch headquarters on Callum Creek.

9   New Walrond Ranche papers, M8688–5, Warnock to McEachran, 3 September 1900.

10 Scrip, he said, is the "cheapest method … under any circumstances," and it would enable you to acquire "all the land required without bargaining with Ottawa officials."

11 New Walrond Ranche papers, M8688–5, Warnock to J.G. Ross, 30 September 1900: "I am glad we have at last been able to get the land surveyed and I trust the sections we have decided to apply for may be secured on easy terms. Dr. McEachran left here enroute East on Wednesday, and was going to see the Land Agent at Lethbridge"; Warnock to McEachran, 14 November 1900: "Pleased to know that you had made application for purchase of land. After all, Sifton will be the man you have to deal with. I expect now that he is returned he will set about throwing open water reserves and endeavour to settle the country as much as possible." See also M8688–8, J.G. Ross to Clifford Sifton, 8 October 1900.

12 Ibid., M8688–5, Warnock to McEachran, 5 February 1901.

13 Ibid., Warnock to McEachran, 16 April 1901.

14 Ibid., M8688–8, McEachran to Clifford Sifton, 4 November 1901: "I beg to make application for the purchase of the following lands on the land leased to me on the terms of the Order-in-Council, 22nd April 1893, viz: – in township 9, range 1, West of the 5th M[eridian]." See M8688–8, J.G. Ross to McEachran, 24 December 1901 for land purchases through the G. and M. Land Company and real estate broker Osler, Hammond and Nanton. See also M8688–6: Warnock to McEachran, 7 December 1901.

15 Ibid., M8688–6, Warnock to McEachran, 6 January 1902; see also Warnock to McEachran, 17 February 1902. In the latter letter Warnock told McEachran that he was "very glad that you have succeeded in arranging about he land.… We are pretty well protected from Heath Creek to the Winter Camp East of Callum Creek, but we ought to get more land in the forks of Heath Creek, also in Big Coulee and up the river above the grade. I am looking up the mounds on government sections now, and will prepare a list for you and make application at Pincher Creek." On 27 February, he wrote: "I mailed my letter, enclosing copy of applications, on Saturday the 22nd at Pincher Creek and I expect it reached you.… The telegram re making application for C&E lands direct to Winnipeg was too late, but as the land Agent at Pincher Creek is district agent for both C&E and Hudson's Bay lands it would save time to make the applications at Pincher Creek. From your letter of 29th January, I understood that you wanted the application made at Pincher Creek for C&E lands as well as Government." On 4 May, he wrote: "two or three new settlers have located in Tennessee Coulee above the corral. I do not think they own cattle and I expect are going to farm. Five Mile is getting so crowded that Plaskett is moving down to the Big Bow. Ferguson too has got to get out of there and, I hear, intends going to Fort Steele to start a dairy. All the water rights on Five Mile are thrown open. I have not heard whether any of the W[ater] Reserves here are open but will see the Land agent at Pincher Creek tomorrow. Three different parties from Montana and Wyoming have been up here looking for a location to run cattle, but I think they found the country too small, and have gone to look at the Medicine Hat district."

16 37,966 x $2.28 per acre = $86,562.48. 34,000 x $2.28 per acre is about $77,520.00. Years later, after selling two quarters of land (320 acres), the company still owned 37,806 acres. The ranch had owned one quarter section from the beginning. Therefore the amount purchased was 37,806 plus one quarter (160 acres). See New Walrond Ranche papers, M8688–2, "Sixth Annual Report for the Walrond Ranche Company," for the year ended 31 December 1903.

17 $86,857.48 ÷ $44.00 = circa 1975.

18 $86,857.48 ÷ $40.00 = 2171; $86,857.48 ÷ $35.00 = 2,481

19 Above, p. 170.

20 GA, New Walrond Ranche papers, M8688–2: "Sixth Annual Report of the New Walrond Ranche Company, Limited," for the year ended 31 December 1903.

21 Below, p. 219.

22 Based on the calculations on page 157 above the average per head value in 1898 would have been about $19.10.

23 It is unclear exactly when McEachran actually paid for the land. At the end of 1903 he still owed over $66,000.00 to the Department of the Interior, the Calgary and Edmonton Land Company, the

real estate broker Osler, Hammond and Nanton, and to "Bills payable" (New Walrond Ranche papers, M8688–2, "Sixth Annual Report of the New Walrond Ranche Company," for the year ended 31 December 1903). However, when he did pay for the cattle his numbers might have been something like (7,842 − 1,975 = 5,866). At $32.00 apiece that number of cattle could be evaluated at $187,744.00. This, of course, was under what was owed the shareholders. However, since the count of 1901 clearly did not confirm the 1901 book figure, McEachran probably believed he had no more than 5,000 head after the cattle were paid for. At $32.00 apiece that would have left him with a herd value of only $160,000.00, which, of course, was *substantially* less than what was owing.

24 See note 16 above. The ranch had owned one quarter (160 acres) prior to the purchases of 1903/04.

25 New Walrond Ranche papers, M8688–8, McEachran to Clifford Sifton, 16 January 1904; J.G. Ross to McEachran, 25 April 1904.

26 Ibid., McEachran to [Arthur] Walrond, 21 October 1905.

27 D.H. Breen, *The Canadian Prairie West and the Ranching Frontier, 1874–1924* (Toronto: University of Toronto Press, 1983), 72; LAC, RG B2a, vol. 159,141376, Part 1, box 1, file 25, McEachran to William Pearce, Commissioner of Dominion Lands, 5 August 1887.

28 In 1901 McEachran had taken a lease on sections 31 and 29 on the Upper Ranch to pasture bulls in the spring and, ostensibly, section 19 on Beaver Creek to locate the horse ranch on as he went back into that business. Presumably he foresaw at that point that he might have

to use the land along Callum Creek strictly for pasturing cattle; see New Walrond Ranche papers, M8688–6, Warnock to McEachran 18 November 1901; M8688–8, McEachran to Clifford Sifton, [1900].

29 M8688–8 McEachran to [Arthur] Walrond, 21 October 1905.

30 New Walrond Ranche papers, M8688–6, Warnock to McEachran, 17 February 1902.

31 To ensure that he could rely on some of the lease land he had lost in 1896 McEachran had taken a new lease on 2,500 acres of land in the foothills. "I note that you have decided to locate the horse ranch near Beaver Creek and have applied for a lease there. I doubt whether you will be able to get a lease as holders of scrip have been looking over that country with a view to purchasing government land," Warnock told him in 1901 (ibid., M8688–5: Warnock to McEachran, 18 November 1901).

32 Centigrade.

33 Elofson, *Cowboys, Gentlemen and Cattle Thieves; Ranching on the Western Frontier* (Montreal and Kingston: McGill-Queen's University Press, 2000), 85.

34 H. Dempsey, *The Golden Age of the Canadian Cowboy, an Illustrated History* (Saskatoon and Calgary: Fifth House, 1995), 145.

35 These cattle did not have the numbers to put great pressure on the fences and few escaped.

36 GA, A.E. Cross papers, M1543–470, C. Douglass to Cross, 20 January 1907.

37 Ibid., M1543–471: Douglass to Cross, 16 March 1907.

38 Ibid.

39 Canada, *Sessional Papers*, 42, no. 14 (1907–08), n. 28, 56, Report of the

Northwest Mounted Police, Annual Report for D Division, 1 November 1907.

40 Beaver Creek flows east and south out of the Porcupine Hills.

41 "A Famous S. Alberta Ranch; The Walrond or 'W.R.'" *Lethbridge Herald*, 2 February 1963.

42 D.H. Breen, *The Canadian Prairie West and the Ranching Frontier, 1874–1924* (Toronto: University of Toronto Press, 1983), 147; see also "A Famous S. Alberta Ranch; The Walrond or 'W.R.'" *Lethbridge Herald*: "During the summer of 1906, it was estimated that there were 20,000 head of stock on the Waldron [*sic*] range, but after the terrible winter toll there were scarcely over 10,000."

43 New Walrond Ranche papers, M8688–9, C.W. Buchanan to Shareholders, 6 April 1923.

44 See below, chapter 11.

45 It had owned 38,126 acres up to 1917, when 320 acres in the lower block were sold (New Walrond Ranche papers, M8688–2, "Twentieth Annual Report of the New Walrond Ranche Company," for the year ended 31 December 1917).

46 "Perhaps the best measure of the havoc visited upon the ranching community during the 1906-7 winter is the number of ranch sales during the summer and autumn of 1907," writes David Breen. "For some the winter simply took what little enthusiasm that was left to continue in face of difficulties which seemed to press from all sides; for others, cattle losses represented such a reduction in working capital that there was no alternative but bankruptcy and sale" (*The Canadian Prairie West and the Ranching Frontier*, 147).

47 The contract with Burns is in New Walrond Ranche papers, M8688–29: "Memorandum of Agreement made in duplicate this 13th day of June, 1907, between the New Walrond Ranch Co. Ltd., of Pincher Creek, Alberta..."

48 New Walrond Ranche papers, M8688–9, J.G. Ross to the Shareholders, 29 April 1908. "Supplementary Letters patent having been issued to this Company, dated the 22nd day of April, 1908, whereby increased powers have been granted to the Company and the Capital Stock reduced to $208,243.71, being 5041 shares of a par value of 8 pounds10s or $41.31 per share, and as the Company is now in a position to disburse upon Capital Account the equivalent of $7.29 per share, notice is hereby given that Shareholders upon return of the certificates, at present held by them to the Company, new certificates will be issued upon the new basis and forwarded accompanied by a cheque at the above rate per share."

49 48.60 x 5041.

50 The people still holding shares in the company at that time were paid back $7.29 for each of their 5041 shares (New Walrond Ranche papers, M8688–9, J.G. Ross to Sir, Madam, 29 April 1908).

51 See, for instance, New Walrond Ranche papers, M8688–2, "Fourteenth Annual Report of the New Walrond Ranche Company Limited" for the year ended 31 December 1911: "Your Directors are still of the opinion that the construction of a Railway through the Company's Lands would greatly enhance their value, however, in deference to the wishes of some of the shareholders that an effort be made to dispose of the property, an agreement has been entered into with Mssrs. Lougheed and Taylor, of Calgary, to place it on the market, in London, in

terms highly advantageous to the Company."

52   3 men x $480.00 x 3 years.

53   New Walrond Ranche papers, M8688–2, "Twenty-fifth Annual Report for the New Walrond Ranche Company Limited," for the year ended 31 December 1922.

54   $4,320.00 + $24,000.00 + $4,000.00.

55   New Walrond Ranche papers, M8688–9, C.W. Buchanan to the shareholders, 6 April 1923. "To pay off our indebtedness for accrued salary and loans to Dr. McEachran and other charges and to give the shareholders their money back *without interest* from 1907 when the last dividend was paid, it would be necessary to sell our 37,000 acres for about $8.00 per acre net to the Company." At this time the ranch was indebted mainly to McEachran to the tune of $56,008.54.

56   $70,000.00 ÷ 26; see New Walrond Ranche papers, M8688–29.

57   New Walrond Ranche papers, M8688–20, inventory for the New Walrond Ranche as of 31 December 1907. The 1908 figures have been inked in beside the 1907 figures; M8688–7: McEachran to Messrs Aitken and Co. Glasgow, [1912].

58   Ibid., M8688–7, McEachran to Arthur Walrond 17 November 1908.

59   Ibid., M8688–20: inventory for the New Walrond Ranche as of 31 December 1907.

60   On 17 October 1911 he told J.G. Ross that he had just sold "the whole of the cattle now on hand… the Bulk at $40 each, calves not counted." These cattle had brought in a total of $4,120.00 (ibid., M8688–7). $4,120.00 ÷ $40.00 is about 103.

61   Ibid.

62   See above, p. 3.

63   Quoted in L.V. Kelly, *The Range Men*, 75th anniversary ed. (High River, AB: Willow Creek Publishing), 199–200. For losses in general see Canada, *Sessional Papers*, 42, no. 14 (1907–08), n. 28, 56, Report of the Northwest Mounted Police, Annual Report for D Division, 1 November 1907; ibid., 69, Annual Report for E Division, 31 October 1907; ibid., 75, Annual Report for K Division, 31 October 1907.

64   According to the Mounties, who lived amongst the ranchers and got to know them well, the loss in that area was about 25 per cent (ibid., Annual Report for K Division, 31 October 1907). This included the smaller ranchers, however. The Walrond undoubtedly took a worse beating than many ranches in the area because of the size and diminished state of its grasslands.

65   New Walrond Ranche papers, M8688–20, inventory as of 31 December 1907.

66   $75,000.00 + $8,050.00 + $5,000 + $97,3815.00.

67   $130,000.00 – $75,192.00.

68   $54,808 – 43,372.60.

69   New Walrond Ranche papers, M8688–7, grazing lease to W. & R. Lloyd for section 31, township 10, range 2, West of the 5th meridian, for $132.00, 23 May [1908]; ibid., grazing lease for one year of section 31, township 10, range 2, west of the 5th meridian, dated 23 November 1908.

70   Ibid., McEachran to W. & R. Lloyd 17 October 1909. McEachran kept back a section or so of land in these years to run a few cattle and what was left of his commercial horse herd. Thus as late as 1922 he showed a livestock inventory worth a few thousand dollars (M8688–2, "Twenty-fifth Annual Report of the

New Walrond Ranche Company Limited," for the year ended 31 December 1922).

71 Ibid., M8688–2: "Fifteenth Annual Report for the New Walrond Ranche Company," for the year ended 31 December 1912.

72 Ibid., "Nineteenth Annual Report for the New Walrond Ranche Company," for the year ended 31 December 1916; M8688–8, C.W. Buchanan to Shareholders, 15 February 1923; GA, Burns papers, M160–224, Royal Trust Company to Burns, 5 April 1923.

73 New Walrond Ranche papers, M8688–2: see the annual financial reports of the company from 1911 to 1922. Burns paid $3,000 a year from 1913 to 1914 and then $4,500 in 1915, $6,000 in 1916 and 1917 and $7,000 thereafter.

74 Ibid. First between 1911 and 1916 he cut it in half and then in 1917 he reduced it to $2,000. Thereafter he only took payment when he incurred expenses in the company's name.

CHAPTER 11 – CONCLUSION

1 He was sixty-nine years old in 1908.

2 GA, New Walrond Ranche papers, M8688–7: McEachran to Walrond, 17 November 1908.

3 Ibid.

4 *Dictionary of Canadian Biography Online*: /www.biographi.ca/EN/ShowBio. asp?BioId=42417&query=Duncan%20 AND%20McEachran.

5 As we have seen, Strathcona was Donald Smith, who had made his fortune building the Canadian Pacific Railway for the Conservative government of Sir John A. Macdonald. He was also mar-

ried to the aunt of Joseph Hardisty, who was himself a shareholder in the Walrond Company.

6 See, for instance, New Walrond Ranche papers, M8688–7, McEachran to Messrs Aitken and Co., Glasgow, 19 July 1912.

7 New Walrond Ranche papers, M8688–7, McEachran to Walrond, 17 November 1908.

8 P. Voisey, *Vulcan; the Making of a Prairie Community* (Toronto: University of Toronto Press, 1988), 53–74.

9 New Walrond Ranche papers, M8688–7, McEachran to Harbard W. Hooper, 6 July 1912: "In 1882–3 the late Sir John Walrond and I started a ranche here having leased 300,000 acres later purchased outright 37,000 acres selected land in the most attractive part of this beautiful country unsurpassed by its many advantages...On the map you will observe a town site on section 12, tp 10, r 2, W. 5, one of the finest town sites imaginable and once the railway is running it will fill in building lots readily and net a considerable sum.... I look for great activities here almost immediately, a ... Bridge is to be built over the river. The Railway surveyors are busy in full force completing the staking out of the line towards Calgary"; McEachran to John Stewart, Commissioner of Irrigation: "I beg to apply for permission to use water for irrigation purposes for the streets of the Town of Walrond which we intend soon to lay out on the following lands."

10 Ibid.

11 Ibid., McEachran to G.C. Fielding, 28 June 1909.

12 Ibid., McEachran to G.L. Lennox, 22 June 1909.

13 Ibid.

14 Ibid., McEachran to A.L Sifton, 24 October 1911.

15 Ibid., M8688–9, C.W. Buchanan to the shareholders, 15 February 1923.

16 5,484.64 ÷ 6.5.

17 Government of the Province of Alberta, Office of the Registrar of Joint Stock Companies, Forty-sixth Annual Report of the New Walrond Ranche Company Limited, 2 February 1944.

18 Ibid., "The New Walrond Ranche Company, Limited, Statement of Receipts and Disbursements for the year ended 31st December 1943."

19 E. Brado, *Cattle Kingdom: Early Ranching in Alberta*, 2nd ed. (Surrey, BC: Heritage House, 2004), 135. See also Company Records, Alberta.

20 37,806 – 10,600 – 840.

21 $159,490.52 ÷ 5,041.

22 After the turn of the century each share was valued at $48.60 (above, p. 210).

23 Government of the Province of Alberta, Office of the Registrar of Joint Stock Companies, Forty-sixth Annual Report of the New Walrond Ranche Company Limited, 2 February 1944: the list of shareholders with their total number of shares, titled simply "The New Walrond Ranche Company Limited," is attached to "The New Walrond Ranche Company Limited, Report and Balance Sheet as at 31st December 1943."

24 Above pp. 87, 104.

25 He took some salary after 1911 as well but at least some of it was offset by money he loaned to the company.

26 New Walrond Ranche papers, M8688–2: see the year end reports, in particular, "Nineteenth Annual Report for the New Walrond Ranche Company," for the year ended 31 December 1916; and "Twenty-second Annual Report for the New Walrond Ranche Company," for the year ended 31 December 1918.

27 S. Evans, *The Bar U and Canadian Ranching History* (Calgary: University of Calgary Press, 2004), 109–47.

28 Ibid., 181.

29 Until six or seven years ago most of us took for granted that the great cattle barons of the frontier period instigated a prosperous industry and were forced to shut down one after the other early in the twentieth century largely because settlers flocked into their grazing lands, fenced off the open range, and crowded them out. In the year 2000 I challenged this view, arguing that large-scale, open range ranching was inherently uneconomic on the northern Great Plains. Wolves, rustlers, winters storms, and disease decimated the herds, and all the big outfits we know about experienced major financial hardships. For George Lane see S. Evans, *The Bar U and Canadian Ranching History*, 109–202; For the others see W.M. Elofson, *Cowboys, Gentlemen and Cattle Thieves; Ranching on the Western Frontier* (Montreal and Kingston: McGill-Queen's University Press), 90, 147–48.

30 At the time when McEachran purchased the 34,000 acres at Callum Creek it grew to 8,600 acres of deeded and 2,500 acres of leased land.

31 At its height it reached 64,000 acres (B.H. McIntyre, *A Brief History of the McIntyre Ranch* (s.n. 1948), 14.

32 Ibid., 25.

33 Respectively the owners of the Bar S, Rocking P, and A7 ranches.

34 Interview with John Cross and Shelley Wilson-Cross on a tour of ranches sponsored by the Glenbow Museum and Archives on 11 June 2008.

INDEX

character, 43–46
"greenhorns" from the East and
    Britain, 43
Irish, 109
pay, 39
rustling, 46–47. *See also* cattle, rustling;
    Walrond ranch
Craig, J.R., 194
Cross, A.E., 5, 76, 175, 176, 179, 180, 215
    cattle losses, 87–88
    cattle operation, 149
    heavy horse business, 149–50, 151
Cross, John, 230
Cross S horse ranch, 149
Crows Nest Pass Railway, 163, 171, 173,
    181, 187, 198
Cullompton, Devonshire, 1, 36, 169
Cunfer, Geoff, 3–5, 11

D

Dakota, 88
Damien, 48
Dans, Jeffrey, 45
Dawes, James Ponley, 102, 169
Deloitte and Company, 103
Deloitte, Touche, Tohmatsu, 103
Department of Indian Affairs, 48, 60, 82,
    91
Devon Record Office, 159
Dewdney, Edgar, Minister of the Interior,
    66
Dickie, Mrs. I., 169
Dimmer, J., 149
Dixon, Anthony, 64
Dixon, James, 64
Dominion Cotton Mills Ltd., 168
Douay, Walscin de, 36
Douglass, Charles, 215
Dublin, Ireland, 38
Duggan, C.J., 174
Dunbar, Robert, 65–70
Dunbar family, 65–70
Duncan, A.H., 169

E

East Devon Constituency, 36
Edgbaston, Birmingham, 103
Edinburgh Courant, 8
Edinburgh Veterinary College, 39
Edmonton, 149, 173
Elbow River, 173
Elgin, John, 69
Elton, Mr., 200
Emerson, George, 194
environment, 2, 3–4, 6–7, 8, 14, 15,
    63, 77, 83–84, 84–91, 95–98,
    141–45, 149, 151, 154, 170, 171,
    172, 179, 192, 193, 195–96, 197,
    198, 201–3, 210, 213–16, 224.
    See also Cochrane ranch, cattle
    losses; Cross, A.E., cattle losses;
    Walrond ranch, cattle diseases,
    environmental attributes, rustling,
    winter losses, wolf predation;
    women on the ranching frontier
Essery, R.A., 149
Europe, 168, 177
Evans, Clinton, 6
Evans, Simon, 6
Evans, William Herbert, 38, 169
Exeter, Devonshire, 159

F

Fallis, Clay, 46, 48
Fares, William, 6, 149
    and the beef cartel, 172–88
Farmer, William, 108
Fergus, Andrew, 75
Fergus, James, 5, 51, 75–76, 95, 230
Fergus, Pamelia, 51–52, 75, 230
Fergus, William, 75
Fergus County, 51
Fergus ranch, 5
Ferguson, John, 169
Fish Creek, Alberta, 174
Five Mile Creek, 23, 30–31, 196
Five Mile ranch, 23, 148
Fort Benton, 41, 42, 43
Fort Macleod, 1, 23, 43, 44, 46, 47, 65,
    146, 173, 176, 194, 198, 214, 215
Fort William, Ontario, 173

Illinois, 13
Imperial Bank, 186
Indians, 52
  beef contracts for, 22, 42, 82, 90–91,
    157, 158, 170, 184, 186, 194
  Blood Nation, 22, 48, 49, 60, 91, 137,
    155
  cowboys, 48
  Peigan Nation, 21, 22, 48, 49, 60, 91,
    137, 155, 196
  Stoney Nation, 143
  wolfers, 48, 49, 143, 161–62, 197
Ingraham, Prentice, 8
Ireland, 8, 38, 109
Ironsides, Robert, 6
  and the beef cartel, 172–88

J

James, Archibald Herbert, 169
Johnson, Mr., 76
Jones, Frank, 47
Jones Creek, 108
Judith Cattle Company, 41

K

Kelly, L.V., 47, 68, 88, 174, 181
Kenora, Ontario, 173
Klondyke, 163
Knox, Charles, 175, 180
Kohrs, Conrad, 34

L

Lachine, Quebec, 102
Lamar, John, 44, 45, 48, 65–66, 109, 155,
    171
Lane, George, 6, 70, 95, 173, 178, 181, 183,
    184, 185, 186, 194, 229
Laramie, Wyoming, 5
Latham, Hiram, 8, 77
Lathom, Lord, 1
Law, Thomas Pakenham, 38, 169
leafy spurge, 136
Lethbridge, Alberta, 71, 202
Lister-Kaye farm, 10
Little Bow River, Alberta, 195, 202
Liverpool, 34, 176, 178

Livingstone Mountain Range, 21, 30–31,
    56–57, 121, 128–31
Lloyd, R., 220
Lloyd, W., 220
London, England, 34, 37, 38, 103, 109, 149,
    167, 178, 223
Loring ranch, 23

M

Macoun, John, 12
McCoy, Joseph S., 8, 77
McCullough, A.B.
Macdonald, D., 169
Macdonald, Sir John A., 1, 2, 34, 39
  government of, 39, 42, 63, 65, 76–77,
    91, 113
McEachran, Dr. Duncan McNab, 2, 3, 22,
    23, 37, 46, 49, 53, 60, 81, 83, 90,
    101, 102, 105, 110, 112, 113, 121,
    168, 170, 179, 188, 192, 193, 194,
    196, 197, 198, 200, 213, 216, 220
  agreement with first Walrond ranch,
    38–39
  agreement with second Walrond ranch,
    101, 103–4
  and Cochrane ranch, 34–35, 39
  and large-scale ranching, 9, 13, 17
  and heavy horse business, 109, 141–64
  and third Walrand ranch, 153–64, 167,
    191
  and Walrond family, 35, 102, 160, 164
  cattle and other purchases from
    Montana, 40–43
  conflicts with squatters, homesteaders
    and others, 63–67
  confusion about cattle numbers on the
    Walrond ranch, 95–98, 155,
    192, 195
  disdain for Indians, 49
  dividend payments to shareholders,
    94, 138, 182, 203. See also
    Walrond ranch
  eternal optimism, 76–79, 84, 85–87, 91,
    94, 163,
  financial mistakes, 138
  financial rewards from years with
    Walrond companies, 226–27
  land purchases, 207–11

T

Tanner's Crossing, Manitoba, 173
tariffs
    Canadian, 41, 42
    American, 176
Thompson, Mr., 45
Tiverton Division Constituency, England,
    36
Tennessee Creek, 49, 116, 196
Texas, 2, 8, 13, 44, 134, 143, 163
Todd Creek, 208
Toronto, 39, 104, 180
Trefusis, Gertrude Albertina, 36
Troyte, C.A.W., 102, 160
Turkey Track ranch, 229
Turner, John, 148
Two Bar Ranch, 173
Tyson Foods, 16

U

Uffculm Parish, 36
United States, 3, 10, 11, 18, 45, 157, 163.
    See also Americans; cowboys
    in print media, 8, 42
Upper Canada Veterinary School, 39

V

Voisey, Paul, 6, 7, 10

W

Walker, Major James, 68
Walrond, Arthur Melville Hood, 35, 38,
    101, 102, 103, 153, 159, 160, 211,
    218, 223
Walrond, Lady Charlotte, 35, 101
Walrond, Lady Francis Caroline, 38, 160
Walrond, Sir John Walrond, 1, 2, 9, 35, 37,
    38, 39, 60, 78, 81, 94, 101, 102,
    103, 160, 169
    and formation of second Walrond
        ranch, 102–3
Walrond, Lionel, 36
Walrond, Margaret, 160

Walrond, William Hood, Lord Waleran,
    35, 36, 101, 102, 104, 153, 160
    financial predicament, 158–59
Walrond family, 164
    shares redemption, 158–60, 227
Walrond ranch, 34, 63, 81, 167, 171, 173,
    175, 178, 199, 201, 202
    as model for study of large-sale
        ranching, 10, 14, 19
    birth of first ranch, 35–39
        shareholders, 35–37, 38, 101–2, 231
    birth of second ranch, 101–3
        shareholders, 102–5, 231
    birth of third ranch, 153–64
        shareholders, 167–69, 170, 216,
        226, 231
    British defections from, 169
    cattle
        calving rates, 17, 54,
            81–89, 111, 112, 192,
            196–200, 203, 210,
            218
        diseases
            blackleg, 200–201
            mange, 67, 171, 201–3,
            204–5
        numbers, 54, 81–82, 134,
            156, 157, 170, 192,
            200, 209, 210, 216–
            19, 22
            confusion about. *See*
                McEachran, Dr.
                Duncan McNab
        purchases, 40–43. *See also*
            cattle, doggies
        quality, 82, 90, 91
        sales (*See also* cattle, prices)
            directly to Britain, 176,
            177
            to A.J. Mclean. *See*
                Mclean, A.J.
            to government for Native
                bands, 22, 48,60,
                74, 82, 89, 91, 137,
                158, 160, 170, 171,
                184, 185, 187,
                192, 194, 195.
                See also Indians, beef
                contracts for

to Patrick Burns, 182–88, 193
timed breeding, 83–84, 191–92
cowboys and other hired help, 42–47, 53, 72–75
dividend payments to shareholders, 38, 39, 78–79, 92–95 , 97, 104–5, 110–11, 138, 160, 170, 181, 203, 216, 227, 228, 231
environmental attributes, 21–33
farming practices, 108, 212–13
feeding practices, 17, 54, 55, 60, 97–98, 107–12, 141, 142, 162, 191, 197–98, 200, 202, 203, 212, 219
financial position, 153–59, 209–11, 216–20, 225–27, 228
grazing practices, 11, 92, 113, 118–20, 121–38, 143–44, 171, 183, 192, 207, 209, 213–14
heavy horse business, 141–64
infrastructure, 54, 108, 141, 142, 154, 162
land purchases, 207–11, 217
land sales, 224–25
operating costs, 105–12
record keeping, 85–87
roundups, 47, 53, 86, 118–19, 171, 195, 202
rustling, see cattle; horses
sell off of cows, 82, 90–91
settlers crowding in on, 196, 207–9, 213
size, 1, 5, 21
squatters on, 63–67
winter losses, 199–200
  generally, 83–84
  winter of 1886–87, 85–86, 89–91
  winter of 1906–07, 78, 153–54, 210, 213–20
wolf predation, 161, 162
  on cattle, 4, 11, 15, 74, 109, 112–13, 155, 195, 196–97
  on horses, 113, 115, 142–43, 149, 195
women, 49–53. See also women on the ranching frontier
Warm Springs, Montana, 41, 96

Warnock, Annie, 50
Warnock, David, 45, 46, 49, 70, 71, 84, 108, 109, 110, 112, 137, 141, 142, 143, 145, 146, 147, 148, 149, 155, 161–61, 163, 170, 171, 175, 184, 186, 187, 191, 192, 193, 194, 196, 197, 198, 199, 202 , 203, 207–8, 210
  effectiveness as an onsite manager, 73–74
West, Elliott, 15, 18
wheat grass, 117, 136
Willow Creek, 84, 85, 135, 148, 192, 193, 195, 202, 209, 213
Wilson-Cross, Shelley, 230
Windsor-Clive, Lieutenant Colonel George Herbert, 36, 169
Wing, Wam, 50
Winnipeg, 35, 37, 47, 71, 146, 172, 173, 174, 176, 177, 178, 179
Wintering Hills, Alberta, 173
Wister, Owen, 8
Wiston, Sussex, 36
wolves, 4, 11, 75, 109, 150, 151. See also Indians, wolfers; Walrond ranch
women on the ranching frontier, 49–53
Wood, C.E.D., 64, 66, 67
World War I, 173, 181, 202, 217
Worster, Donald, 3–4
Wright, Charles, 45
Wyoming, 92, 93, 163
  cattle losses, 88
W.W. and A.W. Ogilvie Company, 167

Y

Yellowstone Journal, 3, 219
Yukon River, 163